ACTIVE FAITH

How Christians Are Changing the
Soul of American Politics

RALPH REED

THE FREE PRESS

NEW YORK   LONDON   TORONTO   SYDNEY   SINGAPORE

THE FREE PRESS
A Division of Simon & Schuster Inc.
1230 Avenue of the Americas
New York, NY 10020

Manufactured in the United States of America

10 9 8 7 6 5 4 3 2 1

Library of Congress Cataloging-in-Publication Data
Reed, Ralph, 1961–
     Active Faith: how Christians are changing the soul of American
politics / Ralph Reed.
          p.   cm.
     Includes bibliographical references and index.
     ISBN 0-684-82758-1
     1. Christianity and politics—History—20th century.   2. United
States—Church history—20th century.   3. Christian Coalition.
4. Reed, Ralph, 1961–   .   5. Conservatism—Religious aspects—
Christianity.   6. Conservatism—United States—History—20th
century.   7. United States—Politics and government—1993–
I. Title.
BR526.R43   1996
320.5'5'0973—dc20
                                                                96-5784
                                                                CIP

To my parents

CONTENTS

ACKNOWLEDGMENTS

Writing this book has been a labor of love, and I wish to thank those who helped to make it possible. Keith Korman, my literary agent at Raines and Raines, first prodded me into writing, and guided me through the publishing world like the expert he is. For their invaluable research and editorial assistance, I thank David Kuo, Jeff Peck, and Cathleen Ueland. They contributed mightily to translating my ideas into a coherent manuscript. I continued running the daily operations of the Christian Coalition throughout the writing of this book, and I could not have done it without their help.

A number of people at the Christian Coalition read the manuscript and offered invaluable suggestions. I am most indebted to Pat Robertson. He read every word, offered unique insights, and encouraged me during the editing process. I shall never forget our phone conversations from Switzerland in which he helped me revise the last several chapters. Furthermore, this book is about a vision and a social movement that Pat helped to birth and build. This is my book, but it is as much his story as mine. I thank him for his kindness and generosity to me and to my family.

Mike Russell, D. J. Gribbin, Brian Lopina, Heidi Stirrup, and Marshall Wittman reviewed the manuscript and gave me the benefit of their good judgment and sound advice. Patsy Greene, my very talented and able assistant, made sure the trains ran on time. They and the dedicated state and local leaders of the Christian Coalition deserve the credit for the success of the pro-family movement that is described in these pages. Although this story is told from my perspective, it is really about them and how they are transforming America. I thank them not only for allowing me to tell our story, but for enriching the life of our nation. They are part of the greatest team in American politics today.

Adam Bellow and David Bernstein at The Free Press are two of the finest editors in the country. They inspired me with an uncompromising standard of excellence and shared my vision of a book that would tell the truth about a social movement that is often misunderstood. They greatly improved the expression of my ideas through gifted editing, for which I am deeply grateful.

Finally, and most importantly, I express my gratitude to my beautiful wife, Jo Anne, and our three children, Brittany, Ralph III, and Christopher. For the third time in two years, they have patiently endured the intrusion of a book in our lives. To them, I promise my unfailing love and devotion, and pledge not to write any more books . . . for a while.

1

HOW WE GOT THERE

The sun was setting over central Florida as the plane carrying me and my colleagues banked right and descended toward Orlando International Airport. It was November 17, 1995, the day before the Republican party straw poll in Florida known as Presidency III. It was the last preliminary bout in the "long primary" that stretched from the announcements of the presidential candidates earlier in the year until the Iowa caucuses in February 1996. Ronald Reagan had won it in 1980, and George Bush won it in 1988, so the press corps and party professionals looked to the straw poll as an early barometer of organizational muscle and a reliable predictor of the eventual presidential nominee.

With me in the plane were Duane Ward, a former aide to Jerry Falwell and Oliver North, and the Texas-based religious broadcaster John Hagee, who had come along just to see the Christian Coalition at work up close. Beneath us rushed the pine trees, occasional palms, and expansive flatness that I remembered from time spent growing up in Florida. As the plane landed and came to a stop on the runway, I glanced at my watch. We had exactly fifteen minutes to make it to the junior high school where nearly two thousand clapping, foot-stomping Christian activists were packed into a gymnasium, awaiting the start of our presidential candidate forum and rally.

I jumped into a waiting van driven by one of our county coordinators, and we screamed off the tarmac behind a police escort. The van careened through the streets of Orlando as two motorcycles with sirens blaring and blue lights flashing cut their way through the night. As the minutes ticked by, our driver reported the startling fact that more than two-thirds of the delegates attending the straw poll from her county were members of the Christian Coalition.

"When we first showed up at the local meeting of the Republican party, we were treated like pariahs," she said. "It was almost like we had leprosy. That was two years ago. Last week we went to a meeting and were surrounded by candidates and legislators seeking our help. We're no longer outside looking in. We're on the inside looking out." As the van screeched to a stop, its burning tires lifting a cloud of blue smoke in the air, we scrambled through a back door of the junior high school, where the rally was just beginning. Greeting my entrance were the animated faces of Pat and Bay Buchanan, who were upset about his spot in the lineup of speakers.

"A candidate trumps a spouse," Bay screamed over the noise. "A candidate always trumps a spouse."

"I have to get ready for the debate tonight," exclaimed Pat. Because Bob Dole and Phil Gramm were stranded in Washington for a budget vote, they had sent their wives—Elizabeth and Wendy—to fill in for them. Pat was upset because the spouses were ahead of him on the program.

"I just walked in the door," I protested. "I don't have anything to do with the order of the speakers. Why don't you take it up with our Florida people?"

"They've already said no," laughed Pat. "That's why I'm coming to you." Pat was a no-holds-barred street fighter who had won a large grass-roots following from his perch on CNN's *Crossfire* program. We had teamed up many times against liberal opponents on television, and I was happy to help him, even if it only meant juggling the schedule. But his request to speak first probably had less to do with debate preparation and more to do with outmaneuvering his opponents.

Rather than argue, we agreed to let Buchanan go first, which sent the other campaign staffs into an apoplectic fit. As the screaming and finger-pointing continued backstage, a singer belted out "The Star-Spangled Banner." On cue, I stepped to the podium to deliver preliminary remarks. A large gold Christian Coalition logo sparkled beneath hot klieg lights behind me while the audience spread out before me like a human blanket in the darkened auditorium.

"If the Republican party wants to retain the majority it won in 1994 and add to it in 1996," I predicted, "it should not, cannot, and must not retreat from the pro-life and pro-family agenda that made it a majority party." The auditorium erupted in applause as those in the bleachers stomped their feet, waved banners, and blew horns.

"In politics, as in romance," I continued, "you dance with the one who brung you. And the Republican party has reached majority status with the votes of evangelicals, pro-family Roman Catholics, Greek Orthodox, and their allies."

As I stepped from the stage, I couldn't help but reflect on how far we had come since we had held the very first meeting of the Christian Coalition in Orlando in late 1989. At that time we had fewer than five thousand members, and our first rally drew only six hundred supporters. Now, less than six years later, we had 1.7 million members and supporters, more than a third of the delegates to Presidency III, and almost two thousand local chapters influencing legislation from school boards to the halls of Congress. In political terms, we had arrived.

Backstage, Lamar Alexander greeted me, minus his trademark red-and-black checkered flannel shirt. He wore a conventional blue suit and tie, the official uniform of presidential candidates. Lamar was flanked by Mike Murphy, his media guru, and Dan Casse, his chief policy wonk. We had talked on the phone earlier in the week, and Lamar expressed his desire to make a strong run at the pro-family delegates in spite of his moderate views on abortion. I suggested that he stress his opposition to federal funding of abortion. That night, Lamar cut the air with his fist and pledged to a rising crescendo of applause that under an Alexander administration, Planned Parenthood would not receive a dime in federal grants.

"Have you ever met Naomi Judd?" Lamar asked. I replied that I had not. My wife was a big country music fan; she would just die if she knew I had met one of her favorite stars.

"Well, she would like to meet you," Lamar said. I was led into a small holding room, where Naomi sat on a bench. Her hair was fiery red, her eyes deep blue, and she looked like a little China doll in an Oriental tunic and yellow silk pants complemented by sparkling white-and-gold sequined shoes. We could hear the crowd roaring in the auditorium behind us. It was almost surreal, as though someone had parachuted a geisha girl into the middle of a battlefield.

"I don't care much for politics," Naomi said, "but I do believe in what the Christian Coalition is doing. So even though I don't normally go to political rallies, I wanted to be here."

I thanked Naomi for coming and then headed to the back of the hall as Elizabeth Dole, looking poised and attractive as always, held forth from the podium. As a committed Christian who spoke openly about her faith, Elizabeth was one of Bob Dole's greatest assets. The Dole campaign often sent her to address pro-family audiences, where she pledged her husband's fidelity to the conservative cause and spoke movingly about her own religious beliefs. Particularly given the contrast with Hillary Rodham Clinton, many at the grassroots hungered for a conservative, pro-family First Lady who would be a symbol for their values the way Mrs. Clinton had served as a symbol for liberal values.

"Bob Dole supported the pro-life plank in 1980, 1984, 1988, and 1992, and he will support it again in 1996," she promised. The crowd cheered approvingly.

Michael Barone of *U.S. News* and Ron Brownstein of the *Los Angeles Times* sauntered over and asked how our members would vote in the straw poll. I replied that they were spread all over the map, with Dole, Gramm, Buchanan, and Keyes all receiving a healthy chunk. Alexander was also making a surprising run. Many remained undecided on the night before the vote. By declining to endorse a candidate, we had avoided the trap of appearing to dictate the nominee to the party. There was no "Christian

Coalition" candidate for president. We had dodged the bullet that brought down organized labor in 1984, when the AFL-CIO made the mistake of endorsing Walter Mondale early and then was blamed when he lost forty-nine states. In 1996 we were being courted by all the candidates, and like a debutante at the cotillion, we refused to surrender our heart (or our chastity) to any of them.

After the rally the crowd scattered, and the candidates hustled to a live televised debate scheduled for that evening on *Larry King Live*. Sitting cross-legged on a metal chair in a back room with bare concrete walls and with electrical cables strewn about, I was surrounded by a blur of noise and confusion. I marveled that our participation in the pageantry of politics was now treated by the media as almost humdrum. Our rally had featured every major presidential candidate or his spouse, dozens of state legislators, the state commissioner of education, the governor of South Carolina, and two thousand grassroots activists. The majority of the delegates to a preliminary straw poll that might well determine the nominee of one of the nation's two major political parties were religious conservatives. Yet no one viewed our presence with alarm any longer. What a contrast from the Republican national convention in Houston in 1992, where many of the same delegates were treated as if they were horned monsters rising from the swamp.

These activists are not seeking to win government goodies or curry favor with politicians. They are reluctant political actors. After two generations of self-imposed retreat from political involvement, they have reentered the political arena with a common purpose and an uncommon enthusiasm. They look out upon a society they see as torn asunder by explicit sex and violence on television, rampant divorce, skyrocketing illegitimacy, epidemics of crime and drugs, and a million teen pregnancies every year. Their way of life and their values are under assault. For these activists, the most important issue in the nation is not "the economy, stupid," as the sign in the Clinton campaign headquarters proclaimed. It is the culture, the family, a loss of values, a decline in civility, and the destruction of our children.

Most politicians miss the heart and soul of this concern. They debate issues like accountants. As they headed into the 1996 elections, two of the most hotly touted topics in American politics were the flat tax and the balanced budget amendment. Those are important issues. But a flat tax will not teach a child right from wrong when a friend offers drugs or easy sex. A balanced budget amendment cannot provide a male role model to a young boy in the inner city who has no father. The nation is hungering for public figures to address these moral concerns—Hillary Clinton has called them "the politics of meaning," Dan Quayle called them "family values," while Bill Bennett has termed them the "politics of virtue." But it is not on such labels but rather on the root causes of moral drift that our national politics will turn in the coming years. On that there is little disagreement. What makes religious conservatives controversial—and essential—to the debate over values is their insistence that, in the end, the answers to moral decline can be found only with a return to faith in God.

From the moment the religious conservative movement burst upon the national political scene in 1979 with the dizzying ascent of the Moral Majority, the press and political establishment reacted with horror. Jerry Falwell, James Robison, and a cadre of preachers and religious broadcasters had awakened the slumbering giant of the American evangelical church. Their supporters poured out of the pews and into the precincts, becoming the most formidable grassroots army since the rise of the labor unions. When the movement played a central role in electing Ronald Reagan and giving Republicans control of the Senate in 1980, their critics reacted ferociously, calling them "fascists," "extremists," and "fanatics." Falwell later found himself embroiled in the financial mess of the PTL scandal and beat a quiet retreat from the political scene. The embarrassing sex scandals that rocked religious broadcasting in the late 1980s, culminating with the collapse of PTL and the fall from grace of Jimmy Swaggart, robbed the movement of the power of the electronic church that had once been its mainstay. The movement seemed dead, and the cultural elites danced on its grave.

For believers, however, the grave is always followed by resurrection. The silent and plodding return began with the founding of the Christian

Coalition in 1989, a year that saw the pro-family movement fighting a desperate (and losing) rearguard action. The Supreme Court upheld a Missouri pro-life law, sparking a vicious counterreaction from the pro-abortion lobby. The National Abortion Rights Action League targeted pro-life state legislators across the country and poured millions into their opponents' campaigns. Two pro-life Republican gubernatorial candidates—in Virginia and New Jersey—waffled on the abortion issue and lost to pro-choice Democrats. Plans to legalize school prayer were quietly shelved. The number of conservative votes in Congress dwindled to barely enough to sustain President Bush's abortion vetoes.

How could the pro-family movement recover from the body blows it had suffered and regain the momentum of the early Reagan years? The way they chose was to focus on local politics and local issues. Thus the Christian Coalition began quietly building a formidable network of grassroots activists, who organized their neighborhoods, sponsored training workshops, identified friendly voters, and passed out voter education literature. A number of independent pro-family groups began to sprout up across the country, gaining newfound clout by lobbying state legislatures and producing well-researched policy papers. The media mostly ignored those changes. For three years we breathed new life into the movement, all with little fanfare. When the Christian Coalition showed its new strength in the successful Clarence Thomas confirmation struggle, the media attacked once again. Our opponents clearly hoped that we would repeat the mistakes of the old religious right, overplaying our hand, using overheated rhetoric, and becoming an easy target for the left. But they were swiftly disappointed. The grassroots were smarter, tougher, and wiser. They were seasoned veterans of many political battles. Now, nearly two decades after the first religious conservatives broke into national politics, we are a part of the scenery, a permanent fixture on the political landscape, treated with respect by our allies and grudging admiration by our foes.

The candidate forum in Orlando that balmy November evening underscored a central reality that will shape American politics in the 1990s. No longer a bipolar world dominated by Republicans and Democrats,

America has become a fragmented, fractious republic of what James Madison called "factions"—citizen movements held together by shared values rather than party loyalty. Perot voters, property rights advocates, term limits supporters, environmental "greens," antitax activists, gays, gun lobbyists, home schoolers, and evangelical Christians are transforming politics in a dramatic fashion. The most effective among these citizen efforts is an emerging coalition of evangelicals, Greek Orthodox, and traditionalist Roman Catholics. Their goal: to limit government, reinvigorate the family, and restore the culture's Judeo-Christian principles. Their hierarchy of loyalties is uncompromisingly simple: They are people of faith first, Americans second, and Republicans or Democrats third. And they are proving yet again that man does not live by bread alone. The real battle for the soul of our nation is not fought primarily over the gross national product and the prime interest rate, but over virtues, values, and the culture.

There are those among the dominant elites and opinion makers who treat these religious convictions and the people who hold them as a danger to be feared. I believe they are a solution waiting to happen. For we must never forget, as George Will has observed, that the case for democracy is not aesthetic—it is philosophical. A dictatorship is efficient, quiet, and inhumane. In the chilling phrase about fascist Italy, Mussolini made the trains run on time. In a democracy, the trains sometimes run late, the conversation is loud, and disputes can turn contentious and occasionally downright nasty. But that dissent is a small price to pay for freedom. Indeed, this noise is not a sign of weakness; it is a sign of strength. And among the noisiest disputes are those introduced into the body politic by people of faith. Sure, the mixture of religion and politics sparks controversy. But this nation's thirty million religious conservatives are forcing us to talk about things that must be talked about. They are not going to be silent or go away. Nor should they.

The case for democracy is that the rights of government derive from the consent of the governed, and the surest antidote to tyranny is a free people that believes it owes allegiance to a Higher Power, not the government. The consent of the governed rests upon faith in a sovereign God to which government itself is subject. In this greater moral context, faith as political force is not undemocratic; it is the very essence of democracy.

Over the past six years, as executive director of one of the nation's leading public policy organizations, I have traveled an average of 200,000 miles a year, living out of a suitcase in a string of anonymous hotels and by-ways, crisscrossing the country and delivering hundreds of speeches to the faithful in hotels, churches, and meeting halls. This endless travel has required the commitment of my wife Jo Anne and our three young children, who have provided emotional support in the struggle. They are also a constant reminder of the reason why I and so many are engaged in it. On this frenetic schedule I have been sustained by the inescapable conclusion that our time as people of faith has finally come.

The reasons are clear: To look at America today is to witness a nation struggling against forces as dangerous as any military foe it has ever faced. The threats, however, come not from without but from within. Families are disintegrating, fathers are abandoning their children, abortion is the most common medical procedure in the nation, and young people attend schools that are not safe and in which they do not learn. In the inner city illegitimacy is rampant, drug deals are openly conducted on streetcorners, hopelessness is the norm, and children are shot by marauding carloads of juvenile gang members. There is no economic solution to this social chaos—it is a collection of moral problems that require moral solutions.

The pro-family movement grows and prospers by addressing these problems. Our solutions are so morally compelling that we can no longer be denied our place in the conversation we call democracy. We shall experience triumph and disappointment, victory and defeat, leaps of progress followed by frustrating setbacks, but we will not be denied what is right. I believe in the unforgettable words of the abolitionist preacher Theodore Parker: "The curve of the moral universe is long, but it leads towards justice."

Whittaker Chambers wrote in his autobiography *Witness* that when he left Communism he felt as though he had passed from the winning side to join the losers. Those were chilling words for anyone who lived during the Cold War. The American revolutionaries in their day, the Communists in their time, and the left in the 1960s all possessed a unique and powerful conviction that history was on their side. Today that conviction no longer belongs to liberals or their allies, but to the right and, more particularly, to religious conservatives. The once morally persuasive and politically powerful left has lost its voice. Where once it was a vanguard on behalf of minorities and the downtrodden, today it is a special-interest polyglot of quotas and set-asides. Its eloquent defense of voting rights and economic equality for women has been drowned out by the extremist demands of the abortion lobby. Its voice for the have-nots has been garbled by a shameful defense of a bloated and unresponsive poverty industry.

But more than any other failure, it is their myopic rejection of religion as a "fanatical" intrusion into politics that has paved the way for the success of the pro-family movement. For today, religious conservatives are poised to enter an era of American life in which moral issues, and the pro-family agenda, will predominate.

Those social undercurrents are far more important than the outcome of the 1996 elections. If the Republicans can make the election a referendum on Clinton's record, he will be a one-term president. But Clinton is a gifted politician who will borrow shamelessly from the rhetoric and campaign themes of conservatives in order to get reelected. His campaign is plagiarizing the Reagan reelection strategy of 1984. That will make the presidential contest competitive and close. But no matter what the outcome in 1996, Clinton is already governing on conservative terms, agreeing to a balanced budget in seven years, delivering homilies in support of school prayer, promising to "end welfare as we know it," dumping Joycelyn Elders and other left-wing lightning rods, and abandoning the pet causes of liberalism.

Bill Clinton cannot win the debate over ideas, but the Republicans could lose, especially if the party abandons its unapologetic pro-life and pro-family policies. If its presidential nominee chooses a running mate or runs on a platform that sends a signal of retreat on issues dear to pro-family voters, support for the party among its religious base will bleed away as if from a slashed artery. The "big tent" will collapse, and a third party featuring an evangelical Ross Perot figure could mushroom from the dank soil of compromise. If the GOP hopes to win back the White House in 1996, it must be the party of Main Street, not Wall Street, and it must be viewed as a pro-family party, not narrowly pro-business.

It is one of the ironies of our time that as society has become increasingly secular, religion has become a more potent force than ever in a cynical and alienated electorate. More than by the Perot movement or the independent voter, the destiny of American politics will be determined by the energized evangelical, the devout Roman Catholic, and the observant Jew.

· To many, this reality comes as a profound surprise. In 1989, when Jerry Falwell closed down the Moral Majority, many declared the religious conservative movement dead. Editorials and columns gloated that after generating much heat, it had simply fizzled out. According to some it was like a "summer flower" that blossomed once and quickly faded. Few believed there was any future for the movement at all. Dark forebodings of irrelevance abounded. Even some evangelicals agreed. Christian groups had campaigned for years on issues like abortion and school prayer "without achieving one piece of legislation," one prominent evangelical theologian observed. And David Frum, author of the 1994 book *Dead Right*, proved that sometimes the conservative chattering class can be as wrong as their liberal counterparts. In his book and in later columns and articles, Frum wrote that a "poor, relatively uneducated group" would not "win very many fights, and is hardly in a position to start them." He wondered how a group "so few in number and so politically weak" had ever "generated so much fuss."

How did the Christian Coalition rise from the rubble of the televangelism scandals and political defeats of the late 1980s to become one of the most effective grassroots political organizations in the country? The answer may surprise you.

After his bruising 1988 presidential campaign, Pat Robertson returned to rebuild the battered finances of the Christian Broadcasting Network, which had suffered more than $100 million in lost revenues in his absence. Robertson had come in third in the Republican presidential primaries, trailing George Bush and Bob Dole. The financial network and grassroots army he had built during this presidential campaign provided a ready-made base for a new political movement. But what form would it take?

In the spring of 1989 Robertson received a phone call from Billy Mc-Cormack, his Louisiana state coordinator, that would prove fateful. "You brought hundreds of thousands of people into the political process," Mc-Cormack said. "Unless you provide them with leadership now, all you have worked for will be lost, and all the blood and treasure you have spent will be for nought." Robertson agreed and some time later sent out invitations to a meeting of key campaign operatives and other pro-family leaders to discuss the future of the religious conservative movement.

In late September 1989 Robertson convened the meeting at a downtown hotel in Atlanta. Many of the most prominent pro-family leaders in the nation attended. They groused about having been asked to carry water in presidential campaigns for Reagan and Bush while being given little input into policy or personnel. That reinforced the feeling among the leaders that they were like urchins with their hands out. Their level of political maturity—and frustration—was rising. They now understood that all the pro-life platforms in the world were a poor substitute for committed conservatives serving in government.

The movement was at a turning point. Unless it did something to reassert its strength, it would continue to be taken for granted by Republican politicians and discounted by the press. It needed to build a permanent, lasting political infrastructure. Two ideas dominated the discussion. Several leaders proposed a large convocation to call for a rightward turn in government and a return to traditional values—a kind of political Billy Graham crusade that would fire up the troops and draw massive media attention. The proposed name was the American Congress of Christian Citizens. The idea was to fill the Houston Astrodome or some other huge arena in the South or West with twenty thousand to thirty thousand supporters. Such a meeting, it was felt, would be a tangible expression of the movement's political clout.

The second idea was for a grassroots citizen group that would "give Christians a voice in government again." Robertson passed out a proposed mission statement with a five-fold purpose, which included training Christians for effective social action, combating antireligious bigotry, alerting Christians of issues and legislation on a timely basis, speaking out for pro-family values in the media, and representing people of faith at every level of government. The reception to this plan, the brainstorm of Robertson, was less overwhelming. Many leaders, like Beverly LaHaye of Concerned Women for America or Don Wildmon of the American Family Association, already had large and formidable organizations. They wondered if another group was necessary. Grassroots leaders were also nervous. Many had launched small, struggling state-based or community-based groups bearing innocuous names like the Family Policy Network. Did they want another national organization that would compete for dollars and moreover could become a lightning rod for the national media, as the Moral Majority had been in the 1980s?

Robertson had invited me to attend the meeting after I bumped into him at an event at the Bush inaugural in early 1989. At his request I had sent him a memorandum on how to organize a grassroots organization—a group that had no name but would later become the Christian Coalition. My background was as a Republican political operative and a historian, though I was a committed Christian. I did not consider myself a "Christian activist," but I shared many of the values of the movement and wanted to see religion play a more vital role in the public life of the nation. The memorandum recommended that the new group focus on building a state-by-state, county-by-county grassroots organization that reached all the way down to the neighborhood level. It also advocated teaching those pouring into the political process how to be effective citizens by launching an ambitious training program modeled after the leadership schools of Morton Blackwell, a longtime conservative who had served in the Reagan White House and whose political activism stretched back to the Goldwater campaign.

When some present were critical of the idea of launching a new organization, I leaned forward and said to Pat, "I think there is a real need and a huge constituency out there."

Although offered an opportunity to become involved in the project earlier, I waited until I had finished my doctorate in history at Emory University. My real goal was to write and to teach at the collegiate level. I was writing literally the final three pages of my dissertation when Pat called and invited me to attend the meeting. The timing was providential. As attracted as I was to the idea of a life in the cloisters of academe, the opportunity to help rebuild the remnants of the religious conservative movement was more compelling. When Pat introduced me to the others in attendance as the "first staff member" of the new organization, I was as shocked as everyone else. But the sense of adventure was irresistible, and the possibilities for success seemed almost limitless.

The meeting adjourned with a decision to pursue both projects simultaneously. The idea was to begin forming a grassroots network across the nation and to use it to feed into the American Congress of Christian Citizens. I moved to Virginia Beach, and began the arduous work of launching a direct-mail fund-raising effort and making the first grassroots contacts from lists of activists left over from the campaign. Sifting through the wreckage of the presidential campaign, I sat in an old warehouse building surrounded by the relics of its heyday: abandoned mail machines, inflatable elephants, an IBM mainframe computer that we sold for salvage, and thousands of cassette tapes bearing the title, "What I Will Do as President." Phones jangled all day with disgruntled vendors still owed money by the defunct campaign. I was reminded of Winston Churchill's observation, "Politics is almost as exciting as war and quite as dangerous. In war you can only be killed once, but in politics many times."

All that occurred against a backdrop of the deepening disappointment of many religious conservative leaders as the Bush administration assembled a government. George Bush was elected in 1988 as the first incumbent vice president to succeed a sitting president since Martin Van Buren followed Andrew Jackson in 1836. Bush had campaigned as a conservative and had pledged to assemble what would have been in effect the third term of Ronald Reagan. Pro-family voters had played a prominent role in his victory—one-third of all voters listed abortion as their main reason for voting—and they cast their ballots for Bush by a margin of two to one. But after the campaign ended, many Reaganites throughout the government were politely asked to leave. A group of evangelical leaders led by Pat Robertson, Jim Dobson, and Bob Dugan submitted names of qualified conservative evangelicals to the Bush transition team. A number of them met with Bush and Chase Untemeyer, director of White House personnel, just before the Bush inaugural and provided them with a list of individuals and the posts they were seeking. Untemeyer and others promised to give the list full consideration.

The personnel selection process got off to a rocky start almost immediately. When the White House floated the name of Dr. Louis Sullivan, president of Morehouse College Medical School in Atlanta, as Secretary of Health and Human Services, the pro-family movement balked. After delivering a huge vote for Bush in the fall, the last thing they expected was for a pro-choice moderate to head the cabinet department with responsibility for social policy affecting families and children. Sullivan was also weak on other important items in the pro-family agenda, such as funding of Planned Parenthood. Paul Weyrich, a longtime Washington-based conservative activist, and others peppered John Sununu, the new White House chief of staff, with messages of protest. But there was a problem: Sullivan was a friend of Barbara Bush. The post had already been offered to him, and he had accepted. With the assistance of George W. Bush, the president's politically savvy son, Sununu contacted Kay James, an eloquent pro-life spokeswoman and prominent conservative African-American, and offered her a post as Assistant Secretary of HHS for public affairs. Kay agreed to serve in the position, sparing the administration a major explosion on the right. But the entire episode left a bad taste in the mouth of the religious conservative community.

Other conservative Christian candidates for high-profile jobs faced a similar fate. Judge Paul Pressler of Houston, a conservative lay leader in the Southern Baptist Convention and a longtime friend of George Bush, was originally recommended for Solicitor General or federal district judge. He later accepted the newly created post of ethics czar. But Pressler withdrew his name from consideration after he came under attack from liberal Baptists and moderates within the Bush White House, who leaked allegations against him to the *Washington Post*. This pattern repeated itself numerous times. Pro-family leaders also lobbied for Patricia Heinz, who had served in the Reagan White House, for a slot as Assistant Secretary for Education, a powerful post with oversight over much of the department's budget. When Senator Ted Kennedy objected, Heinz instead received a post at the Pentagon overseeing the training of Navy personnel, a job that did not require Senate confirmation. Another strong conservative, Hal Ezell, was serving as a deputy regional commissioner of the Immigration and Naturalization Service. Evangelicals concerned with Jewish emigration from the Soviet Union wanted him reappointed, but he was dumped in favor of a Bush loyalist.

In the end, few evangelicals were appointed or, for that matter, carried over from the Reagan years. By the time the Bush administration held its first cattle call for religious leaders in November 1989, the grumbling was becoming clearly audible. In what was supposed to be a typical hand-holding exhibition at the White House, several rose to challenge Chase Untemeyer, director of presidential personnel, as to why so few evangelicals had been selected for prominent posts. Untemeyer argued that it violated the law to "count" people according to religious beliefs.

Finally, Pat Robertson rose to speak. "Isn't it interesting that you have no difficulty identifying evangelicals and their allies during the campaign," he said, "but you cannot find them after the election?" The room exploded with laughter and applause.

Religious conservatives had grown tired of being patronized. Their leaders gathered for a planning meeting in February 1990 at the Mayflower Hotel in Washington, DC, held in conjunction with the National Prayer Breakfast. Among those in attendance were Tim and Beverly LaHaye, Jerry Falwell, Chuck Colson, the Reverend Charles Stanley, D. James Kennedy, and several prominent Roman Catholic organizers. It was one of the largest gatherings of religious conservative leaders in many years.

Spirits were upbeat, but it was clear that financial resources and grassroots organization were exhausted. Many groups had seen their memberships wither and their budgets plummet following the charge-the-breastworks atmosphere of the past decade. When the subject of contributing money (the proposed convocation would cost nearly $1 million) or lending mailing lists came up, many fell silent.

Were the grassroots ready for another crusade? Some were not sanguine about the prospects. "One thing I have learned about Christians, having organized them for years," Jerry Falwell said. "When they lose, they quit. And when they win they quit. We are just quitters." We knew we needed to propose a long-term vision that would stretch not for one election cycle or a single decade, but for an entire generation. To that end, we targeted the fall of 1990 as the date for the American Congress of Christian Citizens, just prior to the elections.

A few days later I flew to California for my first organizing trip for the Christian Coalition on the West Coast. In Orange County I spoke to a packed breakfast meeting with an overflow crowd spilling into the halls. The electricity in the room showed that the grassroots desperately wanted a new vehicle for affecting public policy. Later I dropped by the headquarters of Focus on the Family, headed by influential Christian radio psychologist Jim Dobson, where the public policy staff grilled me on our intentions. Did Pat Robertson plan on running for president again? No, I replied. Were we planning to start a Christian third party? No again. We parted on good terms, but clearly there were suspicions about whether or not the Christian Coalition was simply a front for another Robertson presidential bid.

About a month later, Pat Robertson and I were flying to another Coalition organizational event when I laid out for him the time and effort that would be necessary to put on the Christian Congress event in Atlanta. It was taking more and more of my time, pulling me away from my grassroots activity.

"Pat, we have to decide to do one or the other," I said. "We are either going to do one extremely well, or both poorly. If you want an effective grassroots network, we may need to put the idea of the political rally on the back burner."

Pat looked out the window of the airplane and nodded. "We have to have the grassroots organization," he said. "It is the hope of the country." After that the Congress project quietly died for lack of attention, and we moved ahead with the most ambitious state-by-state recruitment and training program in the history of the pro-family movement. It was a decision that would have far-reaching consequences for the movement and the country in the years to come.

My arrival at this position of responsibility and leadership was the culmination of a long personal odyssey. It all began in Miami, where I grew up. My childhood was hardly spent in the Bible Belt. Miami was an international city in which whites were a bare majority, with a large population of Cubans, Nicaraguans, Haitians, and African-Americans. It also had a large Jewish population, and I attended more bar mitzvahs than baptisms as I grew up. My father was an ophthalmologist and surgeon, and my mother worked at home. I grew up in a fairly typical middle-class neighborhood, where I attended public schools, joined a local swim club, learned to play golf, and followed the Miami Dolphins. But from an early age my greatest passion was reading. Most children of my generation watched *Sesame Street.* I read the autobiography of Eddie Rickenbacker, Sandburg's *Lincoln, The Rise and Fall of the Third Reich* by William L. Shirer, *The Best and the Brightest* by David Halberstam, and *All the President's Men* by Bob Woodward and Carl Bernstein. The political figures in those books—especially Churchill, Lincoln, and Roosevelt—came to life in my young mind.

Shirer's account of Britain's failure to heed the warnings of Churchill and stop the rise of Hitler chilled my bones. I also recall reading a biography of Woodrow Wilson and being enthralled by an account of his election, which had been made possible by the support of political bosses like James "Sugar Jim" Smith. But in his inaugural address, Wilson had promised to reform the political system and adopt progressive measures, astonishing the corrupt bosses who had mistakenly thought they could control him. I deeply admired these great leaders, sensing that public service was an enormously consequential career and that politics could be a noble calling.

HOW WE GOT THERE

Those stirrings persisted until 1972, when both the Democrats and the Republicans brought their national conventions to Miami. It was unusual for both parties to go to the same place (it has happened only four other times in this century), and the entire city was caught up in the excitement. For a political junkie like me, it was like having front-row seats to the Olympics. In those days, before the advent of CNN and C-Span, the networks broadcast only a few hours of convention coverage each night. But Miami television stations provided gavel-to-gavel coverage, and I watched almost every minute. I was one of the few Americans who watched George McGovern give his acceptance speech to the raucous Democratic convention at 3 A.M. I saw Sammy Davis, Jr., hug Richard Nixon at a rally of Young Republicans. Because Nixon often landed at Homestead Air Force Base, just a few minutes from my home, I watched his helicopter pass right over my neighborhood on his way to renomination. Because of the Vietnam War and the Twenty-second Amendment giving eighteen-year-olds the right to vote, the involvement of young people in politics was a hot topic. I remember the hippies, the yippies, the antiwar demonstrators, and a young Gary Hart in blue jeans and open-collar shirt running the McGovern campaign. I figured: If they can be involved in politics, why can't I?

A friend of my family ran for Congress in Miami in 1976, and I worked on his campaign. I walked door to door handing out campaign literature, stood on the side of the highway holding "Burma Shave" signs, and walked in front of shopping malls wearing sandwich boards. It was hardly glamorous work, but I was hooked.

I ran for student council president at my junior high school on a progressive platform that promised Coke machines in the gym locker rooms and greater student participation in school affairs. Since I was only about five feet tall at the time, I painted campaign signs that read, "Vote for Ralph Reed: The Little Giant." Few of the other students understood the reference to Stephen A. Douglas in his 1860 presidential campaign, but the slogan caught on anyway. During a school assembly where the candidates were supposed to give campaign speeches, I packed the hall early with my sign-waving supporters, spreading them throughout the audience so that when they cheered my applause lines, the clapping would ripple through the audience. Later I learned that this use of what is known in political parlance as a "diamond pattern" is a tried-and-true tactic in campaigns. For me it was pure instinct. When the votes were counted I won in a landslide.

In 1976 my family moved to Toccoa, Georgia, a small town in the rural northeast section of the state. At the local high school I formed a conservative club and campaigned for Gerald Ford, a heresy in then-Democratic Georgia, where Jimmy Carter was the former governor. After betting my math teacher that Ford would win, I had to wear a peanut sign and carry a can of Planter's peanuts around my high school for a day as the price of losing. I was elected senior class president and decided to pursue a career in politics after attending college and law school. I attended Boys State, the American Legion program for young political leaders, and the Youth Assembly, a youth-in-government program sponsored by the YMCA, wherein budding adolescent legislators occupied the state capitol for a weekend, passing bills and debating laws. During my senior year in high school I represented Georgia at National Affairs, a national YMCA debate conference, where it seemed that every other person I met thought he or she would be president some day. There I began making the political contacts that would serve me in the future. (I proposed a bill to eliminate the sales tax on food and medicine and increase property taxes for large corporations, a surprisingly liberal proposal that lost by a single vote.)

Despite my involvement in Christian groups like the YMCA, my faith was not an important dimension in my political involvement until some years later. I had been raised in the Methodist church and generally held to conservative views on most issues because of my upbringing in a Republican household. As the Moral Majority flowered in the late 1970s, I remained a secular political activist. Nevertheless, my political views were remarkably similar to those in the budding religious movement. I traveled to Atlanta in 1980 as a freshman in college to lobby the state legislature to raise the drinking age. On a day set aside for student testimony, I strode to the well and told an audience of several hundred people that lowering the drinking age had led to more traffic accidents that were killing young people on our highways. "The battle will be difficult and the opposition fierce," I said. "But the truth, no matter how softly spoken, will always prevail." I do not know who was more shocked by my testimony, the slack-jawed legislators or the stunned students who packed the gallery. The bill raising the drinking age passed easily, though my involvement played only a minor role.

Occasionally I worked for causes some might consider liberal. When Zell Miller, who was then lieutenant governor, proposed raising the sales tax and dropping the tax on food, I walked door to door and gathered more than a thousand signatures in support of the tax break for the poor and elderly. Miller wrote me a generous thank-you note and offered me an internship at the state legislature, which I eagerly accepted. After attending classes in the morning, I drove to the state capitol building in Atlanta, where I attended committee hearings, tracked legislation, and hobnobbed with state legislators. I was a conservative, but I admired Miller in spite of our ideological differences. When the Equal Rights Amendment came to a vote in the Georgia state senate, Miller stepped down from the president's chair and delivered a stirring speech in favor of equal rights for women. While I opposed the ERA even at that young age, I admired Miller's eloquence. I hoped that someday I too could speak out for what I believed in.

My political baptism by fire took place when Georgia's Senator Herman Talmadge, who was plagued by ethics charges, faced a bitter reelection fight. Talmadge was a living legend in the state, and either he or his father Eugene had served in statewide office since the 1930s. As the chairman of the College Republican club at the University of Georgia, I leafleted the campus with Republican fliers, identified conservative students and registered them to vote, and built a formidable campus organization. We appointed "dorm captains," floor deputies, and apartment building coordinators whose job was to canvass every student in their buildings and ensure that anyone planning to vote for Reagan was registered and received a ride to the polls. We plastered the dormitories with hot-pink brochures tweaking "Herman the Hermit" for refusing to visit the campus and meet with students. In a mock election, we carried the campus by landslides for both Ronald Reagan and the Republican Senate nominee, Mack Mattingly. To poke fun at Talmadge's ethics problems, we decided to dramatize the hearings before the Senate Ethics Committee where the senator's ex-wife had testified that she often found wads of cash in his raincoat. I came up with the idea of hanging a trench coat on a coat rack outside the student center and inviting students to guess how much money was in the coat pockets. The person guessing the closest to the actual amount won all the money—and the raincoat. The stunt gained a load of publicity for our College Republican club.

On Election Day, Mack Mattingly won by only twenty thousand votes out of more than a million cast, a squeaker victory that made him the first Republican senator from the state since Reconstruction. Invited to intern in his office, I came to Washington as an eyewitness to the Reagan Revolution. In 1983 I became executive director of the national College Republicans, mobilizing the youth vote for Reagan during his reelection campaign in 1984, and worked with top Republican operatives like Lee Atwater and Ed Rollins.

Our goal at the College Republicans was ambitious and generational in scope. Just as Tom Hayden and the Students for a Democratic Society had transformed American politics in the 1960s and the early 1970s by turning the youth vote into a potent political force, we hoped to create a generation of committed conservatives that would be a mirror image of the new left. Grover Norquist, a former executive director of the National Taxpayers Union, was the driving force behind this effort. With an MBA from Harvard and uncommon political organizing skills, Grover taught me and dozens of others how to build a campus network that helped make eighteen- to twenty-four-year-olds stronger supporters of Ronald Reagan than any other age group. Jack Abramoff, the national chairman of the College Republicans, was a conservative firebrand from Brandeis University, who later went on to a career as an attorney and a Republican activist. I became friends during the Reagan era with many other conservative college students who are now state legislators, members of Congress, or top party operatives.

During that period I experienced the first stirrings of what would become a religious awakening. As a lifelong Methodist, I believed intellectually in the tenets of the Christian faith but had gradually drifted away from the church. In the rough-and-tumble of politics, I began to sense the need for spiritual roots. While I found much that was good and honorable in politics, I recognized instinctively that the allure of fame and power could not satisfy my hunger for a transcendent meaning for my life. I needed more.

My yearnings could be summed up in the words of Lee Atwater, with whom I became acquainted when he worked in the Reagan White House and later helped run the Reagan campaign in 1984 and the Bush campaign in 1988. "[Y]ou can acquire all you want and still feel empty," Lee later said during his losing battle with cancer. Like Lee, I was a bare-knuckle political operative. And like Lee, my heart would be softened and my political style changed by a faith experience.[5]

In 1983 I made a faith commitment and began to attend an evangelical church in Washington. My religious beliefs never changed my views on the issues to any great degree, because my political philosophy was already well developed. As a conservative, I believed in less government, lower taxes, tougher laws against crime and drugs, and policies to strengthen the family. After my faith experience, I became more skeptical of government's ability to legislate morality or reform people's souls. But I did believe that government should protect children and strengthen families. More than shifting my ideology, my Christian faith caused me to shift my tactics. No longer a tough political arm-twister who would do whatever it took to win, I began to call my former enemies and offer to break bread with them or pray for them, and occasionally tried to bridge differences. For someone trained in the old-fashioned school of political hardball, it was quite a transformation. Some of my old foes were speechless.

Faith to me is not an ideology but a way of life. Someone once asked me if I believed Jesus Christ was a Republican. I answered that he was neither a Republican nor a Democrat. God's motives are higher than ours and His message of love and redemption transcends politics. There are liberals who are good people, who love God as they understand Him to be, and who lead lives of character and decency. They are simply wrong on some of the issues. There were Christian slaveholders, Christians opposed to the

American Revolution, and Christians who supported segregation. That did not make them bad people or mean they were going to hell—but it did mean that they were mistaken.

There have been numerous examples throughout history when people motivated by religious faith did great harm because they were convinced they had a monopoly on the truth. The English Civil War, the Crusades, and the Salem witch trials all showed religion at its most dogmatic and dangerous. But I have never believed that I had all the answers or a special dispensation of God's will. Becoming a Christian doesn't mean you are never wrong, only that you are forgiven.

What does it mean to be a person of faith in the political arena? It is no different from being a Christian in any other vocation. If a Christian is an attorney, he seeks to win his case as aggressively and fairly as possible. If he is the starting middle linebacker for a professional football team, he tries to stop the other team. Politics is a contact sport. I have a job to do, and it involves trying to advance my agenda. In that combat, I play hard and I try to win. But I never hit below the belt, I play according to the rules of fairness and courtesy, and after the game is over, I always help my opponent up off the turf. My faith is not a function of my politics. When the last tackle is over and the game ends, I kneel on the field with other players of both teams and ask for God's blessings. That is the proper perspective of faith in politics—not that I am right and you are wrong, or that I have all the answers and you are an enemy of God, but that we are both flawed human beings in an imperfect world in search of the truth who are asking for His guidance in the struggle.

During the past few years we have heard a lot about the dangers of Christian political activism. The argument goes that we are claiming the imprimatur of God and implicitly damning all of our foes. Some have said that since we call ourselves the "Christian Coalition," we believe it is implicitly "un-Christian" to oppose anything in our legislative agenda—from a balanced budget to restricting abortion. That is nonsense, of course. We can win these issues on their merits; we need not impugn the religious beliefs of our opponents. Others have said that we care more about political power than the traditional Christian concerns of charity, love, and caring for the poor. Our critics scrawl a harsh caricature of conservative people of faith as uneducated boobs who live in trailer parks, wear overalls, drive pickup trucks, eat moonpies, and hate women and minorities—the final and ugly backwash of George Wallace's and David Duke's politics of rage. Some have suggested that our movement is explicitly racist, anti-Semitic or morally intolerant. Frequently this opinion pops up on editorial pages, occasionally on television, and often in the hysterical warnings of groups on the radical left dedicated to stemming the rising tide of religious conservatism. Former Democratic representative Robert Drinan, a Catholic priest, called us "arrogant and ignorant," charging that the Christian Coalition believed that all those opposing its political agenda were "not acting like Christians."

Those claims are not only untrue, but their tone shows a lack of understanding about the central—I believe essential—role that religion has played in our political affairs from the earliest days of our republic. Nor is the demonic image of the pro-family movement matched by the demographics of its supporters. It is a predominantly middle-class, highly educated, suburban phenomenon of baby-boomers with children who are motivated by their concerns about family and a sense of values. The religious conservative community has greatly matured in recent years by broadening its message and narrowing its aspirations to those that are appropriate for any other group in a pluralistic society. Unlike fundamentalist political movements in the Middle East, religious conservatives in the United States are properly understood as an interest group within a democratic order. If they gained power, they would not repeal the Constitution or attempt to impose their religion on others through the state. Yet that process of maturation and growth has gone largely unreported.

Religious conservatives do not claim to have all the answers, but we do think we have identified many of the problems: illegitimacy, family breakup, cultural decay, illiteracy, crime, violence, and a poverty of spirit afflicting our land. For the vast majority of our supporters there has never been an understanding that God is a Republican or even a member of the

Christian Coalition. We are people of faith struggling to do what is right, nothing more. We are sometimes wrong. As Lincoln observed during the Civil War, while I know that God is always on the side of right and that He hates injustice, I am less concerned about whether God is on our side than I am that we be found on His. This is the proper perspective of faith in politics: a fiery conviction of right and wrong tempered by a humility before God and a respect for one's foes.

One reason for the remarkable political strength of religious conservatives is simply that liberals and Democrats have abandoned religion as the basis of their own political activity. A quick look back at the history of religious reform in America reminds us that this is a nation with a vibrant religious background. The projection of evangelical and orthodox faith as a political force stretches back to the founding of the country. In fact, almost every great social movement in American history was founded by people of profound religious faith, and has been deeply at odds with prevailing secular values. This unacknowledged truth underscores the hypocrisy of the intolerant liberal attacks on religious conservatives. In their rush to embrace the secular values of modern American culture and to distance themselves from the "unsophisticated masses" of simple Christian believers, today's liberals have forgotten the religious roots of their own social movement. But as I hope to show in the following chapters, far from being a sharp break with America's political past, the Christian Coalition represents a recovery of its most honored and noble traditions.

2

ALL GOD'S CHILDREN

To many in society today the idea of combining religion and politics is like mixing oil and water—or perhaps kerosene and fire. The two simply should not be discussed in the same sentence in polite company, and the pairing certainly has no place in modern, enlightened America. That is true in our political debate, where our movement is portrayed as out of touch with "modern" and "post-Christian" America, and it is true of the popular understanding of history as well, where it is believed that the great social movements of the past century were largely the result of numerous nice secular people getting together to make the world a better place.

Those beliefs are of a recent vintage and run counter to three centuries of American history and the deeply ingrained religious impulses of the American people. Indeed, from the days of our founding through the great social movements of the twentieth century—suffrage, labor, the New Deal, and civil rights—religious impulses borne out in practical politics have been the hallmark of the American experience. In fact, if America has a national political tradition, it is that of religious activism firmly rooted in millennialism. Christians have been the conscience of the nation, shining a light on every kind of injustice and driving the efforts of ordinary citizens to realize the promise of equality. The Christian Coalition is founded upon the same religious principles that fueled those massive involvements of churches and synagogues, and of pastors, priests, and rabbis, in some of the greatest social reform movements in American history.

For the most part, those movements existed outside the political mainstream and created pressure for change from without. Even Martin Luther King, Jr., spent most of his active years marching and demonstrating, not organizing precincts or electing politicians. The antiwar movement succeeded in sponsoring student boycotts and moratoriums, but their single foray into the high-stakes game of presidential politics in 1972 reduced the Democratic party to a shambles. The Christian Coalition is very different from its predecessors, because it has normalized a religious impulse that has heretofore been treated as abnormal. It represents a new thing in American politics: the marriage of a sense of social justice with the practical world of modern politics. It has mainstreamed the voice of faith through its political effectiveness, challenging the political system to confront issues of moral and transcendent significance that might otherwise be ignored or swept aside by purely economic concerns.

One would never know this from the image of our movement reflected by the mainstream media. David Broder of the *Washington Post*, one of the nation's most respected journalists, faulted religious conservatives in 1993 for a "righteousness that can easily become strident and intolerant." That may be true of some elements of our movement—or, indeed, those on the left. But the salient question is not whether a religious tradition makes universal claims ("my way is the only true way"). We cannot ask evangelicals to surrender their proselytizing impulse or Roman Catholics to betray their belief that their Church is God's ambassador on earth and that the Pope is its head. The real question is whether a religious tradition (in our case Christianity) attempts to impose its universalist theological claims by force of law. We do not. Ours is a public policy agenda, informed by faith but not dictated by any church. It respects the historical and time-honored separation of church and state while affirming the role of faith in politics. Yet the tone of the criticism of the pro-family movement by some suggests that the mixture of religion with politics leads inexorably toward theocracy.

That claim is belied by the vital role religion has played in our political

affairs from the beginning of the American nation. The civil rights movement, the antiwar protest, the Social Gospel movement, temperance reform, and the women's suffrage campaign all owed their distinctive moral
fervor to the religious beliefs of their supporters. Turning to examine the
history of these earlier social movements will be revealing and instructive.
For one thing, it will suggest a number of surprising parallels between past
and present and may illuminate the tension between what is new and
unique about the Christian Coalition and what is really consistent with established traditions in American politics. But the exercise should also provide object lessons for today's religious conservatives, who stand now at a
critical crossroads. If they choose the path of their predecessors, they may
ultimately be seen as just another of those brief, intense bursts of reformist
enthusiasm that burn brightly but for only a short period, and leave little
lasting legacy. Today's religious activists should strive instead to husband
and channel their enthusiasm in a way that can make their movement a
permanent and notably constructive force in American political life.

Religious-based political activism is neither un-American nor undemocratic. There is no religion that is more thoroughly democratic than the
Christian faith, and no nation that has been more amenable to the growth
of Christianity and the acceptance of Judaism than the United States. The
resurgence of political activism by conservative evangelicals and pro-
family Roman Catholics since the late 1970s is thus neither a troubling nor
a particularly novel phenomenon. We are one of the most religious nations
in the world, and it is only natural that the moral beliefs that derive from
the faith of the people occasionally impact our politics. Throughout our
history the pendulum has swung from left to right, depending upon the
forms of social injustice that needed to be addressed. Whether the issue
was slavery and racism, the plight of labor and the poor, or the right to life
for the unborn and aged, the faith community has always been the most vibrant and effective political force in the electorate. That is what makes the
oft-stated concern about people of faith in politics so puzzling—and tempts
one to think that it is really the emergence of this impulse on the right that
is the source of consternation.

On the other hand, those in the faith community who worry that religion cheapens itself by becoming a political force need to broaden their understanding of the true call of faith. When Abraham laid claim to the land that is now modern Israel, that was a political statement. When Christ said "I am," he made a political statement—and was killed for it. When He told tax-gatherers to take no more than was owed and to give to the poor, that too was a political statement. Faith is not meant to be confined to monasteries or to atrophy behind stained-glass windows. It is supposed to change the way we live, how we treat each other, how we organize our own families and, by extension, the national and human family. That impulse always has a political dimension, and it is the very essence of an active faith.

The close relationship between religious outpourings and shifts in American politics has been thoroughly documented by the historian Robert Fogel, who points out that the great spiritual revivals of the 1740s, 1830s, and 1890s all affected our politics through the rise of the revolutionary, antislavery, and social gospel movements. Today, he argues, we are at the tail end of another such spiritual resurgence that began in the late 1950s with increased church attendance and continued into the 1960s with the charismatic renewal, the rise of fundamentalism, and the relative decline of the main-line denominations. This Fourth Awakening, Fogel suggests, has transformed our politics by shifting debate away from purely economic issues toward cultural concerns.[1]

As far back as the Great Awakening, which ignited the democratic impulses of American patriots, religion was the first political institution in the hearts and minds of the people. Courthouses were far away and not easy for most of the population to reach, colonial government was lax and inefficient, and commercial centers outside of the seaboard cities were almost nonexistent, so the church became the center of community and family life more by default than by design. The dissenting religions that were harassed and regulated in England thrived in the fertile and free soil of the colonies. Whether it was the Quakers in Pennsylvania, the Congregationalists in New England, the Catholics in Maryland, or the Baptists in Virginia, the thirteen original colonies evolved into a distinctly religious society without parallel in recorded history. It was this religious experience as much as po-

ALL GOD'S CHILDREN

litical or economic convulsions that propelled America toward revolution and independence.

Religious revivalism smashed social conventions, eliminated distinctions between the landed gentry and the common folk, and called into question the hierarchical social relationships of the day. When George Whitefield arrived in America in 1738, he preached to crowds that some observers estimated at thirty thousand or more (this at a time when the entire population of the colonies did not exceed 1.5 million). Those uproarious revivals sent some spectators into frenzied fits of frothing, shouting, and rolling around in the grass and shrubbery. The established Anglican church frowned upon such outbursts of religious enthusiasm, recognizing that it posed a threat not only to the church but to the colonial rule of Britain as well. Between 1740 and 1760 Whitefield crisscrossed the colonies, preaching fiery sermons that warned sinners of God's impending judgment and called them to repentance and salvation. He transfixed his audiences with three- and four-hour-long sermons, often delivered without notes in a booming baritone voice that could be heard hundreds of yards away. It was said of the power of Whitefield's preaching that the man who would empty his pockets before going to church emptied them into the offering plate after hearing him preach.[2]

The Great Awakening introduced to American colonists new ideas about liberty and government. Debates and discussions about what America would become were no longer confined to the powder-wigged intellectuals. The preachers who popularized notions of liberty which were prime factors that moved an entire populace to revolt. In the colonial mind, Great Britain became associated with venality, corruption, and religious decline, while America came to be viewed as a bold experiment in righteous republicanism. Millennialism reached a fever pitch, expressed in such proclamations as that of one revolutionary who declared America would be "the principal seat of that glorious kingdom which Christ shall erect upon earth in the latter days."[3]

Preachers constituted what the historian Alan Heimert has called "a black regiment," a critical spark to American resistance to British rule.

The Great Awakening achieved its transformational work more than a decade prior to the Revolution. But what mattered was that churches and coreligionists, regardless of denomination or theology, began to align themselves into religious parties that closely paralleled the groupings in the future political uprising. Congregationalists, particularly the "Old Lights," aligned with Federalists; Baptists and evangelicals with Patrick Henry, Thomas Jefferson, and the republicans; and Quakers with the British Crown. Their voices and their votes were not turned away. When the conflict came to bloodshed, evangelical preachers justified the revolt by arguing that liberty came from a Higher Source and that resistance to tyranny was not only permissible but a duty and an obligation.

There are significant parallels between those pious patriots and today's modern religious movement. Foremost among the concerns of the "New Light" evangelicals was education. When Harvard drifted from the Puritan faith, more orthodox preachers founded Yale and later Princeton. They were deeply concerned that education teach their youth not only the basics of knowledge but the elements of the true faith. The same impulse can be seen today in the rise of the parochial and home school movements and in the founding of colleges such as Liberty University, Regent University, and Oral Roberts University. Likewise, Patrick Henry, who combined the oratory of the evangelical movement with revolutionary ideology more effectively than anyone else in his time, opposed the ratification of the Constitution because he feared the central government would become too powerful and threaten liberty. The same distrust of government can also be seen today among religious conservatives who oppose one-world agencies like the United Nations and have resisted efforts to convene a constitutional convention.

The revolutionary movement left one critical issue unresolved: slavery. A fresh spiritual outpouring among the people soon forced the nation to confront that evil. The Second Great Awakening demonstrated that when the hearts of the people change, political change follows. Vast numbers of converts freed their slaves and took up civil disobedience by assisting the Underground Railroad, which conveyed slaves to freedom in the North.

They founded the American Antislavery Society and dispatched seventy itinerant evangelists to preach the new doctrine that slavery was a sin and should be immediately abolished. The chief tutor of the Seventy was Theodore Weld, a disciple of the evangelist Charles Finney, who was also heavily influenced by British abolitionism. By 1836 Weld and his band of antislavery evangelists had worked such a profound change over the mass of newly churched converts that one interdenominational convention of abolitionists proclaimed, "the abolition cause ... must prevail before the halcyon day of millennial glory can dawn upon the world." Finney was nervous about equating his ministry with a political cause, and he quietly withdrew from the rising tide of political agitation. But it hardly mattered. The movement had outgrown its spiritual father.[4]

The more radical antislavery activists were treated as unsettling nuisances or worse. Denounced as fanatics, heretics, and Negro-lovers, they were set upon by angry mobs who resented the disruption of their churches and communities. In the South, where a handful of antislavery teachers and preachers migrated to protest the "peculiar institution," they were victims of beatings and even murder. In 1851 the president of a Presbyterian college in Mississippi was murdered by a drunken States' Rights party worker for casting a ballot for an antislavery candidate.[5] The resulting schisms tore some towns and entire denominations apart. So worrisome to some was the mixture of religious enthusiasm with political activism that the Methodist church actually forbade the election of elders who had not first pledged "to refrain from agitating the church" over slavery.[6]

But brutal resistance could not turn back those "single issue" activists who were driven into politics by their religious commitment. Like other religious folk in later years who poured into the political arena because of their opposition to segregation or abortion, they upset the existing political order and provoked a realignment of political loyalties. An examination of voting patterns in the 1840s reveals that support for abolitionist candidates was highest in areas with the greatest number of evangelical churches, where Finney's revivals had worked their wonders.[7]

The same effects could be seen in political parties. Until the 1850s most Northern evangelicals identified with the Democrats, seeing that party as the best defender of the rights of workers and of a broadly equalitarian ideology. But when the Republican party took a bold moral stand against the evil of slavery, many Democrats (and many antislavery Whigs, like Abraham Lincoln) who felt abandoned by their party voted Republican—and that shift gave the nascent party its first presidential victory.

Those who accuse religious conservatives of "taking over" the Republican party should recall this history. The Republican party was born in revival, was nurtured in the cradle of the Second Great Awakening, and was founded uniquely to speak out for what was right and to oppose slavery as a vast social evil. At its 1856 convention, which nominated John C. Frémont, evangelicals dominated the platform committee and passed an antislavery plank that condemned slavery as a sin and a stain upon society. The involvement of people of faith in the Republican party today and their advocacy of a pro-life plank is entirely consistent with that history. It is not religious folk who deny the best and noblest traditions of the Republican party, but rather those "moderates" who want moral issues dropped from public discourse and demand that people of faith leave their religious beliefs at the entrance to the convention hall.

A second social reform impulse that grew out of the Second Great Awakening was the temperance movement. Largely discredited and considered a failure today, the temperance movement of the nineteenth century and the Prohibitionist political movement impacted politics and society in unprecedented ways. Like today's religious conservative movement, it was not an exclusively fundamentalist phenomenon. It enjoyed support across the political spectrum, from Progressives like Jacob Riis and William Jennings Bryan to those on the evangelical right like Billy Sunday. The social ills they sought to cure, as well, were real and endemic. The nation was drenched in alcohol from its earliest days: the first ships that arrived in the New World carried more whisky than grain in their holds.[8] By the 1820s the governments of New York and Massachusetts were reporting that a majority of the paupers in those states were public drunks, while another report concluded that the sale of "ardent spirits" was "almost the sole cause of all the suffering, the poverty, and the crime to be found in the country."[9]

That conclusion may have been overdrawn, but there was no denying the social pathologies that accompanied alcoholism. Prostitution, crime, poverty, petty thievery, gambling, and family abandonment all flowed from a river of booze. As the Second Great Awakening stirred the passions for personal repentance and social reformation, the upper classes yearned for a more ordered and just society that reflected Biblical beliefs and primitive faith. They were repulsed by drinking habits that had grown coarse and unrestrained in the swashbuckling young republic.

Temperance began as a movement among the nation's elites seeking to tame the wild, carousing working class. Groups like the Massachusetts Society for the Suppression of Intemperance typified those early efforts. Limiting its membership to the upper echelons of society, it sought to educate the public about properly refined behavior and to set examples of civilized decorum and moderate drinking. It did not attempt to pass laws prohibiting the consumption of alcohol. Rather, its upstanding members sought to control the excesses of the lower classes through education, by praising self-restraint and shaming the indulgent. But in a culture rapidly becoming more egalitarian, the average American either ignored or rebelled against such upper-class attempts to reestablish behavioral standards. The Massachusetts Society and other elite groups were swimming against the current of history. While their early effort emphasized a voluntary solution to the drinking problem, it found few volunteers. The "common man" did not want to be told what to do and did not want to be told that he was "common."

Four main organizations dominated the temperance movement between the Civil War and the First World War. In 1865 the National Temperance Society and Publishing House was formed to publish magazines and pamphlets to educate and persuade people about the dangers of drink. Its members essentially eschewed political involvement. The harder political work fell to the National Prohibition Party, a new political party founded in 1869 explicitly intending to influence the legislative process and to promote prohibition laws. Already the emergence of those two organizations represented two poles of the continuing debate over whether voluntary or coercive measures contained the answer to America's moral problems. More influential was the Women's Christian Temperance Union, founded in 1874, which ultimately grew to more than one million and became famous for sponsoring the first Mother's Day in 1896.

In more recent times many have tended to equate the movement of women into politics with liberalism and modern feminism, but the most powerful women's political force in American history was not led by the likes of Gloria Steinem or Bella Abzug. It flowed out of evangelical churches, and its women members viewed their civic involvement as missionary work. The WCTU's white ribbon became the most visible symbol of their power, worn on the lapel of male politicians of both political parties as a tribute to the women's agenda. (After 1900 the movement grew more radical and uncompromising, and leadership passed to the Anti-Saloon League, which won actual passage of the Eighteenth Amendment in a final, furious five-year campaign.)

Frances Willard, the WCTU's president from 1879 until her death in 1898, was a fiery champion of temperance and an indefatigable organizer. She was one of the most visible female politicians of the time and one of the most admired women in the nation. Her matronly appearance masked the cool calculation of a savvy political operator who fought her way to the top by winning many of the internal debates swirling through the WCTU and the larger temperance movement. She clashed with Annie Wittenmeyer, the organization's first president, over whether the WCTU should have a single focus on the alcohol problem or should embrace a broad spectrum of social reforms such as school improvements, children's issues, labor rights, prison reform, and women's suffrage. Willard won, pushing the WCTU into a broader agenda, and her "Do Everything" mantra became the organization's motto and a household ideal for many reformers. In another recurring debate, Willard sparred first with Dio Lewis and later with Ellen Foster over whether the WCTU should emphasize temperance and education in persuading the public about the dangers of drinking or launch an aggressive push for prohibition. Once again Willard won, and her unique brand of "gospel politics" brought millions of women into the political mainstream, using their recently gained votes to wage war against the liquor industry and the politicians they denounced as beholden to the "whisky ring."

But Willard could also be doctrinaire and demagogic. Her political style played to the fears of the white Protestants in middle America who viewed the surge of Catholic immigrants with anxiety. "I am first a Christian, then I am a Saxon, and then I am an American," she declared.[10] In an intriguing drama, Willard attempted to ally the WCTU with the Prohibition Party. In previous years, people favoring prohibition had tended to support the Republican party, but because the Republicans declined to embrace the prohibition agenda fully or to make its candidates pledge their support of the WCTU, Willard bolted the GOP and attempted to become the driving force behind the fledgling third party. Her gambit failed. The Prohibition party fielded weak presidential candidates, gaining only 2 percent of the popular vote and never carrying a single state. Having gambled her political capital and lost, Willard saw her power wane, and the WCTU ceased to be the vanguard of the movement.

Willard's meteoric rise, astonishing political power, and rapid fall provides important lessons for today's religious conservatives. First, Willard showed that any movement built around a single issue (in her case, alcohol; in our case, abortion) must eventually broaden its concerns to address the breakdown of the family and the coarsening of the culture. Second, she demonstrated that moral suasion and cultural change alone are no substitute for direct political action. There are some in the evangelical community today who counsel retreat from constitutional or legal restrictions on abortion. "We must first change hearts and minds," they say. But Willard understood that politics is culture—that the law is a teacher, and that ballots can achieve much in shifting social attitudes. Finally, Willard's failure to build a viable third party around temperance should give pause to those in the pro-family movement who wish to spurn the GOP and launch a new political party. The American electoral system does not reward third parties unless they win 50 percent of the vote, something almost impossible for a single-issue party to achieve. Had Willard remained in the Republican party, as most pro-family voters do in our own time, she would have been more effective.

By 1890 prohibition measures had been placed on state ballots with little success. Division and disagreement within the movement played a part, as did the lack of united public opinion. Even many strong advocates of temperance, like Senator Warren Harding, opposed prohibition as "unwise, imprudent, and inconsiderate," though he voted for it to avoid offending the dry lobby.[11] Out of this confusion and disunity emerged a new organization that combined the lessons of the past with a zeal for the future. Founded in 1893, the Anti-Saloon League focused on the single objective of passing laws to prohibit the sale of alcohol, pledging to support candidates of both parties who shared that goal. Its chief agitator was the Reverend Howard Russell, a Congregationalist minister in Ohio who had long been active in the temperance cause. Unlike the Prohibition party, which in its zeal to embrace politics had shunned the churches, the ASL located its base of support in the evangelical churches. Clergy made up three-fifths of the ASL's leadership, and the ASL described itself as "The Church in Action Against the Saloon."

Local victories paved the way to power. Beginning with the passage of "dry" laws in rural counties, the prohibitionists surrounded the cities with a sea of temperance. In 1913 the prohibitionist cause won its first national victory with the passage of the Webb-Kenyon Act, which outlawed interstate shipment of liquor into dry states. While most historians treat the national prohibition movement as a largely conservative phenomenon, lumping it together with nativism and fundamentalism, it featured Progressives in both leadership and grassroots support.

The "localization" strategy of the temperance movement has been emulated by the Christian Coalition. We now recognize that social change flows up from the precincts, not down from Congress or the White House. The adoption of state restrictions on abortion, such as those upheld in the

Webster and *Casey* decisions, show the wisdom of the local strategy. The pro-family movement of today, like the temperance campaign that preceded it, will advance commensurate with its ability to win and consolidate victories at the state and local levels.

On November 13, 1913, at a Grand Jubilee celebration marking the twentieth anniversary of its founding, the powerful Anti-Saloon League announced a campaign to seek a constitutional amendment banning the manufacture, sale, and distribution of alcohol. By then the local-option strategy had built a formidable political base of support. Fourteen states had enacted prohibition statutes by 1914, two-thirds of the states passed prohibition by 1917, and three-fourths of the U.S. population lived in dry counties.[12] Senator Morris Sheppard, a Democrat from Texas, introduced the constitutional amendment by proclaiming that "alcohol is a narcotic poison, destructive and degenerating to the human organism," corrupting the "character of our citizenship," wrecking "public morals," causing "crime, pauperism, and insanity," and visiting fetal diseases upon "children unborn," thereby threatening "the very life of the nation."[13] The proposed amendment won a majority in both houses of Congress when it first came to a vote in 1916, though it failed to win the required two-thirds majority.

Never discouraged by defeat, the prohibitionists pursued a strategy of bold gradualism, slowly strangling the liquor trade with the passage of a series of incremental laws. They amended the conscription law in 1917 to prohibit the sale of alcoholic beverages on or near military installations. That seemed a noble enough goal: Keep the doughboys sober and morally fit. But as the number of army posts increased during the war, *de facto* prohibition spread to urban areas, and the vast majority of the American people saw their saloons boarded up in one emotional wave of patriotism. Without the wartime hysteria and moralistic zeal of the time, it is doubtful that the prohibition crusade would have succeeded. But as alcohol became associated with immigrants, beer with the Hun and German breweries, and abstinence with Americanism and apple pie, the dry lobby marched to victory. On December 18, 1917, a few months after the first U.S. troops landed in France, Congress passed the Eighteenth Amendment and referred it to the states, and it was ratified in January 1919, as the Versailles peace conference convened in Paris. While American boys fought and died in the trenches of Europe, it seemed petty and unpatriotic to defend something as controversial and nonessential as booze. The Lever Act of 1917 and wartime rationing prohibited the use of grain for distilling purposes in any event. Once the war ended and Woodrow Wilson pledged to "make the world safe for democracy," many Americans saw it as their patriotic duty to restore their beloved country's home front to greatness, making no allowance for liquor.

In 1995 the Christian Coalition and the National Right to Life Committee announced their advocacy of a partial-birth abortion ban, which outlawed abortions performed as the child was partially delivered down the birth canal. Some pro-life groups condemned that bill as a partial solution that surrendered the moral high ground. The local option bans and the shuttering of saloons near military bases eighty years earlier by the temperance movement had demonstrated, however, that great social change does not occur in a democracy in great leaps. The key to prohibition's ultimate triumph was the prohibitionists' willingness to move their agenda gradually and incrementally.

Far from being shackled to their pews, people of faith have, at critical times in our nation's history, been moved to vigorous activism. That is the thrust of most religions: to move adherents out of places of worship to redress the moral drift of modern life. For those living in the late nineteenth century, the challenge was to adjust to urbanization and immigration. The rapid expansion from dirt roads to railroads, from rural villages to teeming cities, from plowing fields to plucking feathers in a factory brought with it bewildering pain, dislocation, and social problems. Religious reformers jumped into the ring, and the resulting Social Gospel movement would help define the social advancements of the twentieth century and help the Democratic party to attain a political dominance it had never before known.

The problems that the Social Gospel attempted to address were the problems of the city. Today Americans take urban life for granted—about two-thirds of our population now reside in metropolitan areas. But to people born before the Civil War and raised in the countryside, the city was a strange and confusing place. As Washington Gladden commented after his first visit to Brooklyn, "The city, from the first day, was a thing stupendous and overpowering, a mighty monster, with portentous energies."[14] The rise of the city from the rural expanse of the nation occurred with frightening speed, fueled by immigration from abroad and a populace driven from the countryside by declining crop prices. Between 1860 and the end of World War I the proportion of the population living in urban centers rose from 25 percent to over 50 percent.

The urban phenomenon, combined with industrialization, transformed the nation more dramatically than anything Americans had seen before. Labor unrest exploded with railroad strikes, the protests of the "Molly Maguires" in the Pennsylvania coal mines, the rise of the Knights of Labor, the Haymarket bombing, and the Homestead and Pullman strikes. Farmers accustomed to the rhythm of the seasons found themselves driven to despair by the endless regimen of the factory and its new invention, the time clock. Men, women, and children worked in sweatshops six or seven days a week, fourteen hours a day. Orphans roamed the streets, opium was the drug of choice, disease was everywhere, and alcoholism was rampant. Josiah Strong called the cities both the nerve center and the storm center of American civilization, and many wondered whether their emergence signaled more peril than promise to the nation. As with today's pro-family movement, the conscience of the church demanded a response to those social pathologies.

Against the backdrop of urban strife, labor unrest, nativism, and antimasonry, American politics became a hotbed of reform. The Social Gospel movement was a crusade for social justice within American Protestantism that merged traditional faith with radical political reform. Its appealing moral purpose attracted recruits from all segments of American life. One proponent described it as "the application of the teaching of Jesus and the total message of the Christian salvation to society, the economic life, and social institutions . . . as well as to individuals."[15] A precursor to the civil rights and women's movements that flowered in the 1960s, the Social Gospel was "a crusade for justice and righteousness in all areas of the common life,"[16] a trumpet blast to the church to get involved with political and private institutions.

The Social Gospel was a radical movement even as it retained many traditional Christian tenets, such as a belief in a sovereign, all-powerful God; the imminent millennial return of Christ; and the power of prayer. Drunkenness was a sin, abortion was unthinkable, divorce was the sign of a moral flaw, and until late in the twentieth century, almost two-thirds of young Americans had attended Sunday school, where they learned a common moral heritage based on the greatest compassion stories ever written, such as that of the Good Samaritan.[17] The revolutionary part of their message insisted that it was not merely man who was accountable to God, but man's social institutions as well.[18] Reinhold Niebuhr and other adherents to the Social Gospel would later take the movement to task for failing to emphasize original sin and the transcendence of God, but the claim that the church had an obligation not only to convert souls but to transform society struck a responsive chord.

The preeminent figure of the Social Gospel was Walter Rauschenbusch, a German Baptist pastor and theologian who became convinced that the only hope for lifting up the underclass lay in evangelization. In 1886 Rauschenbusch gave up a comfortable life as a professor at a Baptist seminary in Rochester, New York, to take over as pastor of a church in the Hell's Kitchen section of New York City, an area with a reputation for crime, alcoholism, and human misery.[19] Here he witnessed the casualties of city life etched in the dirty faces of homeless orphans and the sunken eyes of exhausted factory workers. Given his Baptist theology, he was conservative on such social issues as drunkenness, which he viewed as barbaric and self-destructive, and he expressed alarm at the availability of contraceptives, which made "sin easy and safe."[20] The raw survivalism he saw daily for eight years, combined with his dismay at the lack of caring by fellow believers, altered his life's mission from saving souls to shepherding the victims of social indifference, political corruption, and economic greed.

Rauschenbusch viewed the vagaries of urban life as a commentary not only on the failures of capitalism but on the failure of the church. He called upon Christians to build a just social order based on moral law that would replace social Darwinism's notion of the survival of the fittest. He thought that Christians had failed to carry out Christ's command to build a kingdom of God on earth, a mission that some theologians misunderstood to mean that the church itself should be built up and should amass interests of its own.[21]

Rauschenbusch's publications became the canon for the Social Gospel, and he became a highly sought speaker across the country. His message was simple: The Industrial Revolution and the rise of the city had unleashed greed and avarice on a scale unknown in human history, and it was incumbent upon Christians to make their religion relevant to a newly industrialized nation and an exploited working class by caring for them. He argued that, just as Christ had created an apostolic ministry to reach the peasantry of ancient Palestine, it was God's will to create a new apostolate to reach the teeming masses of modern industrial society. The moral clarity of his message gained admirers in high places. President Theodore Roosevelt consulted him on social policy, promising to borrow the good from socialism while leaving out the bad. Two of his books, A Theology for the Social Gospel and Christianizing the Social Order, gave evangelicals the justification they needed for direct involvement in the political upheavals of the day: labor union organizing, the passage of antitrust laws, temperance and prohibition agitation, and the enactment of minimum-wage laws. No muddle-headed dreamer, Rauschenbusch wrote in 1907: "In asking for faith in the possibility of a new social order, we ask for no Utopian delusion. . . . We shall never have a perfect social life, yet we must seek it with faith."[22] Those ideas helped propel the formation in 1908 of the Federal Council of Churches, which was the forerunner to the National Council of Churches, the enormous alliance of churches that would gain prominence later in the century.

The Social Gospel had a profound impact as an intellectual movement. Influenced by Rauschenbusch, Teddy Roosevelt denounced accumulated wealth as an affront to working people and called upon the government to break up concentrations of power such as the trusts. When his hand-picked successor, William Howard Taft, failed to carry out his Progressive agenda of tariff reform and conservation, Roosevelt founded the Bull Moose Party and ran for an unprecedented third term. The party convention in 1912 made the "infamous" Republican convention in Houston in 1992 look tame by comparison. It featured a heavy presence of evangelical delegates who waved Bibles and paraded down the aisles singing The Battle Hymn of the Republic and "Onward, Christian Soldiers." Roosevelt delivered a stirring acceptance speech in which he declared, "We stand at Armageddon, and we battle for the Lord!" Jane Addams, the pioneer of the settlement house movement, announced that the party platform contained "all I have been fighting for for a decade." It pledged support to most of the Social Gospel's favored causes: child labor laws, women's suffrage, and some system of social insurance.[23]

The use of religious language at party conventions and the support of evangelical reformers for party platforms raised few eyebrows in Teddy Roosevelt's time. Yet today the invocation of God and the involvement of evangelicals in the Republican party is treated as a threat to pluralism and democracy. Imagine the Republican nominee standing up at the next national convention this summer in San Diego and declaring that his campaign represented a "battle for the Lord." The media would pillory him as the captive of the "far right," lacerate him for kowtowing to "the fringe," and portray the convention as a throwback to Nuremberg. In fact, as the Social Gospel movement demonstrated, the influence on political parties and platforms by people of faith is a common American phenomenon. It is another characteristic of an active faith.

There was no greater religious-leader-turned-political-leader grounded in the Social Gospel than William Jennings Bryan. Bryan first burst upon the national scene at the Democratic convention in 1896, when he argued for adoption of a free-silver plank in the platform by proclaiming, "You shall not press down upon the brow of labor this crown of thorns; you shall not crucify mankind upon a cross of gold." In a society steeped in

Scripture, Bryan's peroration on the passion of Christ required no transla-
tor. His fiery oration proved so persuasive that the convention voted for
the free-silver platform and nominated Bryan, then an obscure thirty-
six-year-old representative from Nebraska, for president. Steamrollered in
the fall by Mark Hanna and the well-financed McKinley forces, Bryan
nonetheless made history by eschewing the stand-pat "front porch" campaigns of the day and taking off across the prairie in a barnstorming whis-
tle-stop campaign. And though his electoral fortunes never improved, his
impact cannot be overestimated.

Though belittled later in stage and film productions of *Inherit the Wind*
as the bumbling bigot and half-witted fundamentalist of Scopes trial fame,
he was the same man whose eloquence and power made him the voice and
driving force behind the Democratic party for thirty years. He was nominated as the party's presidential candidate three times, more often than
any person in history except Franklin Roosevelt. He was the "boy orator"
whose honey-tongued preaching style captivated a generation of Americans. He was the "Great Commoner" who became the voice for the rights
of labor and farmers who he believed were oppressed by plutocrats and the
gold standard. He was the "peerless leader" who resigned as Secretary of
State rather than compromise his Christian principles over Woodrow Wilson's decision to violate neutrality laws by sending American doughboys to
fight in World War I.

It is impossible to grasp Bryan the politician without coming to terms
with his evangelical Christian faith. His faith fueled his politics, giving
power to his words and a quiet eloquence to his deeds. Far to the left of the
country and even his own party in his political views, Bryan's staunch defense of orthodox Christianity reassured many who might otherwise have
been repelled by his progressive ideas. For Bryan sought to change the
whole political and social order: among the reforms he advocated (all of
which were later adopted) were women's suffrage, prohibition, a federal income tax, government regulation of the railroads, creation of an Interstate
Commerce Commission and a Department of Labor, the demonetization of
the currency, the direct election of senators, and the abandonment of the
gold standard.[24]

ACTIVE FAITH

A man of profound faith, he considered any threat to the absolute
principles of democracy and Christianity abhorrent. Bryan was never
a cold technocrat discussing social scientific theories in sterile, secular
rhetoric. He advanced his argument with the passion of the prophet and
the sonorous bromides of a frontier preacher. While modern Democrats
are far more likely to think of miracles in political terms (Who can forget
Michael Dukakis and his "Massachusetts Miracle"?), Bryan meant the
parting of the Red Sea, Christ healing the lepers, Lazarus rising from the
dead. Those beliefs were evident in his rhetoric. When he began the long
Democratic tradition of addressing the American Federation of Labor on
Labor Day in 1908, he claimed that the rights of workers was a moral issue.
For him, unlike many of today's liberal politicians, defending labor was
about more than wages and benefits. As he put it:

> This is Bible doctrine; it is common sense, and it is human experience. We
> think in our hearts as well as our heads—out of the heart "are the issues of
> life." . . . I begin my speech with this proposition because I want to impress
> upon the minds of those who listen to me, and upon those who read what I
> say to you. The labor question is more a moral than an intellectual one.[25]

Wisely, the Republicans chose not to attack Bryan or his followers for
injecting religion into politics, a strategy that would later be employed by
the Democrats against religious conservatives with disastrous results. Nevertheless, Bryan was not immune from criticism. His religious campaigns
were mimicked by his opponents, and the mobilization of churches and
preachers was carried out by both parties. In 1896 the Republican party organized its own army of Protestant ministers and evangelists, who attacked
Bryan's inflationary monetary ideas as a demagogic attempt to start a class
war and debase the currency in violation of Christian principles. A Chicago
evangelist denounced Bryan's "Cross of Gold" speech as a heretical use of
the Crucifixion for partisan gain. A Baptist pastor went further, saying of the
Bryan program, "That platform was made in hell." Persuaded by the arguments of gold bugs that the coinage of silver would debase the currency and
would lead to economic chaos, many Protestant ministers viewed the contest between McKinley and Bryan as a choice between civilization and an-

archy, capitalism and socialism. Many preached sermons on the Sunday before the election on the topic, "Thou Shalt Not Steal."[26]

His floundering performance and ill health during the Scopes trial, immortalized by H. L. Mencken, betray what was a lifelong optimism in the crusading politician. It is ironic that while Mencken's historical reputation has grown with the passage of time, his crude caricature of Bryan as a boob and bigot survives in the popular culture. In fact, Mencken was far more prejudiced in his views. While Bryan worked for women's suffrage, Mencken opposed allowing women in voting booths or the workforce. Mencken was a notorious anti-Semite, an anti-Christian bigot, a racist, a fan of Hitler, and a Nazi sympathizer.[27] When Hitler rose to power and the Third Reich began to build the military machine that would plunge the world into World War II, Mencken fell out of favor, eventually suffered a stroke, and died in obscurity. Yet his assault on Bryan's anti-Darwinian views on evolution persists. Sadly for Bryan, the episode etched the final memories of his crusade for righteousness into the American consciousness, because it turned out to be his last. He died one week after the Scopes trial ended.

The same charge leveled at Bryan is directed at religious conservatives in modern times: that he marginalized his party, sent it to ignoble defeat, and frightened secular voters with his millennialist agenda. But that is only half the story. For while Bryan himself was admittedly a flawed presidential candidate, he created a platform and a constituency (labor, city dwellers, rural farmers) that would be the bedrock of the modern Democratic party. The pro-family movement has transcended Bryan by achieving what he could not. His ideological crusade led to electoral failure. The fusion of a grassroots religious constituency with a major political party is like pouring new wine into old wineskins. Sometimes the wineskins rattle, and often they break. That was apparent at the Republican convention in Houston in 1992. But the 1994 elections demonstrated that the fusionist strategy of the pro-family movement can succeed, particularly when it is broadened with an anti-tax, balanced-budget component and combined with the Perot message of term limits and political reform. The marriage of the religious impulse with a political party here represents the most thorough projection of religion into our politics since Bryan appeared on the scene, and it has proved far more successful.

A vital element in Bryan's political platform and the Social Gospel agenda was labor reform. As with the treatment of so many parts of the American past, most people will probably be surprised to know that the trade union movement and the passage of labor laws was not achieved (initially at least) with the support of secular leaders or the mainstream press. In fact, much of the popular sentiment about labor unions was extraordinarily negative, because many viewed their ranks as harboring Communist sympathizers and threatening private property.[28] Muckrakers like Lincoln Steffens and Upton Sinclair built public support for the labor movement with difficulty, mainly through their gruesome accounts of working conditions in the factories and sweatshops that sprouted up on the landscape of industrial America.

The most persistent and full-throated voices in defense of labor were those of clergymen and churchwomen. Among their numbers were the most prominent ecclesiastical figures of the time: Cardinal James Gibbons of Baltimore, Washington Gladden, Walter Rauschenbusch, Lyman Abbott of the Plymouth Congregational Church, and the Episcopal bishops Frederic Dan Huntington and Henry Codman Potter all helped raise public awareness about the plight of American workers. They were repulsed by the railroad strike of 1877, the Haymarket riot of 1886, and the Pullman strike of 1894, all of which were put down by the corporations with hired guards and shocking bloodshed. Those labor uprisings jolted the conscience of American Protestants and Catholics more dramatically than any social upheaval until the civil rights revolution of the 1960s. While the blood from the Haymarket affair still stained the front pages of the nation's newspapers, Potter issued a letter to the clergy in the influential New York diocese criticizing those who believed that the way to heal the poor was through charity alone. "What the laborer wants from his employer is fair and fraternal dealing, not alms-giving, and a recognition of his manhood rather than a condescension to his inferiority," he proclaimed.[29] And Rauschenbusch wrote of the conflict between labor and the laborer, "Jesus asked, 'Is not a man more than a sheep?' Our industry says 'No.' It is careful of its livestock and machinery, and careless of its human working force. It keeps its electrical engines immaculate in burnished cleanliness and lets its human dynamos sicken in dirt."[30] Gladden preached an "applied Christianity" in which he claimed that unrestrained capitalism had institutionalized sin, consigning the underclass to such unspeakable horror and hopelessness that its only refuge was indolence and lawlessness. Abbott credited the captains of industry with outstanding progress in technological advances but charged that the foundation of capitalism had become "a destructive one."[31]

Another important Social Gospel figure in organized labor was Charles Stelzle, a machinist-cum-minister who had risen from journeyman mechanic to head the Workingmen's Department of the Presbyterian Church. An unapologetic champion of trade unions, he fostered cooperation between the church and unions, wrote extensively for labor publications, and joined the American Federation of Labor. His theology was evangelical and liberal. Rejecting the idea that Christians should be concerned only with the salvation of souls, he argued that "the mission of the Church of Christ today is to consider the social and material needs of the people as well as their moral needs." In Stelzle's formulation Christ was a labor organizer, and his disciples were skilled workers. "When the church was started two thousand years ago, it was organized by a company of workingmen," he asserted. "Its leader was a carpenter. When it spread to other cities, it was received most cordially by . . . the great labor guilds of the day—the labor unions we would now call them."[32]

After the founding of the Federated Council of Churches, Stelzle began the Men and Religion Forward movement, which combined the revivalism of Charles Finney with the labor recruitment tactics of Samuel Gompers. Joining in the movement were such leading lights of Progressivism as Jane Addams, Booker T. Washington, and Rauschenbusch. An army of itinerant evangelists fanned out to fifteen hundred communities, launching weeklong campaigns that featured mass meetings, parades, demonstrations, and door-to-door canvassing. The political program was "a square deal" for workers. The religious emphasis was on personal conversion and individual sanctification. The campaign was always more focused on purifying the moral environment than on collective bargaining. Preachers agitated for the closing down of brothels, saloons, and gambling dens, which they viewed as causing suffering among the poor. Later Samuel Gompers and the AFL borrowed heavily from the Men and Religion Forward movement in forming the Labor Forward organization, which dispatched union evangelists to preach the gospel of trade unions in church pulpits and YMCA halls. A union revival in Syracuse, New York, featured an evangelist and a choir; it brought more than ten thousand workers to the mourners' bench. Using evangelistic techniques and emotionalism, the unions literally "converted" workers. Those spiritual outpourings united worker solidarity and Christianity, giving believers a stronger link to the social justice movement. How far did union activists equate their politics with the Kingdom of God? Consider the pronouncement of a member of the Garment Workers Union who claimed: "The union label is a religious emblem. It is a religious act to buy goods to which this label [is] attached, an act blessed on earth and honored in heaven."[33]

Like the Moral Majority or the pro-life movement, the trade union movement at its outset combined a distinct political agenda with the religious fervor of its followers. Revivals and altar calls built the labor unions, not consumer boycotts and strikes alone. So much for those who claim that religion and politics don't mix.

The consequences for the Democratic party were staggering. By equating liberal politics with Christian religion, the union movement assimilated Catholic workers in the North into the Democratic party. The alliance among Catholics, labor unions, and the Democratic party emphasized growing wages and worker safety, creating a large middle class that was the mainstay for Democratic candidates. The message was overtly spiritual: "Man does not live by bread alone." Without the treatment of labor politics as part of one's religion, the Democratic party could never have gained the votes of millions of Catholics, which made it a majority party. This is heavily ironic, given the secular platform and often antireligious rhetoric of some of today's liberal Democratic politicians. When the national Democratic party attempted to demonize people of faith prior to the 1994 elections, it was turning its back on its own proud and cherished history.

Because so many workers were immigrants of Roman Catholic faith, the Catholic church also added its voice in support of trade union organizers. In 1920 the American Catholic bishops issued a pastoral letter calling for evenhanded justice for capital, for labor, and for the entire community. In their words, "By treating the laborer first of all as a man, the employer will make him a better workingman; by respecting his own moral dignity as a man, the laborer will compel the respect of his employer and of the community."[34] That same year the bishops of the Methodist church denounced "all murderous child labor, all foul sweat shops, all unsafe mines, all deadly tenements, all starvation wages, all excessive hours."[35]

The conditions those religious organizations deplored included seventy-two-hour workweeks, the lowering of children into mines choked with coal dust, and dangerous machinery that wrenched off limbs and spewed boiling hot smelter, permanently injuring workers. Faced with those miserable conditions, Communist organizers and socialist unions like the Industrial Workers of the World found sympathetic ears among American workers, winning recruits to their radical cause. Yet most American Protestants, including liberals, found those organizations anathema. The Federal Council of Churches tried to establish a Christian middle ground between capitalism and Communist agitation:

> Otherwise, we shall have an autocratic management of industry on the one side, and either a kind of serfdom on the other or a militant, bitter, and class-conscious organization of labor growing yearly more revolutionary. . . . The Church must stand for the right of the organization and collective action. . . . The Church cannot allow itself to be stopped from this course either by pressure from reactionary employers on the one hand, or by the manifest evils of the labor movement on the other.

Pastoral letters, however, were not enough. Union organizers picked up where the churches left off, agitating for labor reform laws and electing politicians, leading ultimately to the abolition in 1923 of the twelve-hour workday in steel factories.[36]

Today, liberal churches have forgotten that lesson. They hold conferences, issue pastoral letters, and sit in large buildings in Washington bloated with denominational bureaucracy. They have lost touch with the American majority. The grassroots energy that once belonged to labor and temperance now belongs to the pro-family movement, including not only the Christian Coalition but a proliferation of many other organizations. Like their forebears, they are seeking not a quick fix but a long-term solution. They have the same persistence that could be seen in the generation of revivalism that preceded independence in 1776; the thirty-five years that stretched from Finney's first great revival until the emancipation of the slaves; the temperance campaigns that swept across the nation in intermittent waves for over a century before prohibition; and forty years of social gospel teaching and progressive reform before the legislative capstone of the New Deal.

The debate over whether the New Deal evolved from Progressive impulses or made a revolutionary break from the past is an old one. The differences between the New Deal and the Social Gospel cannot be disputed. The former focused, at least in its first phase, on relief rather than reform, and aimed to provide jobs to the unemployed, while the latter sought more broadly to usher in God's kingdom. But stressing the purely economic goals of the New Deal fails to do justice to the fact that it was also a movement based on a profoundly moral vision of society.

When the stock market crashed on Black Thursday in 1929, many at first hoped that Herbert Hoover's reassuring promises that prosperity was "just around the corner" might still be true. But the scale of the Depression was staggering and left many to look to heaven for an explanation. Many wondered if the catastrophe did not represent God's judgment on a nation of bootleggers, flappers, and speakeasies. Soon all eyes and the weight of history fell on one man—Franklin Delano Roosevelt.

Roosevelt found himself facing not only a collapsed economy but a spiritually wounded nation as well. Best remembered for his wily pragmatism and Machiavellian political instincts, he had profound religious views, which are frequently overlooked. One of Roosevelt's closest aides, Rexford

Guy Tugwell, wrote of his "deep religious faith," observing that while the "Roosevelt religion was consistent with gaiety and intellectual freedom," it was "nevertheless deeply held."[37] Once, when asked by an interviewer for a statement about his "philosophy," he responded brusquely, "My philosophy? I am a Christian and I am a Democrat."[38] The award-winning Roosevelt biographer Kenneth Davis concludes that Roosevelt's faith was an illuminating aspect of life. His upbringing instilled in him an unwavering faith in God the Father and Jesus as His Son. He trusted the Bible's descriptions of an omnipotent God who cared for every individual. He held to the optimistic view that in God's plan America would emerge from the "gloomy mountains of barbarism" into an "increasingly civilized order." In gold lettering over the State Dining Room fireplace in the White House he mounted a line written by John Adams: "I Pray Heaven to Bestow The Best of Blessing on THIS HOUSE, and on All that shall hereafter Inhabit it. May none but Honest and Wise Men ever rule under This Roof!"[39]

On the day he boarded the train that would take him to Washington for his inaugural, he requested the company of James A. Farley, a man known to him as having a "great and simple religious faith," who would soon be considered one of the country's most skillful political forecasters.[40] The two men talked not of the grave economic crisis that threatened to rend the nation, but of the determinative effect of faith in God.[41] More important than any planned political approach to the solution of the present crisis was a great people's religious faith, Roosevelt said. Ultimately, he believed, the salvation of the United States depended upon the American people's active faith in God, in their seeking and accepting His guidance. To that end, Roosevelt determined that he would do several things. First, he would launch the New Deal with a prayer. His first public act on Inauguration Day was to attend a special service conducted at St. John's Episcopal Church across from the White House.[42] His inauguration would be steeped in faith. FDR insisted on being sworn in on his family Bible, and his inaugural address from its first words—"This is a day of national consecration"—was rich with theological themes.[43] He invoked the imagery of Christ driving the money-changers from the temple when he declared that the moneyed interests were responsible for the crisis, explaining, "They know only the rules of a generation of self-seekers. They have no vision, and where there is no vision the people perish."[44] He finished as he began, proclaiming to a troubled nation "that our true destiny is not to be ministered unto but to minister." The words were taken almost verbatim from the Gospel of Mark, where Christ told his disciples, "Whosoever will be great among you, shall be your minister. And whosoever of you will be chiefest, shall be the servant of all. For even the Son of man came not to be ministered unto but to minister and to give His life a ransom for many."[45]

The New Deal did not end the Depression. Partly it was based on a misplaced faith in the ability of government to solve problems through the redistribution of wealth and the erection of the modern welfare state. But my purpose is not to debate the merits of the New Deal, only to point out that Roosevelt succeeded because he presented himself to the American people as both president and intercessor, one who sought to heal not only the nation's economy but its conscience as well. He told America that it could survive by following his lead and by adhering to the faith of its founding.[46] Roosevelt's optimism that America would again return to happier days and his distinctly Christian call to servanthood was the high-water mark of the Democratic party at a critical time in the life of our country. Later, in the darkest days of World War II, as American troops prepared to land on the beaches of Normandy, Roosevelt again called the nation to prayer and consecration. The people responded. Millions of Americans filled churches and synagogues to overflowing, families huddled together around the kitchen table, and children whispered simple prayers for those in harm's way.

Roosevelt's influence on the nation was exponentially greater in his politics than in his piety. It was President Roosevelt who made many of Bryan's "radical" dreams a reality. He was cool and calculating, and he profited from Bryan's success in advancing an agenda wrapped in faith. But the important distinction between the real Roosevelt and the Roosevelt of liberal mythology is found in his simple expressions of faith. On the eve of the D-Day invasion, Roosevelt issued an official proclamation calling the nation to prayer. When he and Churchill met secretly in the Atlantic to pledge the commitment of each to the other's nation, they held church services on the windswept deck of the ship and ended by singing "Onward, Christian Soldiers." This rhetoric, when employed by religious conservatives today, is portrayed by their critics as dangerous and frightening. But Roosevelt justified his activism during the Depression with an overtly religious rhetoric that would make many secular liberals today shudder—even as they claim to be his heirs.[47]

The social concerns of the faith community shifted with the end of World War II and the onset of the Cold War. The Soviet domination of Eastern Europe, the fall of Beijing to the Communists in 1949, and the Korean War all raised the ugly specter of the Red menace. Americans opposed Communism not only because of its Marxist economic system but also because of its atheism. Religious folk were at the forefront in creating a national crusade against Communism. *Time*'s publisher, Henry Luce, a lay Presbyterian leader, helped to found the China Lobby to oppose the loss of China to Mao, primarily because he had been born the son of missionaries in that country. Fred Schwarz launched the Christian Anti-Communist Crusade to build grassroots support for a strong military and an aggressively anti-Communist foreign policy. At the height of the Cold War, the American people defined themselves in opposition to Soviet Communism, and that meant as a religious people. In 1954 Congress placed the words "under God" in the Pledge of Allegiance to signify the emphasis on religion in the battle against atheistic Communism.

The anti-Communist movement featured colorful figures like the evangelist Billy Ray Hargis, who traveled the country holding huge anti-Red rallies that resembled revival meetings. It was a church-based, bipartisan movement that included many conservative Democrats, not unlike today's pro-family movement. Liberals charged after the collapse of the Soviet Union that the right merely replaced the demon of Communism with a new demon of homosexuality and other forms of socially deviant behavior in order to whip up its supporters and sustain its political fortunes. As usual, the truth was altogether more complex and interesting. What happened in fact was that a religiously inspired movement opposing tyranny abroad turned its attention to social injustice at home. Freed from the international threat of Communism, it had the ability to focus on domestic social problems that threaten the survival of the family, the faith, and the culture. As with the Civil War and World War II, the Cold War and its expenditure of blood and treasure over forty years demanded an answer to the question: For what kind of society have we fought?

This same question was answered in very different ways by the liberal religious impulse during the Cold War. The Great Society and the civil rights movement sought to finish the work begun by Roosevelt, who had been preoccupied with the twin evils of the Depression and fascism. While he courted black votes (becoming in 1936 the first Democratic presidential candidate to win a majority of blacks) and supported the passage of a federal antilynching law, Roosevelt left much of the activist civil rights work to his wife. As black soldiers returned from fighting on battlefields to bring freedom to Europe and Asia, they found a society still segregated by race that treated them as second-class citizens.

While today's perception of the civil rights movement focuses on marches, rallies, and the Kennedy brothers, that movement would not have come to pass were it not for the passion and persuasion of the church. And just as William Jennings Bryan had laid the groundwork for the New Deal, so did the struggle for a color-blind society need a prophet and preacher to call the faithful into battle.

The man of the hour turned out to be an obscure twenty-six-year-old pastor of a Baptist church in Montgomery, Alabama, named Martin Luther King, Jr. Barely a year out of divinity school in 1956, King was thrust into the eye of a hurricane, becoming the central figure in an unfolding drama that would occupy every moment of his life until his death twelve years later. While it is popular today to emphasize King the Gandhian, it is important to recall that first and foremost he was a Baptist and a preacher who was descended from a long line of preachers. His father was a preacher. His grandfather was a preacher, and his great-grandfather was a preacher.[48] King was an apprentice to God's word, a living demonstration of the truth so unforgettably captured by W. E. B. Du Bois when he pronounced early in the twentieth century that "the preacher is the most unique personality developed by the Negro on American soil."[49] And it was the word of God preached in King's eloquent and distinctive cadence that moved not only blacks but the entire nation, for as much as the races were divided on political matters, they worshiped the same God and read the same Bible.[50] The language of Scripture appealed to a mutuality that shattered the barriers created by race. That was also how King viewed matters. To him, there was no real separation between the "real" world and the "religious world." As a young seminarian, he wrote, "religion has been real to me and closely knitted to life. In fact, the two cannot be separated; religion for me is life."[51]

King did not create the civil rights movement from scratch. He had a firm foundation that had been praying and singing for a hundred years: the black church. Its hallowed tradition included slaves hiding their Bibles under the floorboards of their quarters (it was against the law for a slave to read), Negro spirituals that celebrated God's goodness, and a theology of oppression that equated slavery in the South with the enslavement of Jews in ancient Egypt. Born in bondage, nursed in adversity, and sustained by hope, the black church became the incubator for the common language and uncommon tactics later employed by the civil rights movement.[52] King was the interpreter who translated this language into the vernacular of white folk. The words and music had been composed and rehearsed for centuries.

Yet King's genius was indispensable. He provided the vision and leadership that renewed and made crystal clear the vital connection between religion and politics. That connection started at the feet of his father, "Daddy" King, a staunch Republican who preached a conservative theological message of personal salvation with a militant demand for social justice. It continued at Morehouse College, where he began to search for a profession that would enable him to help his people. He thought about the legal profession and honed his magnetic oratory by giving trial speeches before the mirror in his room.[53] Reading Thoreau's "Civil Disobedience" planted the first seeds of a major commitment to reform. King was fascinated with Thoreau's provocative theory that a "creative minority—even a minority of 'one honest man'—could set in motion a moral revolution."[54]

King the seminarian was thrilled to discover Walter Rauschenbusch and Reinhold Niebuhr, who articulated and provided a theological foundation and rich intellectual tradition for the social concerns he had nursed since he was a boy. He saw in Rauschenbusch what true religion ought to be about—not limited to the business of belief but concerned with the whole man, body and soul, material and economic conditions. King believed that the job of the preacher was, in Rauschenbusch's words, "to apply the teaching functions of the pulpit to the pressing questions of public morality."[55] Rauschenbusch's condemnation of capitalism found fertile ground in a man like King, who was familiar with economic disadvantage. He remembered Atlanta's bread lines and his own exploitation at several jobs, where he was paid less than whites for equivalent menial labor. At the same time, after studying Karl Marx, he rejected Communism as a Christian heresy that denied God and placed false hope in the ability of man to save himself and make a better world on his own.[56]

In 1954 a newly married King on the verge of completing his Ph.D. faced a bright future. He hoped to land a teaching job at a Baptist seminary, but the call from a small, middle-class Baptist church in Montgomery, Alabama, tugged at his heart. He did not want to return to the South, where he was tired of the racial segregation, the "Whites Only" signs, and hostility that was even worse in Montgomery than in his hometown of Atlanta, the city that proclaimed itself "too busy to hate." It would be hard to raise a family there. Yet his sense of calling won out, and the decision was made. In May he preached his first sermon as the pastor of Dexter Avenue Baptist Church.[57]

Later that month the Supreme Court staggered Jim Crow with a body blow. In a dramatic ruling issued by a unanimous court, *Brown* v. *Board of Education* found that the "separate but equal" provisions that formed the foundation for segregation of public facilities in the South were unconstitutional. King's elation at the news was short-lived, as burning crosses began to blaze across the South, the White Citizens' Councils led massive resistance to the court's ruling, the newly muscular Ku Klux Klan terrorized the countryside, and tension in black population centers like central Alabama thickened. A few months later Rosa Parks, the diminutive secretary for the local NAACP chapter, launched the modern civil rights movement by refusing to give up her seat on a city bus to a white person. The arrest and jailing of Parks sparked a spontaneous boycott of the city bus system; led by the women of local churches, it spread not by radio or newspaper advertisements but by leaflets circulated in black churches. "Until we do something to stop these arrests, they will continue," the circular pleaded. "We are, therefore, asking every Negro to stay off the buses on Monday in protest of the arrest and trial." Alerted by the flyers and encouraged from the pulpit, blacks spent the day organizing car pools and arranging for protection for those walking to work. When the next morning dawned, bus stops were deserted and buses roared through the streets of Montgomery empty. The movement had begun.[58]

As with most activities in the black church, the impetus began with women and then spread to the preachers. Though King had been in town for only seven months, his fellow ministers tapped him as the chairman of the Montgomery Improvement Association, which assumed coordination of the boycott. At the first mass meeting of the new organization, in a statement that came to define the years of protest to follow, King declared, "I want it known throughout Montgomery and throughout this nation that we are a Christian people." The choice was not integration or segregation, he told the congregation, but whether they would have tired feet or tired souls. To cooperate with an evil political system was to deny God and God's higher law. To a chorus of "Amens" and applause that swept over him in waves, he announced that the political cause for which he fought was aligned with Christianity, and opposition to it was blasphemy. "If we are wrong—God Almighty is wrong! If we are wrong—Jesus of Nazareth was merely a utopian dreamer and never came down to earth! If we are wrong, justice is a lie."[59] This rhetoric stoked emotions but tempered behavior, turning the movement in a peaceful, nonviolent, and explicitly Christian direction. King's methods were disciplined and inspiring. Guided by his authentic and authoritative Christianity, he was convinced that persuasion, not violence, was the only path to follow. From his pulpit he proclaimed the movement's goals. In front of television cameras and in private meetings with governors, presidents, businessmen, and police he tried negotiation.

King named the organization he formed after the boycott the Southern Christian Leadership Conference (after four name changes) to connote the spirit of humility and to differentiate his ministry from the black separatist movement. The first major project of the preacher-led SCLC was a voter registration drive called the Crusade for Citizenship, which opened on Lincoln's birthday in 1958. The campaign was modeled after the famous crusades of Billy Graham, the white evangelist from North Carolina whom King greatly admired for his organizational skills and pulpit oratory. Like Graham, King utilized interdenominational committees of pastors, the pooling of mailing lists, mass meetings, training classes for workers, and door-to-door canvassing. Where he differed from Graham was in the explicitly political content of his message. While Graham was made increasingly nervous by political activism of both whites and blacks on the segregation issue (though he did invite King to deliver a prayer at his New York City crusade in 1957), King considered his duties as proselytizer and political player inseparable. "The underlying philosophies of segregation are diametrically opposed to democracy and Christianity," he contended in a sermon during the Greensboro sit-ins, "and all the dialectics of all the logicians in the world cannot make them lie down together."[60]

Today it seems remarkable that no one in the media suggested King was off base in giving his organization the name of "Christian." But the identification of a political movement with the Christian faith is hardly a new idea. The Women's Christian Temperance Union, the Christian Anti-Communist Crusade, and numerous other groups throughout our history have boldly declared their faith by their choice of nomenclature. Today the

ALL GOD'S CHILDREN

Christian Coalition's name—emulating this proud tradition—is portrayed by some as "exclusionary" and "arrogant," somehow suggesting that those who hold to a different view are not Christians or are not welcome in the church. This is a strange conclusion that runs counter to all we are and all we aspire to be. No one should question the right of Jews to call their organizations the American Jewish Congress or the American Jewish Committee. Martin Luther King did not speak for every Christian, but he fought for what he believed was right according to his faith. Beset by legal harassment, manhandled by police, and jailed on trumped-up charges, King allowed his Christian message to conquer the hatred of those who persecuted him. In his "Letter from a Birmingham Jail," he asserted that "a just law is a man-made law that conforms to the law of God."

As the knot of legal troubles tightened around him in Alabama, he returned to Atlanta to pastor the church where he had grown up, Ebenezer Baptist. Most Americans remember the Martin Luther King of the March on Washington in 1963, triumphantly addressing a biracial crowd of 250,000. But in between the peaks of these protests were valleys of despair. The last decade of his life was spent in jailhouses and courtrooms negotiating the gauntlet of the harassment of Southern law enforcement and the intransigence of federal officials who were supposed to enforce the civil rights statutes. Sometimes the results were comical. When the SCLC ran an advertisement in the *New York Times* that criticized Alabama for its mistreatment of Negro protesters, officials slapped King and several other preachers with a multimillion-dollar libel suit. When an Alabama judge predictably ordered the preachers to pay up, one church had its pastor's automobile registration transferred to "the name of Jesus" to prevent its seizure.

Though he soared to international prominence, landing on the cover of *Time* magazine at the age of twenty-nine and winning the Nobel Peace Prize, King's faith kept him strangely aloof from politicians. The editors of *Time* found his commitment to Christianity somewhat disconcerting, and they directed their writers to play up the influence of Gandhi on King while eliminating references to the singing of "Onward, Christian Soldiers" at his mass meetings. But no amount of media packaging could change the centrality of the gospel to his crusade. When he met with President Eisenhower, he urged him to uphold the *Brown* decision and the 1957 Civil Rights Act, to press Congress to pass more effective civil-rights laws, and to protect voting rights in the South. Because his father and many other Negro preachers remained steadfast Republicans out of loyalty to the party of Lincoln, King remained studiously nonpartisan in his political activities.

It was therefore ironic that King played an indirect role in swinging black votes to the Democratic party and helped to elect John F. Kennedy in 1960. Eisenhower had actually won a majority of the black vote against Adlai Stevenson in 1956 because of his support for civil rights and Stevenson's troubling distance from Negro leaders, with whom he refused to be photographed. Richard Nixon, a lifetime member of the NAACP, had accepted a liberal civil-rights plank in the party platform as a condition of support from Nelson Rockefeller. That, combined with the longtime Republican sympathies of many Negroes, made the black community one of the most hotly contested constituencies in the campaign. The turning point came after King's arrest in Atlanta on specious charges, leading a campaign aide named Harris Wofford and the candidate's brother-in-law, Sargent Shriver, to arrange for a courtesy phone call from Kennedy to Coretta Scott King. The Nixon campaign responded to King's imprisonment with a terse "no comment." Seizing the opening, Wofford arranged for the printing of millions of blue pamphlets bearing the provocative title, *"No Comment" Nixon Versus a Candidate with a Heart, Senator Kennedy.* The pamphlets were distributed through a nationwide network of black churches and were passed out in church parking lots and inserted into church bulletins throughout the country on the Sunday prior to the election. The fliers had their desired effect. Kennedy won 70 percent of the black vote, providing his margin of victory in Illinois, New Jersey, Michigan, and Pennsylvania. The loss of any one of those states would have given the election to Nixon. Many have attributed Kennedy's victory to this get-out-the-vote effort in black churches.

Today some on the left criticize the Christian Coalition's practice of distributing voter guides prior to elections in evangelical and Roman Catholic churches as an unseemly innovation. But as the Kennedy episode of 1960 demonstrates, the distribution of voter-education literature in churches prior to elections was not invented by the pro-family movement. And unlike the pro-Kennedy literature passed out in churches, the Christian Coalition's pamphlets do not endorse candidates, are studiously non-partisan, and cover a broad range of issues. Indeed, voter guides, election scorecards, and other tools to increase turnout among church folk have been used by black churches and liberal groups like the National Council of Churches for decades.[61]

King's tactics were extraordinary. He encouraged his followers to battle for civil rights not from well-appointed, comfortable offices in Washington (the SCLC had only one staff member in the nation's capital) but by penetrating to the core of segregation, laying their lives on the line in Mississippi or Alabama, always using nonviolence to advance the cause. He marveled at how "morally refreshing" it was to "hear five thousand Negroes in Montgomery shout 'Amen' and 'Halleluh' when they are exhorted to pray for those who oppose you." He would publicly petition the Lord to grant the protesters strength to remain nonviolent though they might face death.[62] This was anything but an abstract concept when confronting the fire hoses and billy clubs of "Bull" Connor or the army that George Corley Wallace assembled to try to quash the movement.[63] And while King was getting the attention of the Kennedy administration, the national media, the Justice Department, and Capitol Hill, he was also doing something far more important—stirring the troubled conscience of the white middle class. When he led the march on Washington, he promised to "subpoena the conscience of the nation." And so he did.

It would be a clear distortion to compare the recent political involvement of the white evangelical church with the black church as a political force. But the Christian Coalition has adopted many elements of King's style and tactics. Just as he spoke as a black man to a largely white society, we have tried as Christians to speak in a language that could be heard by a secular society. King used the church and the pulpit to give moral force to what was essentially a political movement. He fought against the forces of extremism and compromise among black activists—the Black Panthers and Malcolm X, who denounced him as an "Uncle Tom"; the NAACP and Roy Wilkins, who believed his marches and demonstrations in the streets sometimes made things worse. Most important, King allied himself with the Democratic party in passing civil rights laws, while maintaining strong relationships with liberal Republicans like Nelson Rockefeller to give his movement a nonpartisan cast. We have done the same by building alliances with Roman Catholic Democrats like former Pennsylvania governor Bob Casey and pro-life Democrats in the House of Representatives.

King's movement was a religious movement from start to finish. It influenced an entire generation of future leaders to view their religious beliefs as informing and shaping their political involvement. In 1960 the Student Nonviolent Coordinating Committee adopted a manifesto that read: "The presupposition of our faith and the manner of our action, nonviolence as it grows from the Judaeo-Christian traditions, seeks a social order of justice permeated by love."[64] Though the SNCC would later veer away from the Christian principles of nonviolence, it achieved its greatest results during its early alliance with King. Nor were such religious appeals to end segregation confined to the black church. After an interregnum of internal debate, the U.S. Catholic Bishops threw their support behind integration, declaring that discrimination based on race could not be reconciled with the truth that God created all men equal and with equal dignity. The following year the United Church of Christ agreed, calling for an end to segregation.[65]

Of course, there is nothing like a crisp moral equivalence between the civil rights movement of the 1960s and the pro-life, pro-family movement of today. We can never know the suffering and outrages endured by those who struggled against racism. Some, like the Mississippi NAACP leader Medgar Evers, lost their lives. Others were beaten, jailed, or fired from jobs, had their homes blown up or their children mowed down with fire hoses. But in our own time, religious folk have poured out of our churches motivated by a sense of right and wrong, seeking to impart decency and

ALL GOD'S CHILDREN

healing to a hurting society and bringing to our political involvement a passion that is fired by faith and tempered by humility. If we succeed, it will be because we have followed King's example always to love those who hate us, doing battle "with Christian weapons and with Christian love." If we fail, it will not be a failure of money or methods, but a failure of the heart and soul.

The task will not be easy. The white evangelical church carries a shameful legacy of racism and the historical baggage of indifference to the most central struggle for social justice in this century, a legacy that is only now being wiped clean by the sanctifying work of repentance and racial reconciliation. There are theological obstacles as well. King, Rauschenbusch, Niebuhr, and other theological liberals poured far more of their faith into their politics than fundamentalists or conservative evangelicals, for whom the Social Gospel is anathema and appeals to perfect the society heretical. Religious conservatives still lack a theology of direct political action. They will need to develop one to achieve their full potential over time, a matter to which we will turn in a later chapter.

King's dream of a racially harmonious society eludes us to this day, a sobering lesson on the limits of what politics—even Christian politics— can achieve. But the legal guarantees he sought were enacted by Lyndon Johnson during the period of the Great Society. Johnson was the first president from the South elected since before the Civil War. Because of his Southern roots, his tepid support for civil rights, and his refusal to attempt to break the use of the filibuster by Southern senators during his authoritarian tenure as Senate Majority Leader, Johnson was an unlikely champion of liberal racial policies. But Kennedy's assassination and a massive grassroots organizing effort by the churches broke the logjam that had held up civil rights legislation. Religious activists marched on Washington, organized political workshops across the country, lobbied their representatives and senators, urged churchgoers to deluge their elected representatives with mail, and participated in twenty-four-hour vigils at the Lincoln Memorial.[66]

As in past struggles, moral language and religious imagery dominated the debate. When Johnson addressed the nation on the Voting Rights Act of 1965, he invoked the words of the Negro spiritual that had become the theme song of the civil rights movement, saying "we shall overcome" the nation's "crippling legacy of bigotry and injustice."[67] The Great Society and the War on Poverty brought to full fruition the hopes and dreams that liberal religious reformers had pursued for nearly a century.[68] Those who marched, protested, and petitioned for what they viewed as social justice heard a lot of objections similar to those raised today from those quarters most threatened by reform. It was the tired old line that mixing religion with politics was a dangerous recipe. One senator voiced the same sentiments that liberals in our own time direct at conservative religious activists when he noted with "profound sorrow" the "role that many religious leaders have played in urging passage of [civil rights] because I cannot make their activities jibe with my concept of the proper place of religious leaders in our nation's life . . . This is not, and cannot be, a moral question." Fortunately, this view did not prevail in the 1960s, and it does not carry the day in our own time.[69]

The Vietnam War ended the era of religious reform that began with the antislavery movement and ended with civil rights and the War on Poverty. By that time the progressive religious tradition (or what we may call the "religious left") resembled Disraeli's "spent volcano." Its activists had grown weary, its moral energy was exhausted, its intellectual tradition sapped, and its political program largely codified in law. As with all social movements, the enactment of its reforms signaled its demise. Beginning in the 1970s, a new reform politics would emerge from the right, led by the likes of Jerry Falwell, Pat Robertson, and the burgeoning Southern Baptist Convention. Joining them were a growing number of Roman Catholics spurred on by the pro-life movement, many of whom had wholeheartedly participated in the labor, civil rights, and anti-Communist struggles of the past. Like Theodore Roosevelt, the evangelicals "insensibly connected a life of social reform and charitable service with Protestant doctrine," while the Roman Catholics, acting in the tradition of Cardinal James Gibbon, fused their theology with their politics.[70]

ALL GOD'S CHILDREN

The rise of religious conservative involvement in politics hardly poses a threat to American democracy. Indeed, it is the source of its renewal. This story will never end, but will continue to stutter, then flourish, flower, and fade. The American political landscape is carved from the granite of a religious people. From the Freedom Riders to Focus on the Family, from Lyman Beecher's Moral Society to the Moral Majority, and from the Women's Christian Temperance Union to the Christian Coalition, we see the lasting impact of changed laws and a transformed culture influenced by the compassion of religious folk. From Finney's Rochester to Rauschenbusch's Hell's Kitchen and from King's Montgomery to Jackson, Mississippi (where conservative Christian groups in 1993 protested the suspension of two hundred students for praying over the school intercom), the story of American politics is the story of a slumbering faithful awakening from the pews and flowing into school board meetings, courtrooms, slums, and state capitols. Contemporary liberals would do well to acknowledge this continuity the next time they hurl invective and bitter recriminations at the so-called religious right.

But there is a lesson in this glorious past for conservatives as well. If we are to funnel our political activities in a positive and lasting direction, we must emulate the passion, the long-suffering, and the nonviolence of our liberal counterparts. They may have a moral blind spot when it comes to such issues as the sanctity of human life, but we have had our own blind spots on issues ranging from anti-Semitism and anti-Catholicism to racial injustice. No one can claim a monopoly on righteousness, and those who think they can often find themselves on the wrong side of history, as the Christian segregationists of the South did, and, increasingly today, those on the left. Like the left in its glory days, we must seek to change hearts and save souls first, believing that the laws will change only as the culture does.

The painful truth that religious conservatives must confront in their general disdain of modern liberalism is this: liberals have been correct throughout history on issues of social justice while we have been neglectful or derelict in applying the principles of our faith to establishing justice in a fallen world. When it came to racism, where were conservative evangelicals? They were not only on the sidelines, but on the wrong side of the most central cause of social justice in this century. I say this to the shame of my own community. It is a dark spot on our history and a burden that we must carry to this day.

There has never been a George Corley Wallace or a Ku Klux Klan on the left. The Klan and massive resistance are our white man's burden, a ball and chain of painful history that remains firmly shackled to our legs. It is one of the main reasons why the pro-family movement's message of protecting innocent human life and religious freedom has had a difficult time achieving moral resonance in the broader society. We quote Martin Luther King to great effect, but how many of us marched with him, and how many of us bear the scars of Bull Connor's billy clubs and police dogs? Sadly, the answer is few. For this reason, our repudiation of racism and bigotry in all its ugly forms must become one of our major tenets as a movement. Pat Buchanan discovered the burden of this issue in 1996, when he received the unwelcome endorsement of former klansman David Duke, and had to face tough questions on his own "populist" views.

The conservative evangelical community's moral blinders on issues of race must be confronted with repentance and genuine reconciliation. Jerry Falwell used his pulpit in the 1960s to condemn civil rights protesters and allowed picketers from the Congress of Racial Equality to be arrested at his church. "Preachers are not called to be politicians, but to be soul winners," he claimed. Billy Graham had a friendly relationship with King and insisted upon desegregated seating at his crusades, but he rarely spoke out against Jim Crow. "I must admit that in all those years it didn't cross my mind that segregation and its consequences for the human family were evil. I was blind to that reality," he later admitted. Both Falwell and Graham have since publicly repudiated that past indifference. But their personal experiences with race, like those of so many others in the conservative evangelical community, show why our attacks on liberals today sometimes ring hollow.

In a speech in Dallas to minority activists of the Christian Coalition in June 1995, I asserted that God would never fully bless the pro-family movement until it first repented for this legacy of racism. Today there is

JDH II

much evidence that this work has begun. The Promise-keepers movement, which is sweeping the nation like wildfire, makes racial reconciliation one of the seven promises that its members make. The Christian Coalition and other pro-family groups are making the inclusion of African-Americans and Latinos in their ranks a major priority. We must do more. The sad record of religious conservatives on race gives liberals reason to hurl charges of bigotry and intolerance at us. However, they are wrong in making those attacks today. The modern pro-family movement enjoys more support for its agenda among minority voters than among whites. It is a multiracial movement that is fully cognizant of its past sins and is marching into the future without the baggage of racial hatred. The Bible says that the sons should not be punished for the sins of the fathers. We should not be judged today based on a wrongdoing with which we have no complicity, and which in fact we have repudiated.

The religious impulse gave the Democratic Party the victories it won over half a century with an unlikely coalition of populists, Progressives, Social Gospelers, New Dealers, and civil rights activists. Incredibly, however, the Democrats in recent years have begun to turn on and decry the very religious influences that fuelled their rise to power. Once invoking the Deity to support their political platform, the Democrats now criticize Republicans for doing so. Once a movement of clerics and laypeople, their party now denounces conservatives for emulating their example. Over time, the agencies and organizations that led the moral crusades of the past have become hollow shells of their former greatness, drifting aimlessly in a political coalition that has become simultaneously more secular and less effective at the ballot box. The story of liberalism's moral drift offers a cogent lesson for the Democratic party—and a warning for Republicans as well. We shall turn to the Republicans in subsequent chapters, but first let us see how the liberals lost their religion—and their political power.

3

LIBERALISM'S HOLLOW CORE

T he long and celebrated history of religiously inspired political activism in America seems to be a tradition ignored—and even
scorned—by many liberals. To hear them tell it, religiously motivated, politically active citizens are a threat to democracy. I was stunned
when Governor Ann Richards of Texas, a Democrat, referred to conservative evangelicals during her 1994 reelection campaign as "mongers of
hate"—this in a state where surveys show that 62 percent of the electorate
consists of self-identified born-again Christians. Not surprisingly, Richards
lost her reelection bid. Later Bob Beckel, a Democratic political consultant
and television commentator, told me that he had called the Democratic
National Committee after Richards' broadside and had warned the people
there to be careful: attacks on religion would backfire in the South, where
religiosity is not generally viewed as a character flaw. Those warnings went
unheeded. And the results were devastating to liberals. The 1994 landslide
that turned the Democrats out of power in Congress and many governor-
ships was in part made possible by dramatically increased turnout among
religious conservative voters.

The religious conservative community is one of the best-organized and
most effective constituencies in American politics today. The failure of lib-

70

erals to grasp that fact is one of the main reasons why the Democratic party is a party with a glorious past, a tenuous present, and an uncertain future. The Christian Coalition is a nonpartisan pro-family organization that does not believe God favors any politician or political party. But the question is: Does the modern Democratic party welcome religious values into our politics? Whatever the reality, the perception among millions of people of faith is that it does not. No matter what happens in 1996 at the presidential level, the Democrats are likely to lose seats in the Senate, to fall to the lowest number of House seats in a half-century, and to wake up after the election with 70 percent of the American people still living in states with Republican governors. Why that has happened is a complex story, but the movement of evangelicals in the South and ethnic Roman Catholics in the North out of the Democratic party is a large part of it.

The Democrats have lost five out of the last seven presidential elections. In 1992, even while gaining the White House, the Democrats actually lost seats in the House of Representatives—only the second time in this century that has occurred. In 1994 they lost in the biggest off-year landslide in the twentieth century. Today, for the first time since Reconstruction, a majority of members of Congress from the South are Republicans. More than two hundred Democrats have switched to the Republican party since the 1994 elections, and one has switched to Ross Perot's fledgling Reform party, but not a single Republican federal officeholder has switched to the Democratic party. The Democratic ranks in Congress are being thinned by a rash of retirement. Liberals like Pat Schroeder have given up hope of regaining a majority, and moderates like Sam Nunn and Howell Heflin have grown tired of battling with liberals of their own party. The Democratic party is not about to disappear. It is still the longest surviving party in the history of the Western industrial democracies. It will remain a viable and effective force at the ballot box. But robbed of its religious heritage, liberalism is fighting a rearguard action against the turning tide of political fortunes, not a forward-looking march back to power.

Many thoughtful liberals are beginning to recognize that the vicious attacks on conservative religious folk by the secular left have completely backfired. "Today, fear of the 'religious right' has pushed many secular liberals into opposing virtually any religiously motivated effort to influence the public policy debate, simply because it is religious," Harvey Cox, professor of theology at Harvard University, complains. "I am dead against trying to keep religious conservatives out of the political debate. The tactic of exclusion is self-defeating."[1] Of course, the problem for liberals like Cox is that they are trying to force liberalism to become religious once more, a task that will be like pushing a boulder up Mount Everest. Too many elements of the liberal coalition, such as the organized feminist and gay lobbies, are openly hostile to the invocation of Biblical values as the basis of political action. The reason religious conservatives have risen as an effective political movement in recent years is that the left dropped its use of religious and moral language in the late 1960s and the early 1970s. The religious left lost its soul, and we stepped into the vacuum. As the liberal Christian writer James Wallis argues in his book *The Soul of Politics*, "liberal religion has lost its spiritual center" and has been co-opted by "the liberal power centers of society."[2]

What a stark contrast to the glorious age of liberalism. In the 1960s liberalism was the rage, in large measure because of the moral language it used to advance its agenda. Liberals were, in David Halberstam's phrase, "the best and the brightest," full of promise and hope, their social agenda fully ascendant. Led by John F. Kennedy and a new generation of post-New Deal leaders, they pledged to eradicate poverty at home and oppose tyranny abroad. Even the rising stars within the Republican party embraced their ideas: Governor Nelson Rockefeller of New York, Senator Charles Percy of Illinois, and John V. Lindsay, the mayor of New York City. The most powerful political organizations in the nation were the AFL-CIO and trade unions like the Teamsters. The most influential think tanks were liberal foundations like the Brookings Institution. The most prominent politicians were all liberals: Lyndon Johnson, Robert F. Kennedy, William J. Fulbright, and Hubert Humphrey. The most important religious leaders were Martin Luther King; Theodore Hesburgh, president of the University of Notre Dame and an opponent of the Vietnam War; and key figures in the National Council of Churches.

Most Americans accepted the basic assumptions of liberalism—the federal government had a duty to help the poor, the United States should play an active role in international affairs, the United Nations was an effective vehicle for ushering in a post–World War II peace, racism was wrong, and government had an obligation to ensure social justice for all. The few who questioned such assumptions, like William F. Buckley and the iconoclastic *National Review* magazine, were treated as oddities by the dominant culture. When Barry Goldwater ran a conservative campaign that launched a frontal assault on liberalism in 1964, he lost in the most sweeping landslide in history.[3] Nor did the Republican party usually function as a stalwart conservative alternative to liberalism. When Senator Robert Taft, known as "Mr. Republican," ran for his party's presidential nomination opposing the New Deal and an international foreign policy, he lost to Dwight D. Eisenhower. As president, Ike left most of the New Deal intact and even expanded the welfare state by creating the Department of Health, Education, and Welfare. The two Supreme Court justices who would become synonymous with liberal judicial activism—Earl Warren and William Brennan—were both Eisenhower appointees. So small were the differences between the two parties that one of the hottest issues in the 1960 presidential campaign involved the fate of two obscure islands off the coast of China, Quemoy and Matsu.

Liberalism's intellectual and political hegemony stretched from the New Deal to the Great Society without a successful conservative challenge. To be sure, there were exceptions. The Cold War demanded a united response that brought liberals and conservatives together in opposition to further expansion of Communism in Korea and Southeast Asia. McCarthyism was a brief but ultimately discredited episode in domestic politics that allowed conservatives to gain an upper hand over liberals they deemed too soft on Communism. The 1950s witnessed the drive for the Bricker Amendment, which would have required a national referendum prior to U.S. involvement in a foreign war as a check on the excesses of internationalism, though it never received the required two-thirds majority in Congress. But those conservative efforts mainly sought to trim the ascendancy of liberalism at the margins. Liberalism marched from victory to victory without a significant challenge to its central ideas, ideas that were almost always advanced in moral terms and in religious language. As John F. Kennedy said two weeks before taking the oath of office, "For of those to whom much is given, much is required . . . with God's help [this] will characterize our Government's conduct in the four stormy years that lie ahead."[4]

The Democratic party—and liberalism in particular—was a movement of religious and moral reform. The Republican party, in contrast, was for most of the post–World War II period the party of big business and opposition to civil rights, and it spoke in the dry, austere language of accountants. That set of circumstances continued from the New Deal until the late 1960s, during which time the Republicans won only two presidential elections, both with Eisenhower, a former war hero. Not that the Republicans were about to go the way of the Whigs of the nineteenth century. But unlike the Republican party of Lincoln, the GOP of the twentieth century had become a bean-counting party, talking about fiscal austerity and budget cuts instead of about strengthening the family and eliminating social injustice. Faced with such tepid opposition, liberalism reigned supreme.

But something strange happened on the way from the coronation. The Democratic party and liberalism began a decline into moral malaise and spiritual exhaustion so gradual that it was at first indiscernible—but over time so great as to compromise its integrity. Where liberalism once was the nation's conscience on issues like women's suffrage, child labor laws, political reform, and civil rights, today it is widely perceived to be the ideology that rejects the true modern equivalents of those causes. On euthanasia and abortion it is not only silent but vocally opposed to basic human rights. In the 1960s George Wallace stood in the schoolhouse door to keep minority children out; today it is the liberals who stand in the schoolhouse door to keep them in. They oppose efforts to provide school choice to those who are trapped in schools that are war zones. Some have resisted reforms of adoption laws that would allow for more transracial adoptions to liberate minority children from a foster-home system that rarely gives them a sense of permanence and love. And yet, in the same breath, they advocate adoption rights for transvestites and homosexuals. A hodge-podge of special interests ranging from gays, labor unions, and feminists to trial lawyers, modern liberalism is torn by the loud demands of its contending factions and no longer presents a coherent philosophy. Its answer to every problem is a federal program that devours the income of American families and transfers it to an uncaring and inefficient bureaucracy in Washington.

The progressive impulse was built upon a visceral opposition to social injustice. But today too many liberals are more concerned with protecting government programs than with helping those who are truly suffering. Has welfare measurably improved the lives of the poor and needy? Irrefutably not. Yet the left condemns anyone who genuinely tries to reform it as "turning their backs on the poor." Has abortion ended the lives of more innocent people than all the diseases in our history? Yes, but if you advocate legal protection for those innocent lives, you are "extremist." Abortion, poverty, a failing education system, fatherless households, and a polluted culture are all modern forms of social injustice. But to these injustices the far left all too often shows a callous disregard.

That is not the liberalism I studied and admired from a distance (even as I disagreed with many of its policies). That liberalism sought to bring political power to bear for defined purposes: to provide basic standards of fairness in the workplace, to ensure civil rights for all Americans, to guarantee health care to widows and the elderly, to give women full political and economic equality, and to grant all Americans full access to the promise of the American experiment. The grand theme of modern liberalism, succinctly stated, was to guarantee equal opportunity for all Americans and a level playing field through government assistance to the disfranchised—the poor, the disabled, racial minorities, and women.

Frequently that meant expanding the role of government. In order to guarantee food and medical safety, liberals created the Food and Drug Administration to monitor the content and safety of food and pharmaceutical products. To provide medical care for the elderly and poor, liberals ushered in Medicare and Medicaid. To regulate the massive railroad monopolies of the late nineteenth century, liberals created the Interstate Commerce Commission. But over time the purpose of government, for liberalism, became less to guarantee equality than to solidify the political support of the special interest constituency that benefited. In the case of civil rights, the initial goal of equal protection under the law for blacks became transformed into quotas and set-asides that actually institutionalized inequality. In the case of women's rights, the lofty goal of granting women equal pay for equal work curdled into an agenda of taxpayer-funded abortion and billions of dollars in subsidies to organizations that perform abortions, like Planned Parenthood.

Let me be clear what I am *not* saying. I am not claiming that GOP stands for "God's Own Party," or conversely that the Democrats are godless atheists. No political party can claim a monopoly on God's truth, and religious conservatives do not assert that those who support a different political platform are acting in an "un-Christian" way. There are still many eloquent and devout people of faith found in the ranks of modern liberalism. But as a movement, liberalism today is decidedly discomfited by the invocation of religious faith as a rationale for political action. One rarely hears a Mario Cuomo or a Jimmy Carter invoke Scripture for why he supports abortion on demand. Feminists rarely if ever bring up the teachings of Christ in their cry for equality for women. Liberalism no longer casts its agenda in moral and religious terms, and that retreat from religious values and religious language is the issue that must be confronted by the left if it ever hopes again to win the hearts and minds of the American people.

Such moral dissonance cannot be sustained. That is why liberalism as a coherent political philosophy is unraveling. The first signs of instability came after the assassination of John F. Kennedy, which passed the torch of liberalism to Lyndon Johnson. The Kennedys and many Adlai Stevenson–style liberals viewed Johnson with deep distrust because of his Southern roots and checkered record on civil rights. Johnson won over their reluctant support by selecting Hubert Humphrey, who first rose to national prominence when he championed a civil rights platform at the Democratic convention in 1948, as his running mate in 1964. He also achieved the passage of such Great Society landmarks as Medicare and the Civil Rights Act of 1964.

Then came Vietnam. The war deeply divided liberals, and the moral center no longer held. At the Democratic National Convention in 1968, Hubert Humphrey, who had personified the best hopes of liberalism, found himself the leader of a party torn apart by internal feuding, with the streets of Chicago stained by the blood of youthful demonstrators who had clashed with police. The American people watched the spectacle unfold on their television sets. Here was modern liberalism's first genuine moral crisis. A war begun by arguably the most liberal president in American history—Lyndon Johnson—and sustained by a series of lies (beginning with the trumped-up Gulf of Tonkin episode) had drained the Great Society of all its moral fervor. The soaring dreams of liberalism in its finest moment died in the rice paddies and killing fields of Southeast Asia. Richard Goodwin, a brilliant speechwriter who wrote Johnson's famous "Great Society" speech, concluded bitterly: "Lyndon Johnson's war destroyed Lyndon Johnson's Great Society." Goodwin reflected later that the war "became a weapon for those who, as the price of their support of Vietnam, demanded a reduction, a virtual abandonment, of liberal reforms."[5] Goodwin bolted from Johnson, first to Eugene McCarthy and later to Robert Kennedy's antiwar presidential campaign, reflecting profound liberal disillusionment with the direction of the Democratic party. Humphrey tried in vain to hold those factions together, trailing Richard Nixon badly until Johnson announced a bombing halt just prior to Election Day. It was too little, too late.

There were still many Democratic party leaders who sought to maintain the mainstream morality that had led to liberalism's great accomplishments. But with the exception of the breath blown into liberalism by Watergate, it was clear that the party and the movement had cast its lot with the special interests. Feminism became an increasingly radical political force that gained a strong foothold in the Democratic party, with some feminists arguing that the traditional family was an outmoded institution, "repressive" to women and damaging to children. Liberal attempts to alleviate poverty led to the *de facto* replacement of husbands and fathers by a federal government of unprecedented power. They began by changing welfare laws that had been on the books for thirty years. Instead of providing a rudimentary social safety net for widows, welfare became a program designed to provide a guaranteed income for all Americans, regardless of whether or not they worked, married, or completed a high-school education.

The legacy of those efforts has not ushered in the promised millennium. As Ronald Reagan once said, we declared war on poverty, and poverty won. In the past thirty years, we have spent $5.3 trillion on means-tested welfare spending, more in constant 1990 dollars than we spent on World War II, Korea, and Vietnam combined. The result has been a skyrocketing increase in social pathologies with no significant amelioration of poverty. Bill Bennett has observed that what we do to our children, they will do to society as adults. If federal programs are to be judged by the depth of their failures rather than the height of their aspirations, then liberal welfare policy is one of the most morally bankrupt and discredited domestic initiatives in modern times.

In education policy, similar failures have occurred. SAT scores have declined for twenty-nine out of the past thirty years. Schoolchildren in the United States trail their counterparts in other industrialized nations in math, science, and geography test scores. In the area of sex education, the teaching of a permissive "safe sex" curriculum has unleashed grassroots parental revolts from Texas to New York City, where the most liberal school district in the nation saw many school board seats won by conservatives in the 1993 campaign against the Rainbow Curriculum. Many on the left seemed to believe that teachers or administrators should have more control over the education of children than parents. They decided what values children should be taught, giving the concerns of parents only peripheral importance. Most notions of challenging cognitive learning were left behind. The newfound liberal disdain for parental rights helps explain why many have rejected the liberal establishment, preferring instead to send their children to private schools or to educate their children at home.

In short, liberalism has lost its moral authority, its hold over the hearts of the American people, and its place as the voice for the voiceless and a defender of the defenseless. How did that happen? Who is responsible?

Part of the answer could be found in a room at the National Press Club in June 1994. As the 1994 election campaign unfolded, it was clear that the Democrats were growing increasingly worried about the possibility of a Republican victory. It was just a matter of time before they cracked. Then one day my office received a fax of *Roll Call,* the newspaper of Capitol Hill, reporting that Congressman Vic Fazio of California, the embattled chairman of the Democratic National Congressional Committee, was going to hold a news conference on June 21, 1994, announcing that the central theme of the fall campaign would be exposing the stranglehold of what he called the "radical right" over the Republican party.

Mike Russell, the communications director of the Christian Coalition, immediately called the National Press Club and reserved the room next door to Fazio's, setting up a scenario of dueling news conferences. We also discovered that Fazio was going to hit us hard and refer to evangelicals as the "fire-breathing Christian radical right." That was all the opening we needed.

The next morning Mike and I hopped on an early morning flight to Washington and tapped out a response to Fazio's broadside on my laptop computer. As I pounded away on the keyboard with the Virginia countryside rushing by beneath us, I kept wondering whether Fazio really intended to take such a reckless approach as attacking religious values and religious people. Were it true, I marveled, it would certainly be the archetype of the new, modern liberalism—a liberalism that had lost its moral compass and was now resorting to precisely the kind of religious bigotry that it had historically battled.

We arrived at the National Press Club toting photocopies of a press release that accused the Democratic party of engaging in "Christian-bashing" and decried its use of "the politics of hate, the politics of division, the politics of bigotry." We stood in the back of the room while Fazio droned on listlessly from a prepared statement. In a way, I felt bad for Fazio; it was apparent that his heart was not in it. The Democrats were in a state of near panic, having lost two special elections within the previous month in Oklahoma and Kentucky, where evangelical voters had turned out in record numbers. Fazio did not catch sight of me or our entourage as we entered the room, though a number of reporters nodded and smiled knowingly. For a while Fazio seemed to be going in a different direction, and I wondered if we had heard an incorrect rumor. Then the words "Christian Coalition" left his lips, and our staff immediately dropped a packet of documents on the lap of every reporter in the room refuting Fazio's assertions.

One valuable piece of evidence was a copy of the nonpartisan voter guide we distributed in the Kentucky race. It noted that Joe Prather, the Democratic nominee, was in favor of restricting abortion and legalizing voluntary school prayer. That showed, first, that our voter education literature was not skewed to the Republicans, as the Democrats so frequently charged. Second, it raised a disturbing question: Did Prather's agreement with our stands on abortion and prayer make him an "extremist"?

At a news conference afterward, I called Fazio's attack an example of "hate-mongering, name-calling, and religious bigotry" and compared it to the anti-Catholic prejudice that had haunted John F. Kennedy during his 1960 campaign for the presidency. Such attacks on a person's religious beliefs were "rank hypocrisy" and had no place in our civic discourse. "Thirty years ago, George Corley Wallace played the race card," I said. "Today Vic Fazio and the Democrats are playing the religion card."[6]

Unfortunately for the Democrats, the attempted demonization of religious people and their values was nothing new. In fact, I would have been far more surprised to hear that Fazio was calling a press conference to announce that he was leading a campaign to reinvigorate the Democratic party with the kind of religious passion and fervor that had once helped define it.

If the Willie Horton ads and the race-baiting employed by some Republicans represents a shocking turnabout for the party of Lincoln, Fazio's attack on religion was a thorough repudiation of the religious heritage that had made liberalism a force for good. For much of its history, liberalism's greatest achievements came about because of its insistence that a moral and religious vision of rights and responsibilities took precedence over purely secular claims. The Social Gospel movement challenged the secular demands of the marketplace to remember those less fortunate. The New Deal, the Great Society, and the civil rights movement all bear witness to that tension. But for liberals in more recent times, that tension is gone. The battle between religious sensibilities and secularism is over, and the political results have been disastrous.

One of the critical moments in this evolution came with the issue of abortion. The Supreme Court's ruling in *Roe* v. *Wade* in 1973 gave liberals a stunning legal and political victory, but at enormous moral costs. The long-standing liberal position that life should be protected from conception through natural death was replaced by a permissive notion that abortion was not about the life or death of a child, but about protecting the right to "control one's own body" without regard to notions of right and wrong. Invoking the constitutionally dubious notion of an unlimited right to privacy, the Court ruled that a child in the mother's womb was not a legal "person," faintly echoing Chief Justice Roger Taney's infamous phrase from the *Dred Scott* decision of 1857.

The reason for religious conservative opposition to abortion is our belief in the sanctity of the individual human being. We believe that every person is created by God with certain inalienable rights, among which is the right to life, and that government is established to protect those rights. In this sense, the abortion issue represents the proper mixture of religion and politics and is consistent with the values of democracy. Both democracy and Christianity are based upon the sanctity of each person. From the Declaration of Independence to the Emancipation Proclamation and the Civil Rights Act of 1964, we have declared those rights and protected them with the rule of law. Protecting innocent life is in the finest tradition of that social justice movement. Straying from the tradition threatens liberalism's intellectual and moral viability as a political philosophy.

Abortion on demand is thoroughly inconsistent with what most politicians and most Americans favored for most of our history.[7] Many traditional liberals maintained their historical opposition to abortion until *Roe* created the right by judicial fiat. A letter written by Senator Edward Kennedy in 1971 summarizes the position well. While movingly acknowledging the difficulties and divisions inherent in the abortion debate, Kennedy concluded that "it is my personal feeling that the legalization of abortion on demand is not in accordance with the values which our civilization places on human life. Wanted or unwanted, I believe that human life, even at its earliest stages, has certain rights which must be recognized—the right to be born, the right to love, the right to grow old." Kennedy continued, "When history looks back to this era it should recognize this generation as one which cared about human beings enough to halt the practice of war, to provide a decent living for every family, and to fulfill its responsibility to its children from the very moment of conception."[8]

Kennedy's eloquence captured the essence of his Roman Catholicism. To underscore how far liberals have strayed, one need only recall that as recently as 1972 the Democratic vice-presidential nominee was Sargent Shriver, Kennedy's brother-in-law and a pro-life Catholic. When George McGovern and Shriver stumped through Pennsylvania during that ill-fated campaign, they were joined by state auditor Bob Casey, who would later go on to become governor of the state and a vocal Democrat opposing his party's moral drift on the issue. Indeed, it is difficult to imagine the traditional liberal opposition to abortion, nuclear war, and the death penalty apart from their religious objections to the taking of life.[9]

Roe was a defining moment for liberalism in its growing disdain for the use of religious language to advance political ideas. As Yale law professor Stephen Carter has observed, abortion played a central role in marginalizing the voice of faith in our political discourse, helping to create a "culture of disbelief." Ted Kennedy, who later retreated from his pro-life views, was far from alone in conforming to the demands of his political party. For most of the 1970s there was no more eloquent pro-life voice in the nation than Jesse Jackson's. He opposed taxpayer-funding of abortion through Medicaid, noting that the majority of the victims of abortion were minority babies, and decried the notion that any child was "unwanted" in God's sight.[10] But Jackson found it impossible to accommodate his pro-life morality to his presidential ambitions. In 1984, during his first bid for the White House, he discarded his pro-life stand.

Al Gore similarly backpedaled from his religious beliefs, at least as they affected his political views. As deeply committed evangelical Christians, Gore and his wife, Tipper, made clear their opposition to abortion from his first Congressional campaign in 1976, and, as a member of the House of Representatives, he cosponsored a Human Life Amendment and voted for an amendment offered by Representative Mark Siljander, Republican of Michigan, defining life as beginning at conception. Tipper was equally vocal on other issues, leading a campaign in the early 1980s for the placement of warning labels on records containing sexually explicit lyrics. Reconciling those views to a Democratic party beholden to feminists and the financial contributions of Hollywood record company executives proved impossible. During his failed 1984 presidential bid, Gore and his wife made a pilgrimage to Los Angeles, where they in effect apologized and repented from their errant ways. Tapped as Bill Clinton's running mate in 1992, Gore attacked the pro-life plank of the Republican platform, the identical position he had voted for in Congress, as "extremist." There was no more talk about warning labels, not when contributions from Hollywood were funding his campaign. And in 1995, when Bill Clinton nominated Dr. Henry Foster as Surgeon General, Al Gore flew to Nashville to hold a pep rally in support of his confirmation, dismissing the fact that he had performed elective abortions.

This does not mean that Jesse Jackson and Al Gore are "less Christian" than their pro-life coreligionists. Only God can judge their hearts, and that is not my purpose here. But their remarkable turnabout on the central moral issue of our time shows how unrelenting liberalism has become in its commitment to a secular orthodoxy, an orthodoxy that often demands that people downplay their religious convictions or keep quiet about them.

To be fair, such conversions are not confined to the Democratic party. While running against Ronald Reagan in the Republican primaries in 1980, George Bush was a moderate on abortion, opposing a constitutional amendment and favoring limited taxpayer funding of abortions for poor women. Bush switched his position as vice president, going on to serve as perhaps the most consistently uncompromising pro-life president in modern times. The pro-life activists who participate in the nominating process of the Republican party routinely win conversions of this kind from politicians, just as pro-choice activists do in the Democratic party. But there are profound differences. George Bush was not required to leave his religious convictions at the door as he sought the presidency. Nor was the evolution of his earlier moderate views on abortion necessary to establish his viability in the Republican party—he was, after all, already vice president. But the Democrats have not nominated a pro-life candidate on their national ticket since the *Roe* decision legalizing abortion. Bill Clinton has actually said that abortion was a "litmus test" in the appointment of federal judges and has vowed not to consider anyone for the Supreme Court who is not pro-choice. That would rule out perhaps half of the Roman Catholic jurists in the nation today. Clinton and Gore, both supporters of various pro-life measures in their earlier careers, sitting stone-faced at the National Prayer Breakfast in 1994 as Mother Teresa condemned abortion as "the greatest destroyer of peace in the world today," are metaphors for a liberalism cut loose from its spiritual moorings.[11]

Democrats failed to recognize that while keeping the option of abortion legal in narrow circumstances may well be favored by many Americans, the constant trumpeting of the right to abortion was not viewed by the American people as the moral equivalent of defending the defenseless unborn child. Why, many wondered, did a political movement that had spoken so eloquently for the weak, the vulnerable, and the helpless, seem so callous toward innocent unborn children?

Mario Cuomo attempted to provide an answer in a speech at the University of Notre Dame in 1984. Cuomo announced that he accepted the teachings of the Catholic bishops on abortion and observed them in his own life. But he argued, unconvincingly, that while as a Roman Catholic he could abide by his church's teaching on abortion, he could not take such a stand as an elected official.[12] Acknowledging that "abortion is a 'matter of life and death,' " he insisted that nonetheless "the question whether to engage the political system in a struggle to have it adopt certain articles of our belief as part of public morality is not a matter of doctrine: it is a matter of prudential political judgment."[13]

This raises a thorny dilemma. How can a person of faith tell when an issue is governed by his moral convictions or by "prudential political judgment"? "The community must decide if what is being proposed would be better left to private discretion than public policy," answered Cuomo, "whether it restricts freedoms, and if so to what end, to whose benefit; whether it will produce a good or bad result; whether overall it will help the community or divide it."[14] In the case of abortion, he added, "the breadth, intensity, and sincerity of opposition to church teaching" has made it impossible to "translate our Catholic morality into civil law, a law not for the believers who don't need it but for disbelievers who reject it." This was an astounding argument. In short, he said that religious convictions are not politically operative if those views are "divisive," and if the opposition to them is intense and broad-based. Such instances, of course, are precisely when religious beliefs are most needed and have the most compelling force in a democratic system.

Was there a consensus on civil rights for racial minorities in the 1950s? Of course not. Which is precisely why the marches and demonstrations of the civil rights movement were so "divisive" and the opposition so fierce. Such morally ambiguous moments are not a time to hide one's religious convictions; they are a time to shout them louder.

Amazingly, Cuomo admits that his argument requires religious people at times to remain silent in the face of staggering social injustice. He observes that "few, if any Catholic bishops spoke for abolition in the years before the Civil War." That silence, he argues, was not because they were "hypocrites; they were realists." Far be it from me to accuse persons of faith who remain silent of hypocrisy—that is a matter of the heart that belongs between them and their God. But let us be grateful that William Lloyd Garrison, Harriet Tubman, and Harriet Beecher Stowe were not realists. They advocated the abolition of slavery because slavery was immoral, not because it appeared politically possible. William Wilberforce did not remain silent in the face of the grave evil of the slave trade. Dietrich Bon-hoeffer did not practice political realism in his opposition to the anti-Semitic rantings of the Nazis—an opposition that he ultimately paid for with his life.

Whether one agrees or disagrees with Cuomo's politics, his rationale for remaining silent on great social issues despite one's deep moral convic-tions seems decidedly *unliberal*. He has indisputably been one of the most eloquent and gifted figures in American politics in recent years. But in 1994 he followed his own advice and sacrificed his moral convictions to the demands of political expediency. During the campaign for reelection as governor of New York, Cuomo abandoned his long-standing opposition to the death penalty and pledged not to oppose a referendum legalizing capi-tal punishment. His reversal—another diversion from the teachings of the Roman Catholic church—was clearly designed to boost his flagging popu-larity. But it failed to persuade many voters—liberals felt betrayed, and conservatives remained distrustful—and Cuomo lost, leaving a sad foot-note to a brilliant political career.

Only in recent years have liberals begun to argue that bringing reli-gious convictions into the political arena is somehow undemocratic and dangerous. Indeed, every liberal reformer from Bryan to Rauschenbusch to King practiced the opposite. Had liberalism throughout this century ac-ceded to this argument, where would child labor laws be, which surely of-fended business, or civil rights, which many whites opposed? If this is the test, we would still be living in the eighteenth century, unenlightened by an "American century" that was ushered in and defined by liberal ideas. The truth is that there can be no divorce between moral belief and politi-cal action, as there can be none between moral belief and religious convic-tions. As Alexis de Tocqueville observed, "Despotism may be able to do without religion, but democracy cannot."

There remains great unease within the Democratic party over the in-consistency of its views on abortion with the party's historic role as a voice for the innocent, the marginalized, and the weak. This unease is a sign of the afflicted conscience of liberalism. Its most compelling voice in recent years has been former Pennsylvania governor Bob Casey, who requested an opportunity to address the Democratic convention in 1992 and almost challenged Bill Clinton in the presidential primaries in 1996. Called "out of touch" by Kate Michelman of the National Abortion Rights Action League, Casey believed that the Democrats were making a mistake by including language in their platform that would guarantee the right of a woman to have an abortion at any stage of pregnancy, for whatever reason she wanted, even if it meant using taxpayer funding.[15] In a letter to Ron Brown, the Democratic party chairman, Casey argued, "The platform draft which I have seen has the effect, in my opinion, of placing the national party even more squarely within the abortion-on-demand camp. I believe this is a serious mistake for the party and would like the opportunity to present this point of view, shared by many Democrats, to the convention."[16] But Casey was not allowed to speak.

The dilemma of the former pro-life liberal is not an easy one. Harris Wofford, elected to the U.S. Senate in 1991, headed the Peace Corps under John F. Kennedy and had helped to arrange Kennedy's famous call to Coretta King as her husband languished in jail by order of a Georgia judge. As the issue evolved during the 1970s and 1980s, Wofford gradually reconciled himself to a pro-choice position. But morally and politically, he remained nominally supportive of Pennsylvania's Abortion Control Act, which required parental consent, a woman's right to know, and a twenty-four-hour waiting period prior to an abortion. In 1993 Wofford voted on a straight party line in a closed-door meeting of a Senate judiciary subcommittee in favor of the Freedom of Choice Act, which would have voided laws like the Pennsylvania statute. A Christian Coalition lobbyist was excluded from the meeting but learned from a committee aide how Wofford had voted. We immediately activated phone banks across Pennsylvania and deluged his office with phone calls. Within a few hours, Wofford had issued a press release promising to oppose any federal measures that would weaken Pennsylvania's pro-life law. Caught between his moral convictions and the demands of the pro-abortion lobby, Wofford voted one way in private and talked another way in public. His inconsistency contributed to his defeat by the pro-life Republican Rick Santorum in 1994.

Today it is hard to conceive that there was a time when the election of a Catholic president seemed unthinkable. But it was not until 1928 that the first Roman Catholic received the presidential nomination of a major political party, when the Democrats repudiated the anti-Catholicism of the Ku Klux Klan and nominated Al Smith, then governor of New York. The ensuing campaign became a pitched battle between city-dwellers and rural country folk, Catholics and Protestants, "wets" and drys. More than race, class, or ideology, the cleavage that divided the nation was religious and cultural. Smith was described by one of his confidants as a man who believed that God would guide him, and that it was his duty to follow God's laws.[17]

That faith almost certainly cost him the election. Smith's defeat is widely acknowledged to have been heavily influenced by anti-Catholic sentiment. "The time has not yet come when a man can say beads in the White House," he said following his loss.[18] Some of the more bizarre aspects of this bigotry were evident in the charge made during the campaign that, if elected, Smith planned to build a secret tunnel from New York City to the Vatican.[19] An equally ridiculous charge, though taken seriously at the time, was that Smith would urge the Pope to move the Vatican to the United States.[20]

The legacy of Smith's defeat was a fear of the explosive role of religion in politics that traumatized American Catholics for a generation. Many Catholics feared that unless they separated their religious beliefs from their politics, a largely Protestant nation would never grant them full citizenship. This historical legacy explains, in part, why Catholic liberals like Cuomo and Kennedy have found it so easy to shed their moral convictions as if they were a second skin. It was pounded into their heads that Roman Catholics in America should never invoke religious values as a rationale for their political stands.

It was thirty-two more years before a Catholic would again attempt a run at the presidency, and again it was a Democratic nominee. John F. Kennedy had been haunted by the prospect of running for the presidency as a Catholic, but his father reassured him, "There's a whole new generation out there, and it's filled with the sons and daughters of immigrants and those people are going to be mighty proud that one of their own is running for president. And that pride will be your spur, it will give your campaign an intensity we've never seen in public life."[21] And so it did.

To Richard Nixon's credit, he declined to make religion an issue in the 1960 campaign and repeatedly stated that the discussion should be about the issues. But not all of his supporters felt bound by the same obligation. Some of the nation's most prominent Protestant and evangelical leaders began a systematic campaign to make Kennedy's Catholicism itself an issue, driving a wedge that frightened many evangelical voters, especially in the South. The Reverend Norman Vincent Peale was one of the organizers of the National Conference of Citizens for Religious Freedom, which asked, "Is it reasonable to assume that a Roman Catholic President would be able to withstand the determined efforts of a hierarchy of his church to gain further funds and favors for its schools and institutions, and otherwise break the wall of separation of church and state?"[22]

Kennedy, against the urgings of many of his closest advisers, including his brother Robert, tackled the issue head-on in a speech to the Greater Houston Ministerial Association in September 1960. In that now famous speech, Kennedy said that "because I am a Catholic, and no Catholic has ever been elected President, the real issues in this campaign have been obscured—perhaps deliberately. . . . So it is apparently necessary for me to state once again—not what kind of church I believe in, for that should be important only to me—but what kind of an America I believe in."[23] He then went on to paint in clear terms exactly the kind of America he believed in. One that was not Catholic, Protestant, or Jewish, and one in which the dynamic tension of church and state was enlivened, not enshrined. He concluded by saying, "I do not intend to apologize for these views to my critics of either Catholic or Protestant faith—nor do I intend to disavow either my views or my church in order to win the election. If I should lose on the real issues, I shall return to my seat in the Senate, satisfied that I had tried my best and was fairly judged." But if the critics of his religious faith believed that "forty million Americans lost their chance of being President on the day they were baptized, then it is the whole nation that will be the loser, in the eyes of Catholics and non-Catholics around the world, in the eyes of history, and in the eyes of our own people."[24]

How ironic that a mere quarter-century after John Kennedy's moving speech the Democratic party's strategy for winning the 1994 elections was to attack evangelical Christians as "fanatics" practicing "subterranean" citizenship. In 1993 the Democrats had attacked a Republican lieutenant gubernatorial candidate, Mike Farris, for being too closely tied to Pat Robertson and Jerry Falwell. Farris and Robertson had never met. The charge that Farris had once worked for Falwell was untrue. Yet the attacks on Farris' religious beliefs, the ridicule heaped upon him for educating his children at home, and the charges hurled by the far left about his religious associations were so vituperative that the journalist Michael Barone called them full of "distortion and religious ridicule."

Even John Kennedy's brother, the embattled liberal Senator Ted Kennedy, raised the religious beliefs of his opponent in a bitter campaign in Massachusetts. In a fire-and-brimstone speech, Kennedy attacked his opponent Mitt Romney for having once served as an elder in the Church of Latter Day Saints. Pointing out that the Mormon church had a policy of excluding women from the priesthood and had formerly prevented blacks from serving as priests, Kennedy and his nephew, Representative Joseph P. Kennedy II, raised numerous questions about Romney's views on abortion and civil rights. They demanded to know: did Romney reject or accept the teachings of his church? In the course of just a few days there were attacks and apologies, attacks and more apologies. The attacks were almost identical to those directed at Al Smith and John Kennedy vis-à-vis the Vatican and their own religious beliefs. The only difference was that this time it wasn't the Vatican that was being attacked, but the Mormon headquarters in Salt Lake City. And this time the "obscure and mysterious" religion was not Catholicism but Mormonism. Ultimately Kennedy apologized, but the damage was done, not only to Romney but to the liberal cause.[25]

Unfortunately for the Democrats, abortion and religious tolerance are not the only issues on which liberals have surrendered the moral high ground. On issue after issue they have traded moral suasion for interest-group politics. The rights of workers have been scuttled in favor of deference to labor union leaders, such as in the refusal to enforce the Supreme Court's decision that workers cannot be required to pay union dues that are used for political advocacy purposes rather than for collective bargaining. The rights of minority students to attend safe and successful schools have been shoved aside in deference to powerful teachers' unions that oppose school choice. The Democrats' longtime advocacy of a color-blind society has been compromised by a campaign for quotas and set-asides and by the refusal of many of their leaders, including the Reverend Jesse Jackson, to denounce the anti-Semitism and anti-Catholicism of Louis Farrakhan. The civil rights message has been further blurred by a politically motivated special rights agenda that calls for minority status based on sexual preference. In 1995 President Clinton sent White House aide George Stephanopoulos to a group of gay journalists to pledge the administration's support for a gay rights bill, an act of political posturing for a piece of special interest legislation that had little if any chance of passage in Congress. The contrast between the Democratic party that achieved success for most of this century and the Democratic party that has stayed alive principally by pretending to be something it is not is glaring and, in the long run, unsustainable. It is more than coincidental that Bill Clinton hired Dick Morris, a Republican consultant who boasts among his clients Senators Jesse Helms and Trent Lott, to devise his reelection strategy in 1996.

Liberals have learned to mask their retreat with the rhetoric of values and spirituality. While embracing the counterculture and the radicalism of feminists and gay rights activists, the Democrats maintain the façade of the traditional morality that was their hallmark from Jefferson to Bryan. That shows up particularly in their attempts to win the presidency. For Democrats seeking a way out of the political wilderness, the rhetoric if not the deeds of Jimmy Carter and Bill Clinton provide a significant road map. Their victories—the lone two victories for the Democrats in the past seven presidential elections—both hinged on the popular belief that they were devout Christians and moral centrists.

In 1976 Jimmy Carter, a self-styled "born-again" evangelical, emerged as the savior of the modern Democratic party. After the horror of Vietnam and the scandal of Watergate, Carter sought to address what he called the "sense of quiet hurt in the land."[26] Throughout his campaign, Carter pounded home two simple points. First, he asked if government could work. He quickly followed that up with another, more important question: "Can government be decent, honest, truthful, fair, compassionate, and as filled with love as our people are?"[27]

All this was wrapped up in a candidate who said that he prayed frequently, "about 25 times a day, maybe more," and who concluded every day by reading the Bible—in Spanish.[28] Carter pledged that he would bring to the office the kind of honesty and integrity that had not been found in the preceding administration. "I would join the nearest Baptist church and go there every Sunday and play down any sort of show about it," he said. "I wouldn't hold a Catholic service and a Jewish service, and a Moslem service in the White House."[29] A broad part of his political success came as a result of the faith he wore on his sleeve. In this humble evangelical peanut farmer from Georgia, the American people found an old-fashioned Democrat, far removed from the special-interest liberalism of George McGovern. One legislator said, "Jimmy Carter's a spiritualist . . . and that's what this country needs."[30]

Carter spoke openly and convincingly about his conservative religious beliefs, which today are viewed with alarm when espoused by a pro-family Republican. In one of his first speeches to government workers, he delivered a sermon against adultery. His sister, Ruth Carter Stapleton, was a Baptist evangelist who worked Iowa and New Hampshire for her brother like a foreign mission field. Carter's entire campaign in the Iowa caucuses was modeled after a project called "pioneer mission," in which his Baptist church in Plains in 1967 had used phone canvassing to identify unsaved, unchurched persons in various Northern cities. Carter and other church members spent months traveling to those lost souls as "home missionaries," staying in their houses, converting them to the faith, and planting a church.[31] Carter also actively cultivated the support of the emerging religious conservative community. Pat Robertson, then still a Democrat, endorsed him prior to the Pennsylvania primary, and Carter pledged to provide appointments in his administration to evangelicals.

Carter defeated Gerald Ford by the narrowest of margins. He reunited much of the New Deal coalition—the poor, blacks, union families, city dwellers, and, perhaps most importantly, ethnic Catholics and Southern Protestants.[32] In short, Carter made people believe that he was something different, a morally conservative Democrat.

But Carter's presidency bore no resemblance to the religious flavor of his campaign. While his four years in the Oval Office brought turmoil over which Carter had little control—the energy crisis, rampant inflation and unemployment, the crisis in Afghanistan, and the hostages in Iran—they were also years in which Carter betrayed a pledge to the American people, one that they felt he had made on their family Bible. In the course of a few years, Carter the Bible-quoting Baptist cast aside the religious voters to whom he owed his election. In the first months of his administration, he broke a promise to appoint qualified evangelical Christians, his "brothers and sisters," to positions in the federal government. Although he said that he found abortion to be "horrible," he did nothing to stop federal funding of abortions. Though he found homosexuality to be a sin, he advocated gay rights.

To pacify the feminists in his party, Carter stumped hard for the Equal Rights Amendment. It was largely political theater. I recall that, when I was a freshman at the University of Georgia working as a young intern at the Georgia state capitol in 1980, Jimmy Carter and his wife Rosalynn personally called members of the state Senate, where Carter had once served, off the floor so they could lobby them over the telephone on the eve of the amendment's demise. Everyone knew it had little chance of passage, but Carter faced a tough primary battle with Ted Kennedy, and he needed to show the far left that he was committed to their agenda.[33]

Carter had promised that if Kennedy entered the 1980 race he would "whip his ass." But Kennedy handed the president an embarrassing defeat in the New York primary—clear evidence of the emotional attachment of the party's activist liberal wing to the last symbol of Camelot. The party's head may have belonged to its incumbent president, but its heart longed for Kennedy. By then, Carter had thoroughly demolished his relations with religious conservatives, who gravitated swiftly to the Republican party and Ronald Reagan. Their sense of betrayal was palpable. In their view, Carter had betrayed his own faith and an administration of promise and had caved in to the pressure of the special interests.[34] "Even though Jimmy Carter was the evangelical favorite in 1976," the Falwell biographer Dinesh D'Souza observed, "by 1980 he was viewed as a dangerous apostate. The hapless Georgian found himself denounced for immoral views on the social issues by hordes of groups."[35]

Carter returned the favor by heaping vitriol on his conservative Christian brethren. As far as he was concerned, he later stated, "Jerry Falwell can go straight to hell—and I mean that in a Christian way." After Carter's defeat, his evangelical faith disappeared from Democratic party rhetoric as though it had never existed. Walter Mondale won the 1984 presidential nomination in a textbook special-interest campaign fueled by an early endorsement from organized labor. The only candidate who displayed a willingness to discuss his faith in God openly was the former Florida governor Reuben Askew, a pro-life Democrat who by all accounts was one of the finest governors in the nation. But in a party dominated by a secular, liberal ethos, Askew had no chance. During the fall campaign, Mondale alleged that the support of Reagan by religious conservatives threatened the separation of church and state. In 1988 Michael Dukakis had even less use for religious language to advance his technocratic agenda of efficient government. "For many Americans," Garry Wills concluded, "the coldly technological 'Massachusetts Miracle' was not only Godless but the enemy of God."[36]

It remained for Bill Clinton, a Southern Baptist and the governor of a small Southern state, to resurrect the lost language of religion. Like Carter, he attempted to reconcile the rhetoric of his religion with the demands of his party's activist wing. And, like Carter, he has failed.

It has not been for lack of effort. Bill and Hillary Clinton attended worship services regularly at the Foundry Methodist Church in Washington, where the president can often be seen emerging from his limousine with a leather-bound Bible under his arm.[37] Prior to becoming president, Clinton was a member of Immanuel Baptist Church in Little Rock, where he sang in the choir and engaged in extensive theological discussions with the Reverend W. O. Vaught, a Biblical scholar and committed liberal. He also made annual treks as governor to Pentecostal revival meetings in Redfield, Arkansas, where more than two thousand worshipers sang, clapped, danced, and prayed in tongues.[38]

Whatever one thinks of Clinton's politics, there is no denying his interest in spiritual matters. He has spoken openly about reading the entire Book of Psalms, originally written by King David as a cry to God for deliverance from his political enemies, for solace at times of personal and political turmoil. He has invited Christian clergy to the White House for off-the-record discussions of the issues, though with abortion and gay rights pointedly excluded. While most of those in Clinton's religious circle hold liberal views, he has also sought out Bill Hybels, the pastor of the conservative evangelical Willow Creek Baptist Church, as a jogging partner and counselor. Hybels is a former member of the board of directors of Jim Dobson's Focus on the Family. In 1993, while on a shopping spree in New York City in conjunction with a Democratic fund-raiser, Clinton made an unannounced visit to St. Patrick's Cathedral for a moment of solitude and prayer. In response to religious conservatives who denounce such exhibitions of faith as political posturing, Clinton has said, "I think the truth is that there are people who don't believe it's genuine because they disagree with me politically."[39]

Clinton has regularly expressed sympathy for the role of religion in the political arena. "There is a great debate now abroad in the land which finds itself injected into several political races about the extent to which people of faith can seek to do God's will as political actors," he said in November 1993. "I would like to come down on the side of encouraging everybody to act on what they believe is the right thing to do."[40] In a stirring address in the church where Martin Luther King preached his final sermon, Clinton evoked a spiritual rationale for his political agenda. "By the grace of God and your help last year I was elected President . . . I have worked hard to keep faith . . . to restore the economy; to reverse the politics of helping only [the rich] . . ."[41]

Those were remarkable statements for this president—or any president. Yet they were not greeted with applause by conservative religious leaders. Words which, if uttered by a Republican, would have been lauded and praised, went largely ignored. The reasons for the silence are complex.

Clinton has proclaimed his loyalty to the gay lobby, has appointed Joycelyn Elders as Surgeon General despite her controversial statements, has opposed efforts to end late-term abortions through a ban on the gruesome partial-birth abortion procedure, and has allowed his campaign operatives to denounce what they have called "the radical right" (a bigoted code word for conservative people of faith) for their involvement in the Republican party. That record hardly meets the test for civility and respect for the religious beliefs of others. For some evangelicals and Roman Catholics, Bill Clinton is another Jimmy Carter, someone who accedes to a pro-abortion and liberal social agenda and promotes it beneath the veneer of Scripture. A perfect example of Clinton's political use of religion came in 1994, when he spoke before a black congregation in Maryland and claimed that the passage of his pork-laden crime bill was "the will of God."

As hard as it is to remember now, following his nearly flawless campaign of 1992, many Americans believed that Bill Clinton had an opportunity to join the ranks of the most consequential presidents of the twentieth century. Clinton the Comeback Kid had weathered the storms of Gennifer Flowers and the Vietnam draft to become the first Democrat since Jimmy Carter to win the white vote. Clinton the New Democrat had stitched together a winning coalition of minorities, blue-collar workers, and former Reagan Democrats without alienating moderates with the special-interest, tax-and-spend message that sank Mondale and Dukakis. He won the veteran vote, the Catholic vote, the elderly vote, the independent vote, and the youth vote—and broke the back of the Republican party in its most reliable region by winning eight Southern and border states. The press wrote the premature obituary of the Republican party, convinced that it lay in ruins.[42] Clinton, the youngest man to occupy the Oval Office since Kennedy, projected a vibrancy that had been missing from American politics, and the pundits ushered him into Washington with open arms and soaring hopes.

Today those hopes are a distant memory. In fact, if Clinton has any chance to earn historical distinction, it is likely to be a negative one—that he presided over the political demise of modern liberalism. Never before has so much been squandered so quickly by so brilliant a political figure. An election filled with promise and a victory that resonated with hope quickly became an administration without a purpose, adrift in the storm-tossed seas of the presidency and torn between the need to compromise and the demands of hard-liners within the president's own party.

In this sense, Bill Clinton is best seen as the American Gorbachev. Like Mikhail Gorbachev's ill-fated reign over the final days of Communism, Bill Clinton is a remarkably skilled politician who is a victim of circumstances beyond his control. The collapse of the welfare state, the rise of social pathologies like illegitimacy and family breakup, the dramatic movement of the religious vote into the Republican party, and the loss of liberalism's moral center have all dictated Clinton's course. Just as Gorbachev struggled in the 1980s to reform Communism and save the Soviet Union, Bill Clinton has attempted to save liberalism by reforming it from within and has instead witnessed its death as a dynamic political force. Saving liberalism by compromising its central tenets proved an impossible task, even for a politician possessing Clinton's consummate skills and instincts.

As the nation prepares for the final presidential election of this century, one is left with the inescapable conviction that even if Clinton loses, it will be less because of his personal failures than because liberalism collapsed during his tenure. Conversely, if Clinton should get lucky and win—as he is more than capable of doing—it will do little to stem the breakdown of the old liberal political order. Liberalism will continue to survive, of course, but in a muted and much diminished form. It will even continue to win political victories. But as a wellspring of ideas for the nation's future or as a source of intellectual energy and vitality, its glory days are over.

The plain fact is that liberals no longer feel comfortable campaigning or governing in the name of liberalism. This, more than anything else, explained the artful dodge of "liberal on programs, conservative on values" embodied in Clinton's campaign and the party platform.[43] The first cracks in Clinton's attempt to balance the old liberalism with new thinking opened during platform debates at the 1992 Democratic National Convention in New York City. In a platform that largely rejected the social radicalism of the liberal interests, Clinton seemed to be promising that the Democrats would change their ways.[44] "We reject both the do-nothing government of the last twelve years and the big government theory that says we can hamstring business and tax and spend our way to prosperity," the platform asserted. "Instead we offer a third way." Clinton claimed his "third way" would not so much reconcile competing claims by the different wings of the party as transcend them. The platform brimmed with references to "market forces," "free enterprise," and "growth and jobs for all." Instead of calling for higher taxes and greater spending, it resorted to euphemisms like "investing significant resources to put people back to work" and borrowed conservative ideas like urban enterprise zones. None of the reporting by journalists at the Democratic convention prepared the electorate for the inherent contradictions contained in this language. The cognitive dissonance required to promise job training largesse to mayors of big cities while also pledging fiscal responsibility would later surface in the ill-fated "economic stimulus" package—the first major legislative defeat for Clinton in a Democratic-controlled Congress.[45]

Those contradictions reached a boiling point on the social issues. Clinton's platform tipped its hat to the notion of "family values" with such platitudes as, "Governments don't raise children, people do," and "Welfare should be a second chance, not a way of life." But a few pages later it called for "civil rights protection for gay men and lesbians and an end to Defense Department discrimination" and listed "homophobia" in a catalog of evils that Democrats opposed. Clinton had pledged to make abortion "safe, legal, and rare," and even claimed, "I think we can be pro-family and pro-choice." Yet the platform actually toughened the abortion plank by endorsing the radical Freedom of Choice Act.[46] This only foreshadowed Clinton's later problems.

The gays-in-the-military controversy, combined with the Zoë Baird and Lani Guinier flaps, travel-office firings, and Clinton's designer haircut

LIBERALISM'S HOLLOW CORE

by Christophe, provided the impetus for a prairie fire of grassroots protest at the very moment religious conservatives should have been flat on their backs. Clinton had committed one of the cardinal sins of politics: He had allowed a defeated foe to rise from the canvas. No single episode by itself was fatal. But like the Chinese water torture, the constant dripping of controversies threw the Clinton administration off its "new Democrat" message at a critical early stage and revealed that liberalism under Clinton still lacked a moral core. Presidents have only one chance to make a first impression, and Clinton's was a disaster from which he never fully recovered.[47]

But the collapse of liberalism has not really been caused by Clinton's missteps. Valiant efforts by some centrist Democrats to reconcile liberalism with the rightward movement of the country had failed long before Clinton took office. It may well be that the watershed in the unraveling of modern liberalism may be marked historically by the formation of the Democratic Leadership Council (DLC) in 1985, the brainchild of Senator Chuck Robb of Virginia and other conservative-to-moderate Democrats intent on reversing the party's leftward lurch. Led by Southern and Western governors like Clinton of Arkansas and Bruce Babbitt of Arizona, Democratic officeholders joined forces to save the Democratic party from the stranglehold of special interest groups that had dominated its agenda for decades: feminists, labor unions, gays and lesbians, radical environmentalists, and minorities. Clinton's involvement in the DLC signaled a break from his own liberal past, in that he had participated in the antiwar movement and the McGovern campaign in 1972, which institutionalized the New Left's control over the national Democratic party. Clinton's repudiation of the old liberalism on the heels of two Reagan landslides (and his own defeat in 1980 as governor of Arkansas) sent the unmistakable signal that he no longer believed running as a liberal was a viable strategy. And yet the goal was clearly not to supplant liberalism so much as to save it. In the words of Al From, the executive director of the DLC, "Our crusade and his was always to try to modernize liberalism so it could sell again."

Or, more accurately, talk conservative and govern as a liberal. Clinton talked a good game when it came to welfare reform, getting tough on crime, and balancing the budget. When he ran for president, he pledged to present a plan that would bring the budget into balance in five years. Instead, he vetoed welfare reform, presented a budget with $200 billion deficits into the next century, and has appointed people from the far left of his party to prominent posts in his administration. The DLC does not seek to replace the lost moral core of liberalism; it seeks to cut it out once and for all. It eschews labels and disdains ideology.[48] It is "Republicanism lite," stripped of messy moral issues.

It is in this regard that modern liberalism most resembles Soviet Communism in its dying hours and that Clinton must resembles Mikhail Gorbachev. The parallels between the two men are striking. Gorbachev rose through the Communist party by forsaking the sophistication and political intrigue of Moscow and serving as governor of the Stavropol territory, an obscure rural post not much more populous than Arkansas. Both men experienced a meteoric rise to power. Gorbachev joined the Politburo in 1982 at forty-nine, making him twenty-one years younger than his fellow Politburo members. Clinton, likewise, became the youngest governor in the nation in 1979 and, at forty-six, the third-youngest president in American history.[49] Both men came to power pledging to revive sputtering economies. Gorbachev's solution was *perestroika*, an economic restructuring that phased out state subsidies and relied more on market forces, while Clinton, touting a trendy business slogan, pledged to "reinvent government." Both ideas represented a sharp break from the ruling orthodoxy of their parties.[50]

Emiliano Zapata once observed, "A revolution eats its own children." This has been true of Gorbachev, and in the end it will be Clinton's fate as well. Gorbachev was deposed as general secretary of the Communist party on December 24, 1991. In 1996 he tied to make a comeback by running for the presidency of Russia and was hardly a factor. Today Gorbachev is viewed as a transitional and largely irrelevant figure. In his place at the head of the Russian Communist party is Gennady Zyuganov, who talks about turning Moscow into a free-trade zone like Shanghai. Whether his record matches his rhetoric is another matter. But when asked why he continues to call himself a Communist while holding capitalist ideas, Zyuganov shrugs. "If I buy a Coca-Cola plant, why would I change its name to Pepsi?"[51]

I am not suggesting that Bill Clinton should be equated with the Communist party chief in Russia or that liberalism is somehow analogous to Communism. But in purely political terms, Clinton faces the same fate as Gorbachev and other reformers in the former Soviet Union. He is a liberal, though he shamelessly uses conservative ideas and moralistic rhetoric to advance his agenda. He is bright and ambitious. He may survive. But the question for the Democrats is, at what cost? Liberalism should be about more than reelecting a president. If Clinton gains a second term, he would be the first Democrat to serve two full terms since Franklin Roosevelt, a truly historic achievement. But what good is that victory if he accedes to the broad outlines of Republican budget policy, if he allows sweeping changes in Medicare and welfare, if he must submit judicial appointments to Orrin Hatch and Jesse Helms, and if he cannot govern the country without working with the most conservative Congress in a generation? The truth is that it is a personal and symbolic victory that will provide the left with little in the way of either personnel or policy.

True liberals are left feeling understandably betrayed. Lani Guinier, who once had Bill and Hillary Clinton as guests at her wedding, was thrown overboard when she became controversial. Marian Wright Edelman of the Children's Defense Fund, where the First Lady once served as chairman of the board, saw her husband jettisoned for an appointment to a federal judgeship because the Republican-controlled Senate threatened to oppose him. (He later received a consolation prize in the form of a recess appointment to the Department of Health and Human Services.) The gold-plated consulting team of Paul Begala, the pollster Stan Greenberg, and the media adviser Mandy Grunwald had their roles diminished or eliminated. In their place is a Republican consultant, Dick Morris. Democrats in Congress who fought valiantly and risked their own careers to pass Bill Clinton's tax hike in 1993 were left twisting in the wind after Clinton repudiated the tax bill at a fund-raising dinner before an audience of large contributors in Houston. If most Americans thought they were electing a centrist and got a liberal, then liberals feel similarly jilted. This was dramatically demonstrated when Clinton phoned Ben Wattenberg to congratulate him on his book *Values Matter Most,* a manifesto calling on the Democratic party to abandon the pet causes of social liberalism and move to the center on values. Plainly, Clinton is intent on sounding like a conservative and running as a centrist. Whether he succeeds or fails in this effort, liberalism is certain to be the chief casualty.

Clinton's dilemma provides religious conservatives with both a unique opportunity and a grave danger. The opportunity is to build a permanent governing majority for traditional moral values. The danger is the temptation to seek a short-term political victory based solely on antipathy for Clinton. If my thesis is correct and Clinton is the American Gorbachev, then he is a purely transitional figure whose historical significance derives primarily from the political order that will follow his tenure. For religious conservatives, Clinton is not the enemy. He is the prelude, indeed the foreshadowing, of our rendezvous with destiny, a rebirth of the American dream with limited government, lower taxes, and stronger families.

Even liberal Democrats recognize this fact. Norman Lear, founder of the liberal People for the American Way, told a conference on values education, "For all our alarm, it is clear that the religious right is responding to a real hunger in our society" and "a deep-seated yearning for stable values." He added: "When they talk of failures in our educational system, the erosion of our moral standards and the waste of young lives, they are addressing real and legitimate concerns."[52]

The liberal crack-up signals the dawning of a new political age. It can be seen in the dramatic turnover in the House of Representatives, 40 percent of whose members have been elected since 1992. It can be seen in the flurry of retirements in the U.S. Senate—thirteen in 1996, the most since the direct election of senators began in the early twentieth century. It can be seen in the rising number of independent voters, now approaching 30 percent of the entire electorate, a post–World War II record. The Perot movement, the Colin Powell boomlet, and the rise of contending communities of meaning from evangelicals to environmentalists all are signs that a new political paradigm is taking shape.

In this new landscape, liberalism will play an active role, but it will no longer be dominant. In its place is a new social movement that owes its success to the same religious enthusiasm and moral fervor that once fired liberalism in its heyday. Religious conservatives have poured into politics in recent years not out of a thirst for power but out of a sense of right and wrong, seeking to restore values that have been lost and hoping to heal deep spiritual wounds in our society. Lee Atwater, the great Republican political operative, recognized their strength before he died. "Long before I was struck with cancer, I felt something stirring in the American society," he wrote. "I don't know who will lead us through the '90s, but they must be made to speak to this spiritual vacuum at the heart of American society, this tumor of the soul." Liberals have largely ignored this spiritual cancer, and their disdain for religiously based political activism has precipitated their decline. Stepping forward into that vacuum is the modern religious conservative movement, a movement that I believe is the most vibrant and effective political constituency in the nation today.

4

RISING FROM THE ASHES

T he internal contradiction between the liberal agenda of the Democratic party's activist base and the socially conservative views of religious voters finally cracked in the late 1970s. Many think that the
earthquake was *Roe* v. *Wade*, the 1973 Supreme Court decision legalizing
abortion. But that was only part of the story. The truth is that the exodus
of religious conservatives from the Democratic party came later. Pat
Robertson, for example, was a lifelong Democrat who campaigned for
Adlai Stevenson, integrated churches in Tidewater, Virginia, and endorsed
Jimmy Carter at a critical moment in his 1976 campaign. He was generally
more progressive on racial and other issues than his father Willis, who
served in Congress and the U.S. Senate for thirty years as a Democrat.
Robertson's aide Bob Slosser, a former *New York Times* writer, wrote a fawning campaign biography of Carter aptly titled *The Miracle of Jimmy Carter*.
In 1978 Robertson delivered a stirring nominating speech for a Norfolk car
dealer who ran as a conservative Christian for his party's nomination for
the U.S. Senate—at the Virginia Democratic state convention. Robertson
declared that conservative evangelicals were a "great sleeping giant coming into the political process." Those words, uttered to Democrats by a fellow Democrat, would prove prophetic.[1]

Evangelicals and many Roman Catholics may properly echo the words of Ronald Reagan, who once said, "I didn't leave the Democratic party. The Democratic party left me." After the Chicago convention in 1968, where pro-life Catholics like Mayor Richard Daley and union hardhats clashed with the hippies and yippies of the antiwar movement, the Democratic National Committee appointed a commission headed by Senator George McGovern to "open" the delagate process. The result was a quota system for women, minorities, gays, and young people that excluded many of the party's traditional precinct workers. By 1972 conservative Democratic members of Congress were denied delegate seats at the convention in Miami Beach to make way for antiwar protesters. Middle-class Catholics began to leave a Democratic party that had become a special-interest patchwork bearing little resemblance to the great party of their childhood under Franklin Roosevelt and Harry Truman. Evangelicals were not far behind.[2]

The greatest spark of the movement was not abortion but an attempt by the Carter-appointed head of the Internal Revenue Service to require Christian and parochial schools and academies to prove that they were not established to preserve segregation or they would risk losing their tax-exempt status. For the Carter administration, the policy was a ham-handed if necessary demonstration of its commitment to civil rights as it made an aggressive play at the black vote heading into the 1980 elections. For conservative evangelicals it was nothing less than a declaration of war on their schools, their churches, and their children. More than any other single episode, the IRS move against Christian schools sparked the explosion of the movement that would become known as the religious right.

At first there was no single organization or leader at the helm. The religious broadcaster James Robison, a Baptist evangelist with jet-black hair and a fiery preaching style, reached millions through his television ministry. In June 1979 Robison led a march of twelve thousand protesters on a Dallas television station that had banned his program from the airwaves because of his sermons against homosexuality. Bob Billings, a bespectacled, unassuming lobbyist for Christian schools, led the fight against the IRS and later became the first executive director of the Moral Majority. Ed Mc-Ateer, a former Colgate–Palmolive marketing executive and Baptist lay leader from Memphis, founded the Religious Roundtable to encourage co-operation among the various groups that were sprouting up across the countryside. McAteer combined the syrupy speaking style of a Baptist evangelist with the marketing genius of a top sales executive. He spoke as much about "softening the market" and "market netting" as he did about school prayer or abortion.

One of the more colorful members of the original cast of characters in the religious conservative movement was Bob Grant, a former minister and the president of Christian Voice. Grant was a silver-haired dandy with a penchant for double-breasted suits who built a network of 37,000 churches and raised more than $3 million a year to lobby for pro-family causes and candidates. His chief deputy was Gary Jarmin, a seasoned Washington veteran and former Republican operative who ran the Capitol Hill lobby operation and networked together Jews, Catholics, fundamentalists, and charismatics, urging them to transcend their theological differences and work together on political matters. Christian Voice was particularly involved in organizing evangelical support for Israel and Taiwan. In later years Gary encouraged me to build a pro-family student network on the nation's college campuses. On the board of directors for Christian Voice were conservative senators Orrin Hatch of Utah, Roger Jepsen of Iowa, and James McClure of Idaho. Many conservative senators and the activists they mobilized had played a prominent role in opposing the Panama Canal treaty in 1978, a favorite cause of the New Right.

Pat Robertson also began his first political stirrings during the late 1970s. After his father's defeat in a bitter Democratic primary for a U.S. Senate seat, Robertson had focused on evangelism and humanitarian missionary work. But in 1978 his disappointment with Carter (he had actually voted for Ford in the general election) began to take a tangible form. He was approached by John Gimenez, the pastor of a charismatic, nondenominational church in Virginia Beach, with the improbable idea of putting a half-million evangelical Christians on the mall in Washington to call for moral renewal in America. Robertson liked to dream big dreams, and the idea of "Washington for Jesus" captivated him. He turned the resources of his *700 Club* program over to organizing the event, which took place on April 29, 1980, and drew a crowd estimated at a half-million to the nation's capital for a festive day of prayer, repentance, and consecration. While the purpose of the march was spiritual, the political subtext was unmistakable. Gazing across a sea of humanity that stretched down toward the Washington Monument and on to the White House, Robertson realized that if this gathering could be tapped as a grassroots political force, such a movement would have few parallels in history. He called it a "spiritual revolution" and issued a call for political action to turn the nation back from the brink of disaster. "We must ask ourselves again," he cried, "can we endure if we forsake the God of our fathers and strip from our national consciousness the teachings of the Holy Bible?"[3]

Shortly after Washington for Jesus, Robertson founded the Freedom Council, a grassroots organization with a budget of $5 million a year. With coordinators in all fifty states and tens of thousands of pastors enlisted (mostly in the charismatic community), Robertson built a formidable grassroots network. Through this grassroots army and his broadcast empire, Robertson touched an estimated total of 15 million people a week. That outreach would later feed his presidential campaign of 1988. As Falwell would later mobilize the fundamentalists and James Robison the Southern Baptists, Robertson moved millions of charismatics and pentecostals who had previously languished on the margins of political debate into the mainstream and, eventually, the Republican party. Robertson also began some of the earliest work in building bridges to the Roman Catholic community.

Robertson was not alone in seeing the political potential of the millions who populated the parallel universe of evangelical Christianity. Architects of the New Right like Richard Viguerie and Paul Weyrich were battle-tested generals in search of an army, and they found it in the emerging religious right. Neither were evangelicals. Viguerie, a devout Roman Catholic, was a balding, brilliant organizer of conservative causes who catapulted to prominence after building a direct-mail empire from a hand-copied list of donors to the Barry Goldwater campaign. He had tapped Terry Dolan to head the National Conservative Political Action Committee (NCPAC), which in 1978 and 1980 played a prominent role in the defeat of liberal senators who had supported the Panama Canal treaty. Paul Weyrich had drifted from the Roman Catholic church to the stricter Eastern Rite Catholic church. A former reporter from Wisconsin, Weyrich came to Washington in the late 1960s to work for a conservative Republican senator from Colorado and quickly grasped that the Republicans had no outside network comparable to that of liberals to build support for their legislative program. Bankrolled by the Coors brewing fortune, he founded the Committee for the Survival of a Free Congress in 1974 and began networking conservative action groups together with weekly strategy meetings. His weekly "Kingston Group" and "Library Court" meetings brought conservative leaders together around a large conference table over coffee and doughnuts to compare notes, trade ideas, and combine lobbying efforts. But Weyrich and his Washington strategists still lacked the grassroots strength they needed to give their strategy legs. They found it in 1979 in the person of a relatively unknown fundamentalist Baptist preacher from Lynchburg, Virginia, named Jerry Falwell.[4]

Though not yet famous among the general public, Falwell was a familiar face in conservative Christian circles. His *Old-Time Gospel Hour* television program was beamed into 12 million homes, he preached frequently against abortion and homosexuality, and his Liberty University singers had crisscrossed the nation holding "I Love America" rallies in all fifty state capitols. In 1978 the *Wall Street Journal* featured him as one of the pioneers of what it dubbed "the electronic church." It was one of the first times the mainstream media ever took note of Falwell's growing influence. At a meeting in Falwell's headquarters in Lynchburg in May 1979, Weyrich and a group of other conservative strategists urged Falwell to launch a new political organization that would tap into the wave of evangelical activism sweeping the nation. Also present was Howard Phillips, the head of the Conservative Caucus and former head of the Office of Economic Opportunity under Richard Nixon. Phillips, who was Jewish, was a huge man with massive hands, a staccato speaking style, and a shock of black hair that sometimes streaked down across his forehead. After the disappointment of the Nixon years—he had been one of the first conservatives to call for his resignation—Phillips had founded the Conservative Caucus, at first working out of the office of Senator Jesse Helms and later visiting every congressional district in the nation to organize the grassroots for the nascent New Right.

Weyrich had already played a role in the founding of the Heritage Foundation, the most prominent think tank on the right. But he knew that position papers without precinct workers and voters were not enough to build a political movement. Following a lunch break, Weyrich leaned forward in his chair and told Falwell there was a "moral majority" in the nation waiting to be rallied to action. Falwell perked up, and the name stuck. The next month he founded the Moral Majority, drafting some of the most prominent evangelical preachers in the nation to serve on the board of directors, and was soon raising millions of dollars through direct mail. Later the name became a liability, as liberals plastered their car bumpers with stickers that proclaimed, "The Moral Majority Is Neither." But in the heady early days of 1979 and 1980, those times were far in the future.

Darting across the nation in a chartered aircraft with the Liberty Singers in tow, Falwell held rallies and parades and packed halls and churches from coast to coast, always passing the hat among the faithful as a choir belted out "God Bless America." It was a good show, and like a spark tossed into a dry haystack, it swept the nation like wildfire. Falwell was a natural showman. He had a gift for the flamboyant, the baritone preaching voice of a backwoods pastor, and the television presence of the seasoned veteran he was.[5]

Early on, the architects of the Moral Majority vigorously debated whether to pursue a "rally" strategy or a "grassroots" strategy. They opted for the former, a tactical error that soon proved costly; for while the media and liberal politicians were initially terrified of the Moral Majority, their fear was based largely on public perceptions of a wildly inflated membership. Falwell himself claimed that 7 million families were involved. Sadly, strong state organizations were not built, few neighborhood coordinators were appointed, chapter growth was scattered, and training programs were sparse. When the organized left and the press discovered that the Moral Majority in a particular state sometimes consisted of a single person or pastor with a home phone number, they turned on it with a vengeance, pronouncing it a paper tiger.[6]

I met Jerry Falwell for the first time in 1984 when I founded Students for America, a conservative Judeo-Christian campus organization. Falwell was kind enough to sign on as one of the first members of our advisory board. He showed up at many of our meetings and was charitable with his time and genuine in his interest in young people. I found him to be a remarkably driven man who maintained a dizzying schedule. During the height of the Moral Majority, he would leave Lynchburg at daylight on a private jet, give numerous speeches, fly back to Washington to lobby members of Congress in person, and arrive home just after midnight before preaching five services the following day. He later said he never let a day go by without calling at least five U.S. representatives and two senators. With harried, exhausted aides in tow and coattails flapping, he maintained a healthy sense of humor and the leatherneck toughness of any pastor who had built a large church (his Thomas Road Baptist Church had more than twenty thousand members). Once when he came to Raleigh, North Carolina, for a fund-raising event I was ushered backstage and found Falwell in a small anteroom working the phones like a seasoned political pro. He would give orders to a subordinate, hang up the phone, and a moment later would be talking in his soothing voice to another politician. I asked him for a few minutes on the program to promote a local pro-life march and he generously agreed, wrapping his arm around my shoulder as I spoke at the podium. Tough as nails but tender at heart, Falwell was riding a bucking bronco, and neither he nor his supporters were sure exactly where it might carry them.

Weyrich and other New Right strategists would later be disappointed that the Moral Majority had pursued a direct-mail and media strategy rather than doing the dirty work of grassroots organization and training workshops. That criticism was reminiscent of the grousing among some in the civil rights community about Martin Luther King—that he reveled in publicity but rarely did the heavy lifting. But few grasped how little the leaders of the Moral Majority knew what they were getting into. Within the space of two years they were raising $10 million annually, had more than 2 million members, and found themselves on the cover of *Time*, *Newsweek*, and every other major publication in the country. Many of the field and legislative staff were people I knew. After the Moral Majority folded, some of them confessed to being completely overwhelmed by the whirlwind of it all, and punch-drunk after the incessant pounding they took from the media and critics on the left. Some, like Ed Dobson and Lamar Mooneyham, who was head of the North Carolina organization and a Falwell confidant, left politics to return to ministry; many maintain a skepticism about political involvement to this day.

But in 1980 the Moral Majority and its allies were riding high. In August 1980, shortly after the Republican National Convention, Ronald Reagan addressed a meeting of the Religious Roundtable called the "National Affairs Briefing." That gathering would later go down in the history of the conservative movement as the wedding ceremony of evangelicals and the Republican party. Against the advice of his handlers, Reagan agreed to address twenty thousand fundamentalists and evangelicals who packed into Reunion Arena in Dallas. On stage was every major leader in the religious conservative movement: Ed McAteer, Charles Stanley, Adrian Rogers, Jerry Falwell, and James Robison. Robison had been selected to introduce Reagan but instead used the occasion to deliver his own twenty-minute stem-winder, which sent Reagan's aides into orbit. Finally Reagan stepped to the podium and, with characteristic aplomb, delivered the line that brought down the house: "I know that you cannot endorse me, but I endorse you and everything you do." During the question-and-answer period Reagan fielded a question about evolution and expressed his doubts about the scientific theories of Darwin. His answer was hooted down by liberal editorialists, who sought to portray Reagan as a stumbling, Bryan-like char-

acter who believed in creationism and trafficked in the theology of fundamentalists. As with his comment to the American Legion that the Vietnam War was a "noble cause," however, Reagan knew exactly what he was
doing when he allied himself with conservative church folk. After the Religious Roundtable meeting, the burgeoning religious conservative movement went to work, delivering a huge vote for the first divorced man ever
to sit in the White House and helping him defeat two of the most devout Christians in the history of recent politics, Jimmy Carter and John
Anderson.

The 1980 election was to religious conservatives what the 1992 election would later be to H. Ross Perot and his followers: a coming-out party.
The pollster Lou Harris issued a report a few days after the GOP landslide,
which also gave them control of the Senate, and found that Jimmy Carter
had lost the white Baptist vote to Reagan by an astonishing 56 to 34 percent. "Ronald Reagan won his stunning victory," Harris concluded, "not
because the country as a whole went conservative, but because the conservatives—particularly the white moral majority—gave him such massive
support."[7] Among the 28 percent of the electorate following the electronic
church of the moral majority, 62 percent voted for Reagan. Falwell claimed
that of forty-three races involving a local chapter of the Moral Majority,
forty were won by the conservative candidate. Members of Congress trem-
bled with fear at the thought of offending the movement, which many
credited for Reagan's margin of victory. "It was Jesus that gave us victory,"
the wife of one winning gubernatorial candidate in Alabama proclaimed.
"God in his mercy heard the prayers of Christians all over this country."[8]

Some of those conclusions were no doubt overstated. But in politics, perception is often reality. And in the early 1980s no one questioned
the strength and influence of the Moral Majority. This new political phenomenon enthralled—and horrified—the media. Jerry Falwell was featured on the cover of major newsmagazines and along with such
organizations as Phyllis Schlafly's Eagle Forum, which defeated the Equal
Rights Amendment in 1982, the pro-family movement was one of the
most amply funded and formidable political forces in the nation.

Expectations quickly soared to unrealistic heights. Religious conservatives viewed Reagan's landslide as the opportunity to outlaw abortion, end religious discrimination, legalize voluntary school prayer, abolish the Department of Education, and launch a crusade against pornography. But they looked to Reagan to provide something else as well: a sense of legitimacy. By hitching their wagon to Reagan's popular political personality, religious conservatives smoothed out some of their rough-hewn edges and assimilated into the political mainstream in a way that had previously been unthinkable. For decades fundamentalists had waged a losing war against what they viewed as the vagaries of modernity. Since the Scopes trial of 1925, in which fundamentalists won the battle over the teaching of evolution in the schools but lost the war, evangelicals had beat a retreat from the political stage that lasted two generations. The repeal of Prohibition in 1933 signaled the death knell of modern attempts to project theological faith into the political arena. For the ensuing four decades, fundamentalists and their evangelical brethren built a picket fence against the encroachments of what they came to call "secular humanism," a faith in the capacity of man to solve his problems without the help of God. In this Manichaean struggle, the evangelicals did not view politics as a particularly effective weapon. When Pat Robertson's father was running for reelection for the U.S. Senate in Virginia in 1966, his son did not feel at liberty to provide anything more than moral support, sensing that God desired him to remain engaged in full-time ministry rather than muddied by the dirt of partisan politics. Falwell and others similarly eschewed political combat. Through a network of Bible churches and sectarian colleges, they had fought a rearguard action against secular humanism, withdrawing from the dominant culture they believed had wandered from the path of righteousness. But helping to elect a president changed all that; they had reentered the American political mainstream. That, more than anything else, was Falwell's historic achievement.

For the supporters of the Moral Majority, Ronald Reagan was a political messiah. Viguerie described the enthusiasm that many of America's most prominent religious leaders felt for him. "Throughout the summer and fall of 1980 the word went out through these religious Paul Reveres (Jerry Falwell, Ed McAteer, Bob Billings, Adrian Rogers, Charles Stanley, Jim Kennedy, James Robison, and many others) that America was in danger and only Ronald Reagan could cure her." Some sensed the danger lurking ahead. Pat Robertson resigned from the Religious Roundtable, because he felt strongly that evangelicals should not tie the gospel to any single political party or leader. Other evangelicals worried that the movement was taking on a much too partisan cast.

Blind faith in Reagan and in the efficacy of politics as a means of social change proved damaging to members of the religious movement. During the heady days of the 1980s, when conservative evangelicals first began to flex their newfound political muscle, I saw many drawn to the heat of political battle like moths to a flame. They pursued the political grail with the zeal of a new convert. One friend of mine crisscrossed the nation working for various pro-family causes and candidates, hopscotching from one state to another and living in a string of airports and Holiday Inns. The minute one crusade ended—whether in crushing defeat or euphoric victory—she was updating her resume and moving on to the next battle. Ultimately, her faith and marriage suffered, and she and her husband divorced. Another friend became so distracted by his political career that he became involved in a series of business deals with shady individuals, nearly went bankrupt, and spent time in prison. I saw the same sad tale repeated dozens of times. It was one of the main reasons why I left politics in 1985 to begin a new life in academe. A few years later my friend Bill Cobey, who served in Congress for one term before being defeated in 1986, told me that he was actually relieved when he lost. "I was losing my wife and family and did not even know it," he confessed. "Losing my seat in Congress was the best thing that ever happened to me. It saved my marriage."

There was also disappointment. Shortly after his inauguration, Reagan reneged on a promise to appear at the March for Life in Washington. To pacify the pro-life community, the White House arranged a private meeting for pro-life leaders in the Oval Office with Reagan. To many this smacked of tokenism, as when black leaders were escorted through a back door to meet with Eisenhower or Kennedy in an earlier era. Nellie Gray, the head of the March for Life, was so angry she boycotted the meeting. Few if any evangelicals were appointed to positions of influence in the Reagan administration. Bob Billings, the former executive director of Moral Majority, was named an undersecretary for nonpublic schools in the Department of Education, only to find his title changed and his portfolio reduced to traveling the nation as a public-relations figure. Patronized by campaign officials before the election, religious conservatives found themselves treated like untouchables once the ballots had been counted and the confetti swept away.[9]

When Bob Michel, the House Republican leader, and James Baker, the White House chief of staff, announced that the social issues would not be the top priority in the Reagan administration, Weyrich organized a conference call with religious conservative leaders. If they allowed the Reagan White House to put their agenda on the back burner, he warned, they would never be taken seriously again. But Falwell and his allies were not eager to start a fight with Reagan, whom they still viewed as their best hope to move the country. That was a critical turning point for the movement. Respected by some and feared by most, it failed to take the political capital of the 1980 landslide and translate it into a tangible legislative agenda. Instead, the White House threw the pro-family movement consolation prizes like speeches by the Gipper to their annual conventions or schmooze sessions in the Roosevelt Room.

As a young intern on Capitol Hill and later as executive director of the College Republican National Committee, I knew many of these leaders and worked with them on a regular basis. Like any other political operative, I understood the importance of the voting bloc they had organized. After growing up in Miami, my family had moved to the deep South, and I spent my youth driving the highways of rural northeast Georgia, where it was not uncommon to pass a white clapboard Baptist or Methodist church every few hundred yards. Each of those churches held a hundred registered voters, most of whom were socially conservative but voted like yellow-dog Democrats. For those voters, the pro-family movement was a political midwife of sorts—educating them, training them, prodding them to put their values first and their party affiliation second. I believed the religious conservative movement was the only hope to build a Republican party in the South. But the marriage of politics and religion was also fraught with hazards. I saw it create in many of the activists of the so-called religious right an arrogance and a self-righteousness that was poorly suited to the rough-and-tumble of politics, which required give and take and some compromise to win. Many were unprepared for the hostility of the media and the angry counterassault of the left that began in the mid-1980s. Sensing that the movement was running out of gas and suffering from basic flaws in strategy, I decided to leave politics shortly after becoming a Christian myself and to go to graduate school, fully intending to pursue an academic career and never to return to politics as a full-time vocation.

After all the promise and successes of the Reagan years, we were still left with this problem: his eight years in office did little to transform a political culture that had become insensitive to religious values and uncaring about innocent human life. Like a little child on Christmas morning who hopes to find a new bicycle under the tree and instead receives only a new scarf, we woke up the morning after Reagan's two terms to discover that many maladies still afflicted our nation and many pathologies had grown worse. That was a tough thing to admit for many in the movement, and it was just the beginning. This is not to say that religious conservatives were disillusioned by Reagan. He had led them out of the wilderness, giving their concerns a viability in the political system they had never had before. He was the midwife of a new political movement, and for that evangelicals were extremely grateful. But they had much to learn about how politics really worked.

As Reagan's advisors prepared for the 1984 reelection campaign, they realized belatedly that they had tossed only a few morsels to the Moral Majority. They thus decided to stage a battle over one of the religious movement's most coveted agenda items: a constitutional amendment legalizing school prayer. From the beginning the battle was uphill. The measure needed a two-thirds vote in both chambers of Congress. One of my good friends worked on Capitol Hill for a conservative senator and was asked by the White House to work up a preliminary vote count in the Senate. When he brought back the bad news to the Reagan legislative staff that the most they could hope for would be a little more than fifty votes—far short of the sixty-seven required for passage—one of the aides replied, "Good, we just wanted to make sure that it could not pass before we began the battle."

The main organizations of the religious right were called to action, with the White House promising the direct involvement of President Reagan in strong-arming wavering votes. But it was all a mirage. The votes were never there, the battle was purely political theater, and the school prayer amendment fell eleven votes short of passage in the Senate.

I later attended a meeting on Capitol Hill where one conservative leader banged on the table in disgust. "We'll turn this into another Panama Canal treaty vote," he shouted. "Anyone who voted against school prayer will be defeated." I sat in the back of the room, wondering if he knew that he had been rolled. It was all rather sad and poignant. Much blood and treasure had been spilled in a futile effort that served to solidify Reagan's evangelical base but did little to advance the pro-family legislative agenda. The religious conservatives had been rolled by the White House and didn't even know it. Later, when the Christian Coalition played a similar role in the 1994 elections, that bitter experience played a major role in our decision to propose an amendment or statute in support of religious freedom rather than voluntary school prayer. Religious freedom would guarantee the right to expression for people of faith in all public settings, while the school prayer issue was narrower in scope and replayed many of the battles that had already been fought in the 1980s.

The religious freedom issue represented a subtle yet seismic shift in the thinking and strategy of the pro-family movement. In the 1980s, its leaders proclaimed the Christian roots of the nation and trumpeted the Biblical basis of their faith. Few demonstrated any uneasiness or sensitivity about the fears of Jews, agnostics, and unbelievers about being forced to say Christian prayers. The religious freedom statute and amendment addressed these concerns. Rather than compel others to recite a prayer led by a teacher, the pro-family movement today is more concerned with ensuring freedom of speech for all. They are most interested in defending young people like Brittney Settle, a fifteen-year-old in Tennessee who turned in an essay in a sophomore English class on the life of Jesus Christ and received a failing grade because of the essay's religious theme. A federal court upheld the right of the school to flunk Brittney because of her faith. The free-speech rights of students like Brittney would not be measurably guaranteed by legalizing school prayer. A religious-freedom amendment would protect her, along with unbelieving students who are nervous about being compelled to participate in mandatory religious exercises in public schools.

The school prayer debate showed how the Republican party sometimes used its religious conservative activists to their own detriment. Bob Dugan, chief lobbyist for the National Association of Evangelicals, once pointed out in another Washington strategy meeting I attended that the religious conservatives had never really sought out the Republican party as much as the GOP had sought them. This began in 1980 and continued throughout the decade, as the Republicans tried to use the social agenda as a wedge to drive Catholics and evangelicals away from the Democratic party. In sharp contrast to the view of evangelicals trying to take control of the Republican party, it was always Republican operatives who wanted them because of their proven strength at the ballot box. That, however, gave the movement an unfortunate partisan flavor that was hard to shake, and it engendered among some the irresistible temptation to be power brokers within the Republican party.

The hard lessons of the Reagan and Bush years, the Moral Majority's meteoric rise and dramatic demise, and Pat Robertson's presidential bid helped teach us which pitfalls to avoid and the right formulas for success in the future. Above all, it was a lesson that mistakes made in a noble cause are the first step to victory, not the last chapter in defeat. "We fight for lost causes because we know that our defeat and dismay may be the preface to our successors' victory," T. S. Eliot wrote. If trailblazers like the architects of the Moral Majority appeared at times to espouse losing causes, their set-backs paved the way for the movement's arrival as a permanent fixture on the American political landscape.

One of the first things we learned was that the red-hot rhetoric that sizzled in direct mail and on cable television may drive core supporters to their checkbooks but ultimately limits one's effectiveness in the broader society. The idea behind direct mail as an organizational tool, as pioneered by Richard Viguerie, was to bypass the hostile press corps and the media by communicating directly with one's supporters. That worked fine for fund-raising purposes, but evangelical pastors who were used to preaching to the faithful found that their high-octane message stuck in the throats of the general public like a chicken bone. "I'm sick and tired of hearing about all the radicals and perverts and liberals and leftists and Communists coming out of the closets," the evangelist James Robison thundered. "It's time for God's people to come out of the closets, out of the churches, and change America."[10] Falwell asserted that by bowing to "libertarians, the New Agers, the abortionists, the feminists, the radical homosexuals . . . we are allowing a tiny little minority, three, four, five percent of radicals in this country in all those areas to literally rewrite American history and totally obscure the fact that America is a Christian nation."[11]

The "Christian nation" rhetoric was rarely intended to imply a theocracy. Religious conservative leaders meant to celebrate a nation in which people loved their neighbors, cared for those less fortunate, honored God, took care of their families, and obeyed the law. But the cognitive gap separating evangelical speakers and secular ears made the translation difficult. Similarly extreme and overheated rhetoric had issued forth from the podiums of the labor and civil rights movements, especially from the raucous leadership of the Student Nonviolent Coordinating Committee, which rejected integration and flirted with the separatist designs of the Black Muslim movement. The difference was that the religious right lacked friendly media to interpret the nuances of the community and elevate its more responsible leaders. For that reason, the most intemperate remarks of pro-family figures tended to dominate headlines throughout the 1980s.

ACTIVE FAITH

That kind of language, while useful in sparking those in the pews to action, has the tendency to frighten almost everyone else. Part of the problem in the past was a fusion of direct mail and media as organizational tactics. Media coverage enhanced direct-mail fund-raising results, raising millions of dollars for evangelical television ministries and political groups, but it further marginalized the movement within the broader political culture.

We learned that lesson the hard way at the Christian Coalition. Early in the 1990s, I occasionally used military metaphors for effect. When they were quoted out of context by the left, they sounded frightening and were a liability. After the 1992 elections I realized that such language had allowed the media and the organized left to caricature our movement as intolerant and uncaring. Moreover, I felt such rhetoric was inappropriate for a Christian organization because it lacked the redemptive grace that should always characterize our words and deeds. I sent out a memorandum to our grassroots leaders urging them to avoid military rhetoric and to use sports metaphors instead. We also assiduously avoided calling our opponents "anti-family" or "anti-God," charges that had been hurled in some of the more heated debates of the 1980s. Vern Kennedy, a brilliant pollster who had helped to defeat David Duke in Louisiana in 1991, conducted several surveys for the Christian Coalition to help us find effective language that motivated our supporters without turning off voters sitting on the fence. We began to concede that our opponents' intentions were good, but that their agenda was leading to skyrocketing illegitimacy and crime, that their proposals were extreme and their ideas out of the mainstream. Such rhetoric—far more than the storm-the-barricades variety that had once flamed forth from evangelical pulpits—set a standard of basic civility that allowed secular ears to hear our message of stronger families and traditional values.

Critics were quick to charge that the dropping of military language amounted to hypocrisy. But that was nonsense; they did not know their history. The apostle Paul said, "I am a Jew to the Jews, a Greek to the Greeks, I have become all things to all men that I might lead all to

Christ." This does not mean hiding one's true faith. It means expressing it in a way that those from different cultural backgrounds can understand and receive it.

Related to those rhetorical problems was the fact that the old religious right never truly developed a coherent and broad-based legislative agenda. On foreign policy, religious conservatives were strongly pro-Israel and anti-Communist. On domestic issues, they opposed abortion and homosexuality, favored school prayer, and called for the abolition of the federal Department of Education. Most of those issues were constructed in oppositional terms. Everyone knew what the religious right was against; few knew what it was for. In the area of homosexuality, for example, they stressed their moral revulsion at a sexual practice that they viewed as unnatural and proscribed by the Bible. But many Americans lacked their Biblical worldview, making such appeals unpersuasive to the general population, and the religious right never broadened this concern by emphasizing a more positive agenda of strengthening the two-parent family. The agenda thus tended to be perceived as narrow and negative. When it did address broader issues, the religious right was often artless. One organization printed a biblical scorecard that rated members of Congress based on their support for the Strategic Defense Initiative, which it justified by quoting a verse from the New Testament about protecting one's household.

A second adjustment has been a shift from a clergy-based leadership class to lay men and women, which has tended to shift the rhetoric of both leaders and their supporters from the evangelical idiom to the less apocalyptic vernacular of the legislative arena. The original board of the Moral Majority, formed in 1979, included the pastors of some of the largest evangelical churches in the nation: Jerry Falwell of Thomas Road Baptist Church in Lynchburg; Charles Stanley of First Baptist Church in Atlanta; D. James Kennedy of Coral Ridge Presbyterian Church in Fort Lauderdale, Florida; Greg Dixon of the Baptist Temple in Indianapolis; and Tim La-Haye, associated with the Scott Memorial Baptist Church in San Diego.[12] LaHaye's wife, Beverly, had founded Concerned Women for America, which provided evangelical women with a conservative alternative to the

ACTIVE FAITH

National Organization for Women. Stanley and Kennedy reached huge television audiences through national broadcasts of their church services. Stanley later served as president of the Southern Baptist Convention, which passed from liberal to conservative hands in a series of bitterly fought conventions in the 1980s. Kennedy was the most prominent Presbyterian minister in the nation and a leader in the conservative Presbyterian Church of America.

The Christian Coalition, by contrast, has only one ordained minister on its national board of directors, and only one of its fifty state chairmen is a pastor. More common among the new leadership of religious conservatives are small-business men and women, political operatives, physicians, and attorneys. Our state leaders include a fund-raising consultant in Texas, a real estate developer in South Carolina, an insurance executive in Georgia, a small-business owner in Illinois, and an investment consultant in Indiana. Their business contacts and extensive experience in secular pursuits have greatly reduced the fear of others in the Republican party and the broader political community about their involvement.

A lay-based movement, we discovered, was far more effective than the old preacher-led model of the past. Of course, what is true of the black community is also true to a degree in the white evangelical community: If you get the preachers, the flock will follow. But as the basis of a long-term strategy, it was inadequate. Pastors and ministers are not politicians. Their primary job is to serve their congregations, to save the lost, and to minister to the needy. Pastors are still critically important. They teach, exhort their members to be good citizens, facilitate the distribution of nonpartisan voter-education information, and serve as important role models for proper political involvement. But by drawing upon the skills and talents of lay leaders, we freed the pastors from having to spend half their time on political activity and allowed them to do what they did best: build the church.

This idea first struck me when I was a graduate student at Emory University and attended Mt. Paran Church of God, a large evangelical church in Atlanta. With a congregation of ten thousand members, the church and its pastor, Paul Walker, were deluged with requests for assistance from a variety of causes and candidates. To screen out the good from the bad, the church established a Moral Concerns Ministry with lay leadership headed by a Chamber of Commerce executive. The result was a professionalization of the church's civic involvement. I later carried that important innovation with me to the Christian Coalition, and it became an essential element in our national strategy. It was one of the main differences between the old religious right and the new pro-family movement.

Another lesson was the importance of avoiding an attitude of arrogance and triumphalism. In the past, religious conservatives attempted to compensate for their weak grassroots organizations through a combination of bluster and bombast. The fact that they believed they possessed God's Truth caused them to ignore the pressing need to be civil—and professional.[13] Religious conservative political figures never grew tired of boasting that they represented 40 million to 50 million born-again evangelicals and 30 million traditionalist Catholics. But further examination revealed that the numbers were often overstated. Moreover, religious voters are hardly monolithic. Studies of the voting behavior and political views of self-identified born-again voters indicate a diversity not only in party affiliation but even in the number holding centrist to liberal views on social issues. The vast majority of these voters are pro-life and conservative, of course, but being a committed Christian is not the same as being a conservative Republican.

Sometimes the frustration of conservative Christian leaders, who believed they had delivered the votes on Election Day and then received only scraps from the table, had comical results. One pro-family group demanded that Ronald Reagan appoint evangelicals to political posts equal to their numbers in the U.S. population—a kind of quota system for Christians. Needless to say, Jews and those of other faiths viewed such plans with suspicion. Like the redheaded stepchild finally invited to the family reunion, religious conservatives longed to sit at the head of the table and carve up the political spoils.[14] That triumphalism reflected both their feelings of inferiority and the relative inexperience of religious conservatives in the political process. Over time, we have learned to understate rather than overstate our influence, resisting the temptation to shout when speaking in a soft voice will more than suffice.

One of our most important learning experiences concerned the limits of power in Washington, particularly the presidency. Religious conservatives caught a bad case of Potomac fever after the election of Reagan in 1980. Convinced that their moment had arrived on horseback with a dashing, handsome president, they swooped into Washington in droves, opened offices on Capitol Hill, and became a visible part of the political scene in the nation's capital.

Groups like the Family Research Council, a political arm of James Dobson's radio ministry, were joined by other groups like Concerned Women for America (1979), and the American Family Association. The annual meeting of the National Religious Broadcasters became a regular venue for speeches by Reagan and later Bush. Reagan, for instance, delivered his famous speech labeling the Soviet Union an "evil empire" before the National Association of Evangelicals. We were in, and our issues were hot.

Then came the disappointments: the loss of the Senate to the Democrats in 1986, making the movement of pro-family legislation through Congress more difficult, and, in 1992, adverse Supreme Court decisions on school prayer and abortion. Those developments demonstrated that presidential rhetoric was a poor substitute for real influence. We deeply admired and loved Ronald Reagan, who would always remain our hero for his devotion to our values. For my generation in particular, having grown up during the traumatic period of Vietnam and Watergate, Reagan was the first president who ever made us feel proud to be Americans, and who in his warm and generous personality reflected the essential decency of the American people. In that sense he was the booster rocket of the pro-family movement and its emphasis on traditional values. But in spite of Reagan's personal charisma and popularity, we came to understand that no one person could do the work of an entire social movement, even if that person served in the Oval Office.[15] This lesson was further demonstrated during the Bush years, when Republican losses in Congress reduced the power of the presidency to his ability to sustain his vetoes. The social agenda was largely neglected as Bush devoted most of his term to the ill-fated budget deal of 1990 and the Persian Gulf war.

By then, the combined wreckage of the scandals that had rocked religious broadcasting had dealt a death blow to the electronic church and the religious conservative movement. Falwell, consumed by the distraction of the PTL scandal, renamed the Moral Majority the Liberty Federation and turned its leadership over to an Atlanta entrepreneur named Jerry Nims. Without Falwell devoting his full energies to the organization, the mailing list dissipated and contributions plummeted. Jim Dobson, the psychologist and radio-show host with a huge national audience, showed great potential as a future leader, but he largely eschewed the political stage and avoided the white glare of the media. There seemed to be a vacuum, if not a black hole, in what had once been a vibrant and potent political movement. The press and pundits were beside themselves with glee, feverishly (and, as it turned out, prematurely) writing the obituary of a political force they had greeted with a mixture of loathing and fear.

It was out of this apparent debacle that the seed that would become the Christian Coalition sprang forth. The genesis was Pat Robertson's 1988 presidential bid. Robertson's candidacy, like the Goldwater campaign of 1964 and the McGovern campaign of 1972, was a watershed moment that gave the activists and leaders of a previously marginalized community a chance to play in the big leagues. Defeat for them was not a final chapter but the first act in a long play. They made their share of mistakes, of course, but these were valuable learning experiences. Robertson and his lieutenants went head to head with Lee Atwater, Ed Rollins, and Jim Baker in Iowa, Michigan, and New Hampshire. They defeated Bush in Michigan, overwhelmed him in Iowa, and sent him reeling into New Hampshire, where negative ads and missteps by the Dole campaign saved the day. As Robertson once told me, "I was in the ring for twelve rounds with some of the best political operatives. You don't do that and not learn something." Indeed, he and his supporters learned more in two years about politics than many in the pro-family movement had learned in the whole previous decade.

I had long been an admirer of Robertson, having watched his *700 Club* news program for years, and followed his humanitarian efforts. His Operation Blessing program, one of the largest private charities in the nation, shipped tons of food to the inner cities every month. A former Democrat, Robertson had helped to integrate a white Baptist church in Tidewater, Virginia, in the early 1960s and had hired an interracial couple at his television station a few years later—not an easy task in segregationist Virginia, a stronghold of massive resistance. As a native Southerner who grew up in the region when it still bore the scars of Jim Crow, I was attracted to Robertson's tolerant racial views and his strong pro-family stands. I knew his bid for the Republican presidential nomination in 1988 would be an uphill struggle. But I learned a valuable lesson in the growing strength of the movement he led when I attended precinct caucuses in Georgia.

On a cold and blustery day in January 1988, my wife and I drove to the DeKalb County courthouse just outside Atlanta and stepped into a hall packed with charismatic Christians and fundamentalist evangelicals, most of whom had never attended a political party convention in their lives. In our precinct we were the only two Jack Kemp supporters among a dozen Robertson delegates. The chairman of our precinct stood in a semicircle of fellow evangelicals, his hands quivering and his voice shaking as he read slowly from a photocopied sheet of paper, which I later learned was a "cheat sheet" of instructions that had been provided to him by the campaign. The Robertson leaders wore baseball caps to allow their supporters to identify them. If the cap was on a leader's head, supporters were to vote "yes." If the cap was off, they voted "no." The result of those lockstep orders was the political equivalent of a total shutout. The Robertson forces blanketed the party regulars in caucuses across the state. In some precincts, Republican elected officials and longtime party activists were simply swept aside by the religious tidal wave. I was more fortunate. The Robertson folks knew I was a committed Christian, and they allowed me to attend the convention—as an alternate.

As I walked back to my car after the meeting, my head was swimming with ideas. The party establishment had reacted to this influx of religious folk with all the horror of a country club invaded by yahoos. But for me it was an epiphany of a very different sort. My candidate had been trounced, but I was nevertheless euphoric about the outcome. Why? Because my own dream of bringing religious values and conservative principles back into the political arena after two generations of liberal dominance seemed possible for the first time. I had seen the beginning of a new political era in that Georgia courthouse, and its seeds lay in the precincts. More than direct mail or television ministries, the key to giving these religious folk a voice was in grassroots organization. Millions of conservative religious people were coming of age politically, and all they needed was guidance and direction.

For grassroots activists in the Robertson campaign, the race offered the equivalent of a Ph.D. in hardball politics. In Michigan, precinct meetings were moved at the last minute and Robertson supporters found themselves locked out in the snow; in North Carolina, a district convention in Raleigh ended in a brawl that left bloody noses and broken chairs; and in Georgia the Republican party chairman convened a rump convention, disfranchising evangelical delegates and embroiling the party in a bitterly fought lawsuit. Robertson spent in excess of $24 million and came in third (behind Bush and Dole) but ended up with only five state delegations of his supporters: Georgia, Washington, Hawaii, Nevada, and Alaska.

But as with other losing campaigns throughout history, Robertson won in the end. He transformed the culture of one of the nation's two major political parties and changed the broader political culture in the process. As a first-time office seeker and a relative newcomer to the national political scene, he stunned the political establishment. His campaign theme—"restoring the greatness of America through moral strength"—foreshadowed the "values" message that would come to dominate our politics in the 1990s. He called for a flat tax and for reforming entitlements, and predicted the collapse of the Soviet Union. Most important, he stressed that the budget deficit and a sluggish economy were symptoms of a deeper moral problem in America. That was the message that caught fire at the grassroots and that still resonates strongly in an electorate worried about what kind of nation they will leave to their children and grandchildren. As Garry Wills trenchantly observed after the 1988 election, George Bush defeated Michael Dukakis largely by adopting many of Robertson's issues and campaign themes.

After the campaign, a key organizer for Robertson in Texas quoted Christ's statement, "Unless a grain of wheat falls into the earth and dies, it remains by itself alone; but if it dies, it bears much fruit." He added with a touch of humor, "Pat, you died in thirty-two states."

But for Robertson there would be another day. He avoided the trap that Jesse Jackson fell into and wisely chose not to be a perennial presidential candidate. Instead, he decided to take the energy and enthusiasm that I had witnessed in that Georgia courthouse and redirect it toward building a precinct-by-precinct and city-by-city grassroots network that would work primarily on local issues. Just as the Goldwater defeat of 1964 had given the Old Right its next hero (Ronald Reagan) and its best technicians, the Robertson campaign of 1988 cultivated a new generation of leaders and activists who were poised for later victory. Those trained during the campaign and other pro-family organizations spread themselves throughout the political process. Some ran for school boards and state legislatures, others became leaders in their local party organizations, and still others helped to run congressional and statewide campaigns. Among them were Steve Scheffler, Iowa state Republican executive committee member and a Dole campaign operative; Marlene Elwell of Michigan, who assisted the Buchanan and Dole campaigns in 1996; Guy Rodgers, a former national field director of the Christian Coalition and later a Phil Gramm operative; David Miller, chairman of the Kansas Republican Party; and Charles Winburn, a city councilman in Cincinnati. Unlike the first wave of the so-called religious right in the 1980s, which flowed from the grassroots to Washington, this new exodus flowed down from Washington to states and local communities.[16]

My own involvement in the Christian Coalition came about by accident. I first met Pat Robertson following a debate among the Republican presidential candidates at Dartmouth College prior to the New Hampshire primary in early 1988. He had produced a copy of the Intermediate Range Missile Treaty and thrust it at George Bush, pointing out that it did not require the destruction of warheads, as Bush had claimed. At a reception that followed, I asked him how he thought he had done. "I'm a former Golden Gloves boxer," he replied, "and I know the look of a wounded fighter. I think I stunned him."

Stunned or not, Bush swept every primary on Super Tuesday and won the nomination easily. The next time I met Robertson was one year later at the presidential inaugural. Bush was president, and Robertson was trying to determine his next move. He was still sifting through the remains of his presidential campaign, and we discussed both the remarkable successes and some of the errors that had been made. My biggest concern—one that he shared—was how to reduce friction within the party caused by the influx of evangelicals. In Georgia, the mayor of one of the state's largest cities had not even been allowed to be a delegate. I suggested trying to gain influence without casting aside GOP officials and longtime activists. It would be more effective to work from within the party, moving it in a pro-family direction while striking a bargain with the Old Guard wherever possible. Robertson agreed. He told me he was considering launching a new grassroots organization to provide a permanent vehicle for activists who had been mobilized by his campaign, the Moral Majority, and other efforts of the 1980s. As yet, he said, it had no name.

After a meeting in an Atlanta hotel with Pat and key supporters in September 1989, I became the first staff member of the Christian Coalition. We kicked around some alternative names, such as Citizens for a Better America and the Family Values Coalition. I liked the former, but in the end we decided that no secular-sounding organization would pacify either the media or our critics. We were Christians, and we would be wise to wear that label proudly rather than appear to be ashamed of either our faith or our mission. That boldness soon paid off, when our first forays into direct-mail and grassroots recruitment brought in donors and activists by the tens of thousands. Gradually our membership broadened beyond Pat's former supporters to include Roman Catholics, mainline Christians, and many who had supported other presidential candidates in 1988. We were built around no single personality but rather an allegiance to a set of issues and beliefs that transcended both parties and politicians.

Robertson, I soon learned, was not a man of small designs. When I presented a plan for a first-year budget of $2.5 million (which I thought ambitious), he suggested, "This is fine for a first year, but we need a ten-year goal of much more, say one hundred to two hundred million dollars." I had originally projected signing up 3 million members and supporters—making us as large as the National Rifle Association or any counterpart on the left. Robertson wanted 10 million members by the end of the decade. At first I found those expectations a little intimidating, but I soon discovered that I was the one thinking too small. Once we began to build and train, it seemed that anything was possible. Our original ten-year plan had projected a pro-family majority in Congress by 1996. Although that goal seemed unattainable at the time, it was met ahead of schedule following the 1994 elections, when a combination of seventy-three Republican freshmen and conservative "blue dog" Democrats enabled us to achieve many of our pro-family legislative goals.

The first week I came on staff, I mostly sat alone in an abandoned warehouse office that had once housed the Robertson campaign headquarters, drafting a long-term plan for the organization. It called for state affiliates, a national media presence, and a large, well-funded grassroots training effort. Paul Weyrich had once told me that if the leaders of the religious right of the 1980s had been generals, they would have been court-martialed for failing to train their troops properly for battle. The long-term plan of the Christian Coalition projected training up to fifty thousand people a year through church-based seminars by the year 2000. It also projected a Christian Coalition chapter in each of America's three thousand counties and a neighborhood coordinator in all of the nation's 175,000 precincts. Robertson and I met for lunch one day, and he reviewed the plan and suggested several changes. Later the board of directors gave its approval, and we went to work.

RISING FROM THE ASHES

In the beginning our staff was skeletal. I often opened the mail and answered the phones myself the first month we opened our doors. Our humble beginnings gave few hints of the explosive growth that came later. My wife, Jo Anne, worked as my secretary (without pay because funds were so scarce), answering the mail and helping me send thank-you letters to those who sent contributions, which at first came in at a trickle. Our daughter, Brittany, then six months old, played on the floor with a rattle and cooed away while we worked until late in the evening. After dinner I would return to the office and call potential contributors, asking for $100 and $200 at a time. Our Bible study group stuffed the first gift appeals by hand in our living room and ate take-out pizza. Those hardly seemed the beginnings of a political behemoth. I still remember traveling home to Georgia at Christmas that first year, driving through the night as Jo Anne sat in the back, licking and stuffing envelopes while Brittany slept peacefully beside her. Our pro-family efforts were truly a family affair.

Our first membership and fund-raising appeals focused on ending the taxpayer funding of pornography by the National Endowment for the Arts, which had recently funded an exhibit by photographer Robert Mapplethorpe that included explicit depictions of various sex acts and suggestive poses of nude children. The first mailing to 134,000 former donors to the Robertson presidential campaign brought in around three thousand new members. A telemarketing appeal to the same donors soon reaped around forty thousand supporters and built a cash reserve of over half a million dollars at a time when we had only a handful of employees, a couple of desks, and a broken down copying machine left over from the campaign. We were off and running.

Slowly but surely that hard work began to pay off. At the first Christian Coalition event in December 1989, in Orlando, Florida, two hundred people attended a luncheon and six hundred came to an evening rally. In a meeting with prospective county coordinators, we found most of them full of optimism and hope, ready to begin the important work of building a new grassroots network. After consulting with the board, I hired four regional field directors, who roamed throughout the country setting up state affiliates, starting chapters, and holding training seminars. I jumped into my car, a red Subaru station wagon, and drove through Pennsylvania, Virginia, North Carolina, and Georgia, holding early organizational meetings, often staying in homes of supporters or at Holiday Inns. We kept overhead low and expenses down. Meanwhile, the contributions from direct-mail and telemarketing appeals began to pour in. Within a few months we had over half a million dollars in the bank, and we began to expand our operations, adding a microcomputer network to maintain our growing database and publishing a four-color tabloid newspaper.

Robertson was one of the most prominent evangelicals in the twentieth century to seek the presidency, and he maintained a strong friendship with George Bush. Still, there were rumors that the Christian Coalition was a stalking horse for another Robertson presidential bid, which I found slightly amusing. In fact, we focused our energies almost exclusively on the grassroots.

We believed that our best chances for success lay in the heartland of the country. Our values were popular, particularly in the South and Midwest, but also in unlikely regions of the country, and we enjoyed a strong demographic base of support from evangelicals and Roman Catholics. When the Supreme Court ruled in the *Webster* decision in July 1989 that states could pass some restrictions on abortion, it confirmed what we knew all along: the future of the pro-family movement lay in the states and localities, not in Washington. In 1990 Louisiana, Pennsylvania, and Utah passed laws restricting abortion in varying degrees, and across the country declining educational performance led to a rash of education reform proposals and conservative campaigns for school boards. Soon we discovered that it was far easier to win a school board seat than a Senate seat, and far more likely to change the vote of a state legislator than to change the mind of the president.

Some of the innovations we developed occurred without any advance planning. The first voter guides were distributed in 1990 in seven states, mostly through other pro-family organizations. Voter guides had been used in the 1980s by the pro-family movement, and they were hardly a new voter education tool, but we took the technology to a new level by raising the distribution into the tens of millions and distributing voter guides in races for school boards and county commissions. In 1991 the Christian Coalition undertook one of its first major voter education efforts in the Virginia state legislative elections, identifying pro-family voters, distributing nonpartisan voter guides, and turning out the vote with phone banks and telephone trees. The results were astonishing. In Virginia Beach, a state senator who had built his entire campaign around opposition to Pat Robertson and the Christian Coalition lost in a landslide, a defeat that rippled across the region and gave seats to other pro-family Republicans.

The Christian Coalition did not become a factor in national politics until June 1990, when we took out full-page ads in the *Washington Post* and *USA Today* calling for an end to taxpayer-funded pornography sponsored by the National Endowment for the Arts. The agency had sparked a furor by funding the controversial Andres Serrano exhibit portraying Christ immersed in a jar of urine, and the Robert Mapplethorpe exhibit, featuring graphic homoerotic photographs. John Frohnmayer, the Bush-appointed head of the NEA, was a well-intentioned arts bureaucrat from Oregon who was totally unprepared and ill-equipped for the riptides of Washington politics. Rather than reform the agency, he defended many of the controversial exhibits and created a fire storm of protest. We called for Frohnmayer's resignation and lobbied for restrictions on the funding of pornography, which passed the Senate but were bogged down in conference committee by liberal House members. We focused on taxpayer-funded pornography and obscenity because it played into two broad themes that energized religious folk: first, the sense that government no longer shared their values and had lost touch with middle America, and second, the culture's celebration of violence, sex, and the profane at the expense of the sacred and uplifting. In this sense, the NEA's direction was less about politics than it was symbolic of the drift of the culture toward hostility to religious belief and values. Finally, during the 1992 presidential primary campaign with Pat Buchanan, the Bush White House fired Frohnmayer. Later that year I was invited to debate Frohnmayer in his home town in Oregon; we had a spirited and cordial exchange. He was still a little shell-shocked from his stormy tenure. Afterward he came up to me and shook my hand. "Thank you for coming," he said earnestly. "Most of my conservative Christian critics won't even have the decency to talk to me." I found him to be a decent and honorable man, but one who lacked the kind of razor-sharp political skills necessary to head a federal agency plagued by controversy and scandal.

In 1991 one of our biggest victories came with the confirmation of Clarence Thomas' appointment to the U.S. Supreme Court. I crafted our legislative plans after consulting with Robertson and the state leaders, and we all agreed that Thomas' confirmation was a major priority. At the time, many in the pro-family community expected Thomas to be the fifth vote in a decision overturning *Roe,* a hope that turned out to be groundless. Leading the strategy for the pro-family movement during the Thomas battle was Tom Jipping, a gifted judicial strategist at Paul Weyrich's Free Congress Foundation. Jipping believed that if the NAACP supported Thomas, it would be almost impossible for liberals in the Senate to oppose him. But in August we were holding a briefing for our state leaders when word reached us that the NAACP had decided not to endorse Thomas, who would be only the second African-American to sit on the nation's highest court. We viewed this as a storm cloud on the horizon. While we never anticipated Anita Hill's charges of sexual harassment, we knew the organized left would spare no resource to defeat him. We broadcast radio and television ads in Georgia, Louisiana, and Pennsylvania, on the theory that senators Sam Nunn, Wyche Fowler, Bennett Johnston, John Breaux, and Arlen Specter would determine the outcome. Four days before the Hill charges were broadcast by Nina Totenberg on National Public Radio, I huddled at the Heritage Foundation with other conservative lobbyists, and we came up with a nose count in the Senate that showed Thomas winning no more than fifty-two votes—the closest confirmation for a Supreme Court nominee in history. By then our media and grassroots campaign had delivered more than fifty thousand petitions and letters to Capitol Hill.

Like most observers, I do not believe the Anita Hill controversy changed many minds in the Senate or the country at large. Those who were anti-Thomas believed Hill's story and used it for political purposes; those who knew Clarence well and admired him did not. Thomas was always going to face a close vote, and the sexual harassment controversy, while significant in raising the importance of the issue, made little difference in the final tally.

The Thomas-Hill controversy became to the culture wars of the 1990s what the Alger Hiss-Whittaker Chambers dispute was to the Cold War in the 1950s. As in the case of Hiss' trial for perjury (he was ultimately convicted), whether one believed Hill or Thomas tended to be colored by ideology. Liberals embraced Hill as a feminist heroine who faced down a panel of white men in blue suits and ties who had no clue as to the gruesome reality of sexual harassment. Conservatives felt that Thomas was a victim of left-wing McCarthyism, and the target of an ideologically motivated witch hunt in which the feminists and the pro-abortion lobby would do or say anything to defeat a justice they feared might vote to overturn abortion rights. I found Hill's account to be out of character with everything I knew about Thomas. A close member of my family had once been a victim of sexual harassment, and I knew she would never repeatedly call her former harasser to seek career assistance or "just say hello," as Anita Hill did. My relative found the thought of her harasser repulsive and avoided contact entirely.

When Charles Kothe, the former dean of the law school at Oral Roberts University, released a statement indicating that Anita Hill, who had formerly taught at the school, had invited Thomas to speak and had offered to drive him to the airport, I faxed Kothe's statement to the media and to the staff of the Senate Judiciary Committee. Later, Kothe testified before the committee, indicating that her conduct did not appear to be that of someone who felt in the least bit uncomfortable with Thomas. This testimony, along with the powerful character references provided by former female employees, all vouched for Thomas' gentlemanly conduct toward women in the workplace. I have always felt that the vicious treatment of Thomas (and Robert Bork) by the radical left helped to inspire our movement to encourage people of faith to make a difference and become an influential force on Capitol Hill. It is my prayer that nothing like the character assassination that characterized those hearings is ever again repeated in public life.

A month after Thomas' confirmation, we held our first Road to Victory conference at the Founder's Inn in Virginia Beach. More than eight hundred activists from forty states gathered to hear addresses by Senator Jesse Helms, Pat Robertson, Representative Robert Dornan, and Representative Guy Vander Jagt. The featured speaker was Vice President Dan Quayle, who delivered an early version of what would later become known as his "Murphy Brown" speech. "Some 25 percent of America's children live in homes with only one parent," he said. "All of us know the problems, and all of us understand what causes them—all of us, I should say, except those who deem themselves the cultural elite." But the emphasis of the weekend was not on speeches. Delegates attended workshops on voter education, voter identification, running for the school board, parliamentary procedure, and running for delegate to the Republican or Democratic party convention.

Our grassroots strategy had succeeded beyond any of our initial expectations. By 1992 our annual budget had soared to $8.5 million, our total membership had surged to 250,000, and our crackerjack field staff and state coordinators had organized one thousand local chapters in all fifty states. Things couldn't have been going better. Then came the Houston convention.

How religious conservatives got blamed for the Houston convention is one of the great untold stories of 1992. It began the week before the convention formally opened, when a platform committee heavily sprinkled with religious conservatives overwhelmingly approved the same pro-life platform of 1984 and 1988, and also spiced up the document with strong language endorsing choice in education, advocating tougher laws against pornography, and opposing gay rights. The media, which had spent months providing favorable coverage of Republicans for Choice—a group with no significant membership, budget, or organization that wanted the Republican party to be "neutral" on abortion—were plainly dismayed by the outcome. Moreover, the press was bored. The platform was more conservative than anticipated, efforts to dump Quayle from the ticket had ended with a whimper, and Bush was gliding toward a ho-hum renomination. There were twenty thousand reporters trapped in the August heat of Texas, and they needed a story.

I vividly recall standing at a pay phone in the Houston convention center and overhearing E. J. Dionne, a respected political reporter for the *Washington Post,* describe to his editor in animated language the presence of so many religious activists. Dionne, extremely popular among his colleagues, was a good barometer of sentiment among the press corps, and I knew we were in trouble. Several days later I had lunch with a CBS producer who wanted to know how the Christian Coalition had managed to recruit so many members as delegates. Several surveys indicated that one out of six delegates were Coalition members and that 42 percent were conservative evangelicals. When the media wandered onto the floor of the convention and found what more closely resembled a tent revival, they sharpened their quills. Connie Chung of CBS News grabbed Pat Robertson, who was a delegate from Virginia, and stuck a microphone in his face, asking, "Is this platform right wing enough for you?"

The turning point came on the second day of the convention, when the delegates passed the most conservative pro-family platform in the party's history. After months of hoopla and press coverage, a much-publicized campaign to drop or water down the pro-life plank had fizzled. We had worked for months to encourage our members and allies to run as delegates and serve on the platform committee. The result was that about a quarter of the 107 members of the platform committee were pro-family leaders or activists. Those people were not the goobers the media portrayed them to be. Some, like Betsy DeVos of Michigan, whose family owned the Amway Corporation, were major financial supporters of the party and were thoroughly integrated into the party structure. Others, like Representative Henry Hyde, state senator Mark Early of Virginia, and state senator Tim Philpot of Kentucky, were some of the most respected legislative leaders in their respective states.

The Christian Coalition had worked hard to preserve the pro-life plank that Ronald Reagan had run on in 1980 and 1984, winning landslide victories. I testified before the platform committee at hearings held in Salt Lake City in the spring of 1992, presenting tens of thousands of pro-life petitions to Senator Don Nickles, who chaired the platform proceedings. I also strategized regularly with Phyllis Schlafly, a veteran of numerous battles, most memorably that of the Equal Rights Amendment; her political involvement stretched back to the Goldwater years, when her book *A Choice, Not an Echo* became Goldwater's campaign theme. Phyllis is greatly misunderstood by many. No shrinking violet who defers to men or believes that women should take a back seat, she is a no-nonsense, savvy political operator who knows how to count votes, how to build coalitions, and how to compromise when necessary without surrendering her principles. When Henry Hyde offered a preamble to the platform that noted the diversity of views within the party over many issues, a minor concession to the pro-choice lobby, Phyllis agreed not to oppose it.

Nevertheless, the conservative platform adopted in Houston was really due less to our lobbying than to the strenuous efforts of the Bush campaign. Charlie Black, the wily former Reagan operative, worked the phones for the Bush campaign from a makeshift office deep in the bowels of the convention center, cajoling and persuading moderate Republican governors like Bill Weld of Massachusetts and John McKernan of Maine to drop their opposition to the pro-life plank. Both Weld and McKernan acceded to his requests. The Bush campaign—not the so-called religious right—squashed an effort by six states to petition the convention for a minority plank. Mary Matalin and Charlie Black worked the wayward delegations like backroom pols, urging them not to start fisticuffs over abortion. Why? They were playing to the right in an attempt to win back activists within the GOP still disaffected from Bush. I sat in on an early strategy meeting for the platform with Jim Ciccone, the campaign issues adviser, and he indicated that Bush's problems on the right caused by the 1990 tax increase had made it unthinkable for Bush to move left on any other issue, especially abortion. Before the first delegate arrived in Houston, the die was cast. The fact that the Bush campaign was still working this late in the game to get back the core conservative supporters of the party demonstrated Bush's weakness.

We celebrated the passage of the pro-life platform on the Tuesday of the convention with a "God and Country" rally held at the Sheraton Astrodome hotel. As luck would have it, the Sheraton Astrodome turned out to be the headquarters hotel for the national press corps. Because the ballroom was one of the largest in the city, we had wheeled in old-fashioned popcorn machines and large vending booths to fill up what we hoped would not be a half-empty hall. Two hours before the doors opened, I was walking across the vast Astrodome parking lot and saw a line of hundreds of straw-hatted, sign-carrying Christian activists snaking across the hotel grounds under the sweltering Houston heat. "Wonder who they could be," I thought. As I got closer, I realized we were not going to have a problem rustling up a crowd. The mob filled the lobby, jammed the hallways, and spilled out into the street. Hundreds of reporters had already taken seats on the press riser in the back. At 2 P.M. we threw the doors open, and a mass of humanity surged toward the stage. Four thousand people toppled exhibit tables and nearly knocked over the popcorn machines, shouting slogans and singing songs as a jazz band played in the background.

"Pro-life! Pro-family!" they shouted.

Pat Boone, the emcee of the event, strode to the podium wearing a cream suit, a lavender tie, and a purple handkerchief, glowing under the hot lights like an angel on fire. Darkly tanned and virtually ageless, Boone was a kind of evangelical Dick Clark, looking not a day over thirty even though he was recording hits before Elvis was King. Backstage, I paced nervously, worried sick because Vice President Quayle, our featured speaker, was running late. Boone stalled by telling jokes and crooning tunes while we waited for Quayle. The crowd began to grow restless. We presented "Friend of the Family" awards—framed pictures of a bald eagle soaring over a mountain range—to Phyllis Schlafly and Senator Don Nickles in appreciation of their hard work in support of the platform.

"In 1988 they said the Christian conservative movement was dead," Pat Robertson said. "Well, this is a resurrection here today."

At that moment, Quayle burst through a back door of the hotel with

Secret Service agents trailing him like dark-suited robots and his chief of staff, Bill Kristol, in tow. Quayle enthusiastically shook my hand and we exchanged a few quick words. He gazed from behind the curtain at the huge crowd that awaited him. The electricity in the room sizzled. When Quayle, still fresh from the Murphy Brown controversy, bounded onto the stage, the cheers became a deafening roar, cowbells rang, and chants of "We love Dan!" filled the air.

Quayle, in a self-deprecatory reference to his Murphy Brown speech, joked about "my career as a television critic." He pounded away at pro-family themes, and any mention of the media brought a chorus of hisses and boos.

"Do we trust Bill Clinton?" asked Quayle.

"No!" the crowd shouted.

"Do we trust the liberal media?"

"No!" they bellowed, now getting into the rhythm of Quayle's cadence.

"Who do we trust?"

"Jesus!" came back the response. The answer clearly caught Quayle off guard, and for a split second he got a deer-in-the-headlights look. The answer he had clearly expected was "George Bush."

Members of the press corps were in shock, their eyes widening like saucers. They were still adjusting to the large presence of evangelicals on the floor of the convention. Like the spectacle of young antiwar delegates at the Democratic National Conventions in Chicago and Miami in 1968 and 1972, the sight of so many religious conservatives presented an odd profile to the political establishment. The barely restrained hostility between many of them and the media hardly helped matters. Bob Beckel, a television commentator for CNN, was jostled, and his fiancée heckled, by some of the more unruly members of the crowd. Taking personal affront, he later launched into an uncontrollable tirade against us on *Crossfire*. As I left the hotel after the rally, stepping over discarded signs in the empty ballroom, I got the first inkling that we had stepped on a political land mine. And there were more problems ahead.

The media tore into us like wolves. "God and country. What is it about the linkage of those two words, at this time, in this place, to strike the pit of the heart with terror?" a columnist in the *New York Post* asked. "Check your mind at the door and pick up your plastic fetus." The *Boston Globe* quipped: "You know what they say about Houston. It isn't the heat, it's the stupidity."

That evening I conducted a brief interview on the convention floor with Nina Totenberg of National Public Radio. Totenberg was anathema to many conservatives because of her role in the leak of an FBI report containing allegations of sexual harassment against Clarence Thomas. Several hecklers—not members of the Christian Coalition—stood just a few feet away from us, hurling insults and shouting epithets at Totenberg, until I asked them to please be quiet so we could finish the interview. Afterward they stalked her across the convention floor, calling her a "whore" and other unprintable epithets. I found such behavior incredibly juvenile and politically suicidal. I kept wondering: Who are these losers, and where are the sergeants-at-arms to hustle them off the floor? I certainly did not share Totenberg's politics, but I was embarrassed at how shabbily she had been treated. There was no way such clashes with the media could fail to find their way into the coverage of the convention. As the old saying goes, never pick a fight with someone who buys ink by the barrel.

It was against this backdrop that Pat Buchanan's rabble-rousing convention speech echoed through the press corps. The speech was exactly what both Buchanan and the Bush campaign wanted: red meat served up raw to the grassroots conservatives they needed to win back into the fold. I thought parts of the speech were outstanding, such as the amusing line about Bill Clinton's only foreign policy experience consisting of having once dined at the International House of Pancakes. That kind of partisan needling was fair game, and it had the convention hall rocking. Buchanan's candidacy had resonated with the conservative grassroots throughout the 1992 primaries, not because they had expected him to win, but because they hungered to send a message of protest to President Bush, particularly against his 1990 tax increases. Outside of New Hampshire and Georgia, he never received more than a third of the vote in any primary. But the media always overstated his strength among religious conservatives in order to tie us to Buchanan's occasionally hot rhetoric. In truth, his was always a protest candidacy. In New Hampshire, for example, half of the Buchanan vote was pro-choice and liberal. They were not so much voting for Buchanan as against Bush, a trend that portended doom in the fall.

What many of our members admired about Buchanan was his willingness to tell it exactly as he saw it. His razor-sharp wit and stiletto tongue appealed to a populist undercurrent in the grassroots of the GOP. When Buchanan spoke, his listeners could almost be heard asking themselves, "Did he really say that?" As with Barry Goldwater and Ronald Reagan in earlier times, the answer was an emphatic yes. Like Goldwater, who had once speculated about the tactical use of nuclear weapons, Buchanan's rhetoric frightened some, but it energized grassroots activists who had grown tired of the focus-tested pablum of career politicians. When broadcast to a national audience of undecided voters and interpreted by a hostile press corps, however, Buchanan's appeal to the conservative wing of the party was twisted by our foes to sound harsh and unyielding. But Buchanan's use of the "religious war" metaphor was needlessly provocative. And again, part of the responsibility lay with the Bush campaign. One member of the Bush team told me that he did not even see the Buchanan speech until a few hours before it was delivered. When he suggested changes, he was told flatly by campaign manager Bob Teeter that his deal with Buchanan allowed him to give the speech he wrote, unedited, with no revisions. But the biggest downside to the Buchanan speech had nothing to do with its content. The evening program was already running dreadfully behind schedule when Buchanan mounted the platform, and the result was that Ronald Reagan did not address the convention until after the prime time hours had slipped away on the East Coast. It was the greatest blunder in convention planning since George McGovern delivered his acceptance speech at the 1972 Democratic convention in Miami at three in the morning, long after most Americans had gone to bed.

For those and many other mistakes of the GOP, religious conservatives took a beating. Pat Robertson delivered a standard Republican stump speech that celebrated the fall of the Berlin Wall and the end of the Cold War, called for term limits and tax cuts, and reached its crescendo with an emotional tribute to Barbara Bush. "Tonight we say to the American people, a Republican White House gave you victory over Communism and liberated Kuwait," Robertson said. "Now give George Bush a Republican Congress and he will win the war with the budget deficit as skillfully as he won the war in the Persian Gulf."[17] That was not how the press reported it, however. Rather it portrayed his speech as a call for a political jihad, lumping his remarks together with Buchanan's and Marilyn Quayle's, forgetting that he had also addressed the convention in New Orleans in 1988. Robertson had come to address the Houston convention not at his request but at the invitation of the Bush campaign, and he gave the speech at 7:20 P.M., not during prime time. Robertson was also heavily edited by the Bush people, who assigned a very able speechwriter to work with us. Our original draft had one line about Hillary Clinton, which the campaign duly dropped; yet a much tougher jab at Mrs. Clinton survived in Buchanan's speech. Why this happened was not altogether clear.

When it came to the convention rhetoric, there seemed to be no clear theme or message, just wild punches thrown in desperation as the bell sounded. On the opening day Rich Bond, chairman of the Republican National Committee, launched a blistering attack on Hillary Clinton in which he alleged that she had compared marriage to slavery. He said of liberal Democrats, "We're America, and they're not." Who was editing Bond and the other Bush operatives? The answer was no one. I felt a sense of foreboding, thinking to myself that the death of Lee Atwater loomed large at the convention. For one thing, I firmly believe that had he lived, Lee would have prevented Bush from raising taxes in 1990, and a Buchanan primary challenge could have been averted. Unfortunately for the Republican party, Lee was diagnosed with an inoperable brain tumor and died before the campaign began. I was not alone in feeling haunted by his ghost.

As the week wore on, it was obvious that we had walked into an ambush. The television networks broadcast extensive profiles of the Christian

Coalition, crediting us with the rightward march of the party (or, more accurately, blaming us for it). By the time George Bush flew triumphantly to Dallas the day after the convention to announce to the Religious Roundtable that the Democratic party platform had failed to mention the word "God," the long knives were out. I had recommended to one Bush campaign official that Bush either not attend the event or at least deliver a different speech. But by then it was too late.

It was ironic that Buchanan, who had stayed loyal to Nixon when he faced a challenge from the right in 1972, bolted the ranks to oppose Bush. Within the conservative movement, there was division over how to respond to the Buchanan candidacy. Some longtime leaders like Phyllis Schlafly and Pat Robertson remained supportive of Bush as the best hope to preserve the pro-life and pro-family stands of the Reagan era. Jack Kemp, Bill Bennett, and Dan Quayle all campaigned for Bush in New Hampshire, and Bennett charged that Buchanan was "flirting with fascism." Buchanan's campaign was really an intramural struggle between the Old Right of the 1960s, also known as "paleoconservatives," and those "neocons" like Bennett and Irving Kristol who had been longtime Democrats until they switched sides in the 1970s and the 1980s. In this battle, the pro-family movement generally sided with Bush, not because it disliked Buchanan personally, but because Bush had stood firm on the abortion issue. Pro-family leaders also pragmatically understood that if they opposed Bush in the primaries and fatally wounded him so that he lost in the fall, they would be blamed. In the end, Buchanan was rewarded for his campaign against the incumbent president with a prime-time speaking slot at the convention. Conservative evangelicals, who remained loyal to Bush mostly because of his strong pro-life stance, were rewarded by being blamed for his defeat.

There were other significant differences between Buchanan and the pro-family community. While he stressed themes of economic populism like protectionist trade policies and sharp restrictions on immigration, most pro-family supporters were motivated by moral concerns. On U.S. support for Israel, Buchanan had criticized American foreign aid to the

Jewish state, while most evangelicals made support for Israel their top foreign-policy concern.

Later, during his 1996 campaign, the media would do a better job of reporting the substantive differences between Buchanan's "America First" message and the pro-family movement's agenda. There were significant overlaps, especially on the cultural and moral issues like abortion, but the two were never one and the same. While some pro-family leaders climbed aboard the Buchanan express as a means to hold the party's feet to the fire on the social issues, many others remained ambivalent beneath the surface.

In 1996, at the height of the Buchanan surge following his victory in New Hampshire, I received a call from one of the highest-ranking leaders in the Southern Baptist Convention. "I cannot vote for Pat Buchanan if he is the Republican nominee," he told me. I was taken aback. I had come to expect such protestations from more establishment Republicans like Colin Powell or Bill Bennett. But here was one of the most prominent conservative evangelical leaders in the nation saying he would never support Buchanan—even against Clinton. I did not share his views, and expressed surprise.

"Why not?" I asked.

"He is not supportive enough of Israel," the leader told me. "And he wants to build a wall around America and isolate us from the world. Isolationism is what gave rise to fascism in Europe and ultimately dragged us into World War II."

This outlook hardly spoke for the majority of evangelicals, but it did reflect a continuing ambivalence among religious folk over Buchanan's candidacy. The truth is that religious conservatives are neither universally supportive of nor opposed to Buchanan's brand of pro-family populism. There is a diversity of views. In Iowa, religious conservatives split evenly between Buchanan and his opponents. In New Hampshire, they broke heavily in his favor. In the South, Bob Dole won a plurality of Christia Coalition members, defeating Buchanan roughly 48 percent to 26 perce There will always be a part of the religious conservative community admires Buchanan's tenacity, his protectionist economic views, and his anti-establishment rhetoric. These voters are an important part of our coalition. There are also pro-family conservatives who respect and admire Buchanan as a talk-show host and advocate but who feel that his appeal as a candidate is limited. They are drawn to more conventional candidates like Reagan, Bush, Phil Gramm, and Bob Dole. It would be a mistake to suggest that either the pro-Buchanan populist strain or the more conventional activists represent or speak for our entire community. Any social movement representing more than one-third of the Republican primary vote is bound to be diverse. Religious conservatives did not, for example, flock to Buchanan in the same numbers that African-Americans in the Democratic party fueled Jesse Jackson's candidacy in 1984 and 1988. In my view, when the helicopter carrying Ronald Reagan left the Capitol grounds in 1989 following the inauguration of George Bush, we witnessed the departure of the first and last individual who could unite all religious conservatives from the national political stage.

While Pat Buchanan may have made the biggest headlines in Houston, a quick glance back at the program reveals that the convention was a diverse one—far more so than the Democratic convention in New York City, where Governor Robert Casey of Pennsylvania, a staunch pro-life advocate, was prohibited from even addressing the delegates. While the Democrats excluded pro-life speakers (several delegates from Minnesota were roughed up and kicked when they tried to raise pro-life banners), the Republican convention included many pro-choice speakers. Among them were Governor William Weld, Governor Pete Wilson of California, and Labor Secretary Lynn Martin, who gave one of the nominating speeches for Bush. The featured speakers on the evening when Pat Robertson spoke were keynoter Phil Gramm and Mary Fisher, the mother who had contracted AIDS from her husband and who spoke on the need to show greater compassion for those suffering from the HIV virus. "Though I am female and contracted this disease in marriage and enjoy the warm support my family, I am one with the lonely gay man sheltering a flickering candle from the cold wind of his family's rejection," said Fisher. "[W]e do the president's cause no good if we praise the American family but ignore a virus that destroys it."[18]

All the subsequent mythology about the family-values theme bringing down the ticket was nonsense. Bush received a double-digit bounce in the polls from Houston, closing the gap with Clinton to a winnable race. Without the recession and the tax hike of 1990, which Bush later conceded allowed his critics to question his credibility, he would have been reelected. A postelection survey found that voters ranked debate performance very important to their voting decision, while the conventions ranked thirty-fifth out of thirty-eight possible factors. The pro-family agenda was not a liability to Bush; it was an asset. John C. Green of the University of Akron later analyzed the election returns and concluded that without the strong support of conservative evangelicals, Bush actually would have garnered less than 33 percent of the popular vote.

George Bush, one of the most decent and honorable men ever to sit in the Oval Office, was also a president who resisted unveiling a bold domestic agenda, was perceived not to have addressed a stubborn recession, and broke the most fundamental promise of his 1988 campaign—his "read my lips" pledge not to raise taxes. The Republicans limped into the campaign with a president who had signed a tax hike, a quota bill, the Clean Air Act, and a host of other liberal initiatives. All they were left with were a bunch of loyal, happy-faced religious conservatives who would do everything they could for him, regardless of the consequences. In spite of his reputation as a flip-flopper on taxes, Bush had never wavered in his pro-life stand, issuing several courageous vetoes of pro-abortion measures passed by Democrats in Congress. He was arguably the most pro-life president in the history of the country. Out of a sense of obligation and gratitude, the pro-family community stood by their man, as Tammy Wynette sings, and its reward was to be charged with introducing a wave of "intolerance" and "hate" into American politics.

In that sense, Houston was a gigantic missed opportunity. Party conventions are supposed to crown the nominee and serve as unpaid infomercials targeted at ticket-splitters and swing voters. But on the eve of the

Houston convention, the Bush campaign faced a Hobbesian dilemma: energize conservatives and risk alienating the middle, or play to ticket-splitters and deflate party activists. They chose the former, with predictable results. It was not that issues like school choice, stronger families, and traditional values offended voters. To the contrary, these were winning issues. But after the Houston convention, the Bush campaign dropped the family-values message and fell into the trap of playing to Clinton's assertion that the election was about "the economy, stupid," and as a consequence they lost.

Our people compounded this error by focusing on the party platform to the exclusion of other matters, such as personnel and policy. The platform committee produced a document that pressed every hot-button issue dear to conservatives, but it had purely symbolic meaning and all the negatives of overheated rhetoric. The platform had assumed magnified significance after 1980, when conservatives succeeded in adopting a pro-life plank at the Republican convention in Detroit that nominated Reagan. The Reagan White House used the platform as a blueprint for administration policy. But Bush, lacking strong ideological instincts, felt no such constraints. To pacify the right, the Bush campaign gladly turned over the platform to conservatives, with sometimes comical results. The platform subcommittee dealing with the economy adopted a draft that condemned the Bush tax increase, an unheard-of slap in the face to their own president. When the press gleefully reported that rebuke, an angry White House chief of staff, Sam Skinner, called and singed the eardrums of the Bush campaign staff. The campaign hastily assembled an emergency meeting of the platform delegates to amend the document and avoid embarrassing the president. Religious conservatives on the panel showed their influence by lacing the platform with Bible verses and pro-family homilies. One delegate offered an amendment changing a quotation by Barbara Bush that celebrated personal growth to one that honored motherhood. Another changed a statement praising America's "religious pluralism" so that it gave proper due to her "Judeo-Christian heritage," while still another changed a Bible verse from a Living Bible translation to the King James Version, which sent members of the press corps giggling to the pay phones to call in the tidbit to their editors.

This critical mass of problems led to the false and unfair perception that the Houston convention had been the American political equivalent of an Iranian tea party. David Gergen of *U.S. News* wrote that evangelical delegates had "captured the party platform, writing into it flaming denunciations of alternative lifestyles." The clatter of "storm troopers marching in the background" echoed as they cheered Pat Buchanan, "whose talk of cultural and religious wars and bashing of gays and feminists was harshly divisive."[19] The *Boston Globe* found the GOP platform brimming with "puritanical, punitive language that not only forbade abortions, but attacked public television, gun control, homosexual rights, birth control clinics and the distribution of clean needles for drug users."[20]

An estimated 40 percent of the delegates in Houston were self-identified evangelicals, a figure that roughly approximated the percentage of evangelicals among Republican party primary voters. (It was hardly a disproportionate number. One-third of Democrats say they are "born-again" Christians.) The *New York Times* found in the presence of those delegates proof that "the fundamentalist impulses at large in the Republican Party" would soon launch a political battle and "divide the nation along religious lines."[21]

That conventional editorial wisdom hardened the perception that the Houston convention had signaled the opening volley in a holy war for the soul of the Republican party. The GOP "faces a civil war the likes of which it has not seen since the Goldwater and Rockefeller forces self-destructed in 1964," the *Los Angeles Times* commented. "And it could be a decade or more before the looming war between the two camps can be settled."[22] Another press account foretold "the worst round of Republican bloodletting since Barry Goldwater was trounced by Lyndon Johnson" and wondered if the Republican party "can survive in its present form."[23] All of this led to an inescapable conclusion: religious conservatives had infiltrated the Republican party like termites, had seized control of the levers of power, and now aimed to impose their theocratic designs on an unwitting public.

The dire predictions and funeral dirges written about our movement would later be resoundingly refuted. But that knowledge was not so apparent on election eve in 1992. Throughout the evening, somber-faced network anchors proclaimed the demise of the GOP and moralized about the divisive influence of religious conservatives. Ed Bradley of CBS News reported that "there were a number of Republicans who said that they felt let down by their convention . . . that some of the positions of the religious right did not represent the way they felt." Just before Pat Robertson went on the air for an interview with Tom Brokaw of NBC News, I whispered in his ear, "Be prepared for him to ask about whether we are trying to take over the Republican party." Pat laughed, "What is there left to take over?" A good question, I thought, as I began to ponder my own future and the future of the pro-family movement.

5

CHRISTIAN COALITION

After the Fall

A few days after Bush's defeat in November 1992 I boarded an airplane for Jamaica. I had to get away for a few days and reflect on the future. But no amount of rest and relaxation could help me escape the magnitude of the setback we had suffered. We had founded the Christian Coalition as a local and state operation because we had learned after twelve years of Republican rule that winning the presidency in isolation did little to advance our legislative agenda. Now we were being blamed for the Republicans' loss of the White House, the press was demonizing us, and our entire strategy seemed to be in jeopardy.

I sat on the balcony of my hotel room in Montego Bay, staring out over the blue ocean glistening in the sunset, contemplating the presidency of Bill Clinton. The press was in a full-blown fawning mode. The *New York Times* gushed over his "masseur's touch with the English language" and expressed the hope that he could heal the nation with "the balm of rhetoric."[1] Sounding like a teenybopper at a Courtney Love concert, the *Boston Globe* exclaimed, "He can talk in complete sentences!"[2] Meanwhile, the political pundits were sifting through the ashes of what remained of the Republican party, pointing fingers at the chief culprits in the recent defeat. Not surprisingly, religious conservatives were at the top of everyone's list.

In truth, Clinton's victory was not especially deep or wide. He had won 43 percent of the popular vote, about the same as Michael Dukakis in 1988, a little more than Walter Mondale in 1984, and less than Jimmy Carter in 1980. He had won the Democratic party's base vote, and nothing more. The party had lost House seats while winning the presidency, something that had happened only once before in the twentieth century. "We didn't break the Republican electoral lock on the presidency," James Carville quipped after the election. "We picked it."

But those signs of weakness were not apparent in the postelection euphoria surrounding Clinton. The White House and Congress were controlled by liberals, and our chances of advancing the pro-family agenda seemed more remote than when the religious conservative movement first emerged in the late 1970s. I was in no way plagued by self-doubt. I knew the work I was engaged in was important, and I felt we had done a good job in organizing at the grassroots. But I was stunned by the media caricature of the Houston convention, in which advocating stronger families and traditional values had been portrayed as somehow "hateful," and disappointed that it had stuck.

A few weeks after the election I had lunch with Bill Kristol, Dan Quayle's very able chief of staff, and we reflected on the future. Bill was surprisingly sanguine, convinced that a few years in the wilderness would be good for us. As for Dan Quayle, Kristol expected him to pursue a Nixon-like eight-year strategy to the presidency: sit out 1996, assuming that Clinton has a decent chance of being reelected, and position himself for a comeback in the year 2000. He suggested that conservatives were intellectually exhausted from twelve years of governance and needed some time to reflect, think, and rejuvenate. I was less upbeat. I wondered if our critics had not so thoroughly demonized conservatives that our effectiveness would be severely hampered. As things turned out, Bill was right and I was mistaken. But in any case, the task of moving into opposition quickly absorbed all of my time and mental energy. I had additional field staff to hire, a lobbying office in Washington to open, new legislative initiatives to launch, and special elections for the U.S. Senate in Georgia and Texas just around the corner. One upside to losing the presidency was that four thousand experienced political appointees were being dumped into the employment market just as I was looking to beef up our operation. There were so many qualified political people looking for jobs that I almost did not know where to begin. I soon found being in the minority more exciting than I had ever thought possible.

In consultation with our board of directors and local leadership, we began to lay the groundwork for the next chapter in the movement's resurgence. Through the lessons learned and the wisdom gained in the aftermath of the Houston convention and the 1992 elections the foundation of a stronger and more vibrant grassroots organization and a mainstream pro-family message were laid. In the future, we would not seek public policy victories by relying on the patronizing benevolence of a friendly White House. We would advance the pro-family agenda the old-fashioned way: one family at a time, one church at a time, one neighborhood at a time, one community at a time.

Ultimately, I came to see that losing the presidency was not an obstacle to a new rebirth of religious values and the triumph of conservative ideas; it held the key to our long road back. George Bush's defeat had severed the umbilical cord that tied an entire social movement to the presidency, perhaps the most overrated prize in American politics. With our new focus on local issues came phenomenal success and a prize that few could have dreamed of—one of the most extensive grassroots networks in American politics and within two years, conservative control of Congress for the first time in two generations.

In the fall of 1995, as the media remained transfixed by the horse race for the presidency, a former Democrat, Mike Foster, won the governorship of Louisiana by a landslide on a pro-life, pro-family platform. Governor Kirk Fordice, a conservative Christian and former businessman, won reelection by a comfortable margin in Mississippi, the first governor of that state in modern times to do so. Meanwhile, the Christian Coalition did not endorse any of the candidates for the Republican presidential nomination, which meant that there was no single "Christian" aspirant. This freed our membership to remain focused on state and local issues. No matter what happens in the 1996 elections, the pro-family movement is stronger and more effective than at any time in its history.

That lesson was not forgotten as we headed into the 1996 election cycle. How influential it is can be seen with just a quick look at the numbers. In the aftermath of the 1994 elections the pro-family community had a greater level of influence in government than it had after the Reagan landslide of 1980. Religious conservatives accounted for one-third of the entire electorate in 1994, contributing to a staggering 9-million-vote increase in Republican turnout over 1990. About forty-four of the seventy-three freshman Republicans elected to the House of Representatives in 1994 had close ties to the pro-family movement or enjoyed the support of its various organizations. There are twenty to thirty more reliable pro-family votes among the conservative House Democrats. The aggressive freshman class, the most ideologically focused cohort since the "Watergate babies" of 1974, formed the Family Caucus and the Conservative Action Team to advance the family rights message. These groups of social conservative lawmakers are the pro-family equivalent of the Conservative Opportunity Society, which Newt Gingrich and other GOP backbenchers formed in the 1980s to push their message of tax cuts and dismantling the welfare state. No longer outside looking in, we are now an integral part of American politics.[3]

Getting to that place from total defeat in only two years was an arduous process. A few weeks after the 1992 election, we held a private strategy meeting in Virginia Beach with some of our top state leaders: Sara Hardman of California, Dick Weinhold of Texas, Roberta Combs of South Carolina, and Tom Scott of Florida. They confirmed what we already suspected: The state of our movement was much stronger at the grassroots than the pundits suspected. Pro-family candidates had won school board elections, religious conservatives had made inroads into the political parties, and our membership was already surging as the Clinton era dawned. The signs were upbeat and positive. Vern Kennedy, our pollster, presented exit polling data from the elections confirming our belief that the "family values" message had not backfired, as the pundits suggested, but had simply not resonated powerfully enough with an electorate concerned primarily with jobs and the economy. Even evangelical voters were mostly focused on the economy and the budget deficit, with social issues such as crime, education, and abortion ranking lower on their list of priorities. The family values theme had worked to a degree, but it needed to be supplemented by a broader economic agenda.

Our surveys of Perot voters, whom we also desperately wanted to attract, showed that they were not so much social liberals as genuinely unconcerned about moral issues. They did not cast their ballots based on our issues, but on economic anxiety and populist angst at the political establishment of both parties. Therefore, we stressed our support of term limits and other political reforms as a way to let the Perot voters know that we stood with them. As for Buchanan's former supporters, many of them had returned to the fold and were working closely with us at the local level. Those who were not remained active in American Cause, the organization Buchanan had established after his presidential bid. We fully expected Buchanan to seek the presidency again in 1996, and we remained friendly and cooperative with him and top aides like his sister Bay and his press aide Greg Mueller, who also worked closely with us. Privately, we did not expect Buchanan to win the Republican nomination, but we also knew that it was important for us to remain allies. There were too many in the Republican party who had made it clear that they intended to abandon cultural issues. In spite of our relatively minor tactical differences, Buchanan's supporters and ours agreed that we had to stick together if the party was to remain pro-life.

Jeff Bell, a former Kemp operative and a keen political strategist, flew in to share his insights with our state leaders. Bell believed that Clinton's greatest vulnerability would be our strength: the social issues. Clinton had inherited a strong economy, the Gulf war was over, the Soviet Union was gone, and there was a bipartisan consensus on reducing the deficit. But, Bell argued, Clinton now had to deliver the goods to the more controversial elements of his coalition, beginning with the National Organization for

Women, the pro-abortion lobby, and gay rights groups. If Clinton had an Achilles' heel, it was on the cultural agenda. Bell suggested we think in those terms, and his prediction came true in short order.

Notwithstanding the conventional wisdom that the 1992 elections were a major setback for religious conservatives, the loss of the presidency contained within it the seeds of a renaissance of pro-family policies at the state and local level. For while George Bush lost the White House, the number of pro-life members of both parties in Congress actually increased. About five hundred religious conservative candidates of both parties had sought local office, with 40 percent of them winning on election day. After the election I sent a memorandum to local Christian Coalition leaders encouraging them to make such contests a major priority:

> The pro-family movement now shifts to the loyal opposition. No more photo ops in the Roosevelt Room or bill signing ceremonies in the Rose Garden. It will force us to do what we should have been doing all along: building a permanent presence at the grassroots, and returning to the state and local legislative issues that are closest to where people live, and where we are strongest.[4]

These were ideas drawn from a life spent studying political history. After the defeat of George McGovern in 1972, leaders of the New Left and the antiwar movement limped back to their respective states, licked their wounds, and prepared to run for local and state office. Bill Clinton ran for Congress in Arkansas, Gary Hart for the U.S. Senate in Colorado, and Willie Brown for the state assembly in California. David Bonior, a Vietnam veteran opposed to the war, returned to Michigan and ran for the state legislature, eventually winning a seat in Congress in 1976 and rising to a leadership post among Democrats in the House. I proposed that religious conservatives imitate that strategy, a modern form of *narodnaya volya*, in which nineteenth-century Russian agrarian reformers had left Moscow and worked on farms in order to return "back to the people." Like agriculture, building coalitions, crafting legislation, working with the media, and handling constituent concerns can only be learned by doing. The left had become skilled at the art of governing at the local level. Religious conservatives had all gone to Washington to run lobby groups. The paucity of our hands-on experience in government showed, and it needed to be corrected.

Our goal was to transform the religious conservative community from a political pressure group to a broad social reform movement based in local communities. To this end, we focused not just on building a huge direct-mail list but on training activists and leaders. In 1992 we held our first training seminar for state legislative and local candidates, many of whom would later serve as mayors and state legislators. In 1994 we held our first seminars for school-board candidates and members, teaching them how to combat the power of the teachers' unions and pass commonsense education reforms in curriculum and school finance. We increased the number of local chapters from less than one hundred in 1990 to over two thousand in 1996. We also encouraged our state organizations to distribute nonpartisan voter guides and other voter educational information in local races such as those for city council and school board. In such contests, boosting voter turnout was easy and competition from labor unions and pro-abortion groups tended to be lax. We discovered that our opponents on the left could target one or two school-board races and win, but it was impossible for them to focus on a thousand races at once. Someone somewhere was bound to win—and so they did. Our objective was not political power in the rawest sense, for electing people to library and zoning boards hardly brought us power. We were trying to do something far more important and profound: to take a community of millions of people with little hands-on political experience and move them back into the mainstream. It is awfully difficult to demonize individuals for their religious views if they have been elected to local political office and have served their community with distinction.

Christians had not exercised civic responsibility commensurate with their numbers in three generations. We were a little rusty. We needed practice. States and localities would become the "laboratories" for testing our policy ideas, and for building a "farm system" of future candidates, where locally elected religious conservatives could serve "apprenticeships" in government in a low-risk environment less exposed to the hostility of liberal lobby organizations.[5]

Rather than bemoan the loss of the White House, we rolled up our sleeves and set about to solve the nation's real problems. School boards determined what children were taught. State legislatures decided whether there would be school choice or restrictions on abortion. Mayors and city councils had the greatest say in the number of police on the streets. On issue after issue, the pro-family agenda had the greatest impact in local communities, close to the people.

All this still left the question of how to handle our negative exposure at the national level. Two opportunities, each fraught with hazard, presented themselves before the dust from the 1992 election had settled. First, an arcane law in the state of Georgia forced a runoff in the U.S. Senate race between Senator Wyche Fowler and his Republican challenger, Paul Coverdell, because neither had received a majority on election day. With only two weeks before the runoff, we had to make a decision to jump in or sit on the sidelines. Coverdell, a pro-choice Republican, was hardly the darling or first choice of the pro-family community. The Christian Coalition state leadership sent Coverdell a candidate questionnaire containing extensive questions about his views on abortion, gays in the military, religious liberty, and education issues. Coverdell pledged to oppose taxpayer funding of abortion and the Freedom of Choice Act, which would have codified *Roe* v. *Wade* in federal law. The Christian Coalition distributed more than 2 million nonpartisan voter guides and contacted fifty thousand voters by telephone, not telling them which candidate to support but urging them to go to the polls. Just two weeks after Bill Clinton had carried Georgia, Paul Coverdell was elected to the U.S. Senate by only 17,000 votes. He went on to become a conservative stalwart in the Senate, helping to lead the fight against the Clinton health care plan and for welfare reform and family tax relief. Coverdell was a symbol not only of the pro-family movement's remarkable effectiveness in mobilizing evangelical voters but of its ability to build coalitions across ideological lines, even with those who did not always agree with its views on abortion.[6]

The second opportunity was the race for the chairmanship of the Republican National Committee in early 1993. The leading candidates were Governor John Ashcroft of Missouri, Spence Abraham of Michigan, and

Haley Barbour of Mississippi. Lynn Martin, Secretary of Labor under President Bush, also briefly flirted with becoming a candidate but ultimately chose not to run. Several candidates trouped to Christian Coalition head-quarters in Chesapeake, Virginia, or contacted me or Pat Robertson seeking our support. I spoke often with Governor Ashcroft and his staff on the phone during this period, but Ashcroft did not announce his candidacy until late, making it difficult to win endorsements. Bill Kristol worked hard for Spence Abraham, and Bill and I discussed Spence's candidacy in a series of phone calls. At Paul Coverdell's swearing-in ceremony, which was held at the White House, I bumped into Haley Barbour, whom I knew from his service in the Reagan administration, and wished him the best. Even Craig Berkman, the liberal former state GOP chairman from Oregon, visited me at my office and asked for my support. I declined, of course, but we had a pleasant conversation and promised to work together whenever possible.

I was actually sanguine about the party's future, in spite of the finger-pointing that followed the 1992 elections. Haley Barbour, in a speech after he announced his candidacy, pronounced that the party had "squandered the greatest political legacy since Teddy Roosevelt." That was true at the presidential level. But in Congress, state legislatures, and local offices, the party had actually made gains. The Republican party might have needed a face-lift, but it did not need to have massive surgery or any of its limbs amputated. Religious conservatives continued their slow march through the institutions of local government, gradually gaining a foothold and eventually a significant presence in about half of the state Republican party organizations. My greatest hope was that the national leadership of the party adopt a policy of neutrality toward us. As long as they were not hostile, we could continue to make inroads. I viewed Ashcroft, Abraham, and Barbour as seasoned Reagan-era veterans who understood the importance of the moral issues and the huge constituency mobilized by them, and we felt comfortable with any one of them.

I discussed the field of candidates with several conservative members of the Republican National Committee, most of whom were leaning toward Abraham. Then we made an important strategic decision: we decided to sit out the election. We did so not because we were still smarting from 1992, for the Georgia Senate race had more than demonstrated our ability to educate and turn out the pro-family vote. But we were struggling to find our place in American politics and felt that, as a purely institutional matter, injecting ourselves into a Republican party leadership race was unwise, particularly immediately after an election in which we had played a controversial role. The national press corps, still chewing on the "holy war in the GOP" angle, was itching to write more stories about how the Republican party was controlled by the Christian Coalition, which was simply not true. Finally, there was the simple matter of arithmetic. Most of the RNC members were Bush partisans, and many were still bitter about the Houston convention and its aftermath, blaming us for the president's defeat. Why pour salt on the wounds of the party at such a sensitive time?

"Who is your candidate for RNC chairman?" one reporter who called me prior to the vote inquired.

"We do not view it as appropriate for us to attempt to dictate the leadership of the Republican party," I replied. "That is a decision best left to the Republican National Committee."

The silence at the other end of the line was deafening. Just as we had hoped, we played into few stories leading up to the selection of a new Republican chairman. We also did not attend the Republican governor's association meeting in Lake Geneva, Wisconsin, in November 1992, where the governors debated the future direction of the party and heard speeches from the various candidates.

In the end, Haley Barbour won the RNC race and proved to be an outstanding chairman. But by avoiding the contest altogether, the Christian Coalition proved one of the oldest maxims in politics: pick your fights carefully. Our hands-off posture on the RNC race made it clear that we were not a partisan organization, laid to rest fears that we sought to "control the Republicans," and helped to ease tensions in the party.[7]

These and other steps also helped to counter the negative image of the Christian Coalition that had emerged during the 1992 elections. By playing the proper role in the Coverdell and Barbour victories, and in the later triumph by Kay Bailey Hutchison in a special election for U.S. Senate in Texas, we forced the press to take a second look at us. We worried about our public persona enough to consider retaining a public-relations firm, and I even entertained a proposal from some former executives of Hill and Knowlton, the premier PR firm in Washington. But we ultimately rejected that strategy. Instead, I hired Mike Russell, a radio news director in Virginia Beach, to begin to build a more proactive media strategy. We began to conduct surveys and provide the data to the media, churn out press releases on a regular basis, circulate friendly editorials, set up lunches with the bigfeet of the press corps, and provide greater access to our local leadership and training seminars. Our own survey of voters in late 1992 showed that the American people in general divided along ideological lines in their views of the Christian Coalition, with about a quarter in favor, a quarter against, and the rest undecided. But among churchgoing voters and self-identified born-again Christians, we were overwhelmingly popular. This suggested that our base was intact and energized.

This reality gave me a newfound confidence. One evening I met a former press aide in the Reagan administration over drinks at a Capitol Hill bar and restaurant to discuss how to more effectively convey our pro-family message. I was about to go on CNN and debate a critic on the left. "Just remember this," he advised me. "Smile. You're winning."

After the Coverdell and Barbour victories, we increased our visibility in Washington by opening a fully staffed lobbying office on Capitol Hill. We knew the challenges and initiatives of the Clinton administration would require constant vigilance. In addition, many members of Congress and the national press corps knew about the Christian Coalition only from what they read in the newspapers, which meant their view was overwhelmingly negative. My goal was to hire the very best legislative tacticians I could find, preferably with strong credentials outside the narrow confines of the religious conservative movement.

The left had gained its influence over the years on Capitol Hill not only by building a formidable grassroots network, but by erecting a thicket of beltway interest groups to target members of Congress with mail, phone calls, and telegrams. We had a local network that was second to none, but our muscular grassroots presence was disconnected from the conservative think tanks and letterhead organizations on the right that dotted Capitol Hill. The generals inside the beltway needed an army, and our army lacked directions from headquarters. They had never been represented by a phalanx of well-trained veteran lobbyists who bore the scars of decades of legislative battles. We set about to change that.

I received several calls recommending Marshall Wittmann, a deputy assistant secretary for legislative affairs at the Department of Health and Human Services. I met Marshall for a job interview at Bullfeathers, a Capitol Hill watering hole where Congressional staffers network over all-American burgers and draft beer. Marshall is a Jew and former Trotskyite raised in the Bible Belt city of Waco, Texas (pre-David Koresh, as he liked to joke), with salt-and-pepper hair combed neatly across his forehead and dark, intense eyes that stare out from behind John Lennon–style glasses. He had gained his political experience on the left, first as a labor organizer for Cesar Chavez and the United Farm Workers and later as a lobbyist for federal employee unions. Marshall was a brilliant legislative tactician. He talked about the future of the Bush administration, how Ivy Leaguers and social climbers had come to Washington to pick out their windowed offices, which they redecorated with tasteful panache while virtually ignoring policy battles. "The Reagan people came to Washington to do something," he said. "The Bush people came to Washington to be somebody." I hired Marshall about two weeks after our first meeting. He was joined by Heidi Scanlon, a former management consultant with Price Waterhouse, who became director of governmental affairs. I had known Heidi for years, going back to my involvement on the college campuses. She brought a polished professionalism that helped ensure our operations were blazingly efficient and gave the Christian Coalition the kind of no-nonsense reputation that Washington needed to see. Together, she and Marshall made an effective team that began the slow process of meeting with senators and representatives and introducing them to a side of our community that many of them did not know existed.

Our goal was to unite social conservatives and economic conservatives by supporting traditional issues like welfare reform, a balanced budget, and tax cuts for families. We believed that most of the tension between moralists and libertarians was overstated. After all, conservative evangelicals who supported school prayer and pro-life laws were not in favor of higher taxes or deficit spending. In general, social conservatism led naturally to libertarian views on the size and scope of government. Our purpose was not to gloss over differences on the so-called "hot button" issues that divided us, but to put those differences into context by emphasizing the large area of agreement.

Even while opposing Clinton administration initiatives, we avoided a full frontal assault on Clinton, whom we expected would enjoy a rather extended honeymoon. Our state leaders also maintained strong discipline, resisting the temptation to attack Clinton or the First Lady personally, always confining their criticism to policy differences stated in respectful terms. Our self-restraint contrasted sharply with the perception of the incendiary rhetoric of the Houston convention. Frankly, in spite of Jeff Bell's suggestions that the social issues could cause Clinton serious problems, we believed that he would govern as a New Democrat, advocating a modest tax cut for the middle class, avoiding international conflicts, and introducing a middle-of-the-road welfare bill that would be hard for Republicans to oppose.

Clinton was highly regarded for his political skills. We had no inkling that he would hand our movement gift-wrapped issues early and often. Then came the gays-in-the-military and Lani Guinier controversies, followed by the large tax increase and the health care plan that become his and the Democrats' undoing.

The day the gays-in-the-military controversy erupted, I was on my way home from the office when I called Pat Robertson from my car about another matter. Clinton had been in office less than ten days when the White House communications office routinely reported that an executive order was being drafted repealing the ban on homosexuals in the military. Clinton had made this promise to the gay community during the campaign, and we had included the issue on millions of nonpartisan voter guides, but it had generated little interest at the time. The announcement of Clinton's move soon met with a chilly reception on Capitol Hill and grumbling among the Joint Chiefs, some of whom complained to the media that they were not adequately consulted. Republicans announced plans to overturn Clinton's action with legislation. White House spokesman George Stephanopoulos, stunned by the blizzard of controversy, announced that Clinton did not believe anyone should be excluded from military service because of their "status," a euphemism for sexual preference.

Over the next several days, calls began to descend on Washington by the thousands, then the tens of thousands. Some were generated by conservative talk-show hosts or lobby groups, but many were spontaneous.

I reported to Robertson on this development during our phone conversation. "Have you thrown the Capitol switchboard up on screen during the *700 Club*?" I asked.

"Not yet," Pat replied, "but I just may do it tomorrow."

"Everything I hear from Capitol Hill is that calls are coming in by the thousands," I reported. "It is conceivable that enough calls coming in at once would literally jam the switchboard."

The next morning Pat urged his viewers to call Washington and make their voices heard. That day, 436,000 phone calls hit the Capitol switchboard, a record at the time. How many of those calls came from *700 Club* viewers could not be determined, although no doubt the number was considerable.

Two days later I was in Columbia, South Carolina, teaching a Christian Coalition training seminar. When I checked in for messages, my secretary informed me that I had received a call from Michael Weisskopf, a reporter with the *Washington Post*. He had received a tip that Pat Robertson had mentioned the gays-in-the-military issue on his television program.

I called Weisskopf back and gave him some quotations about Colin Powell and Sam Nunn already publicly opposing Clinton's gays-in-the-military policy, along with a host of veterans' groups. I emphasized that we had no intention of leading the fight, which would hand Clinton an opportunity to change the subject by making us the issue. I stressed that this was a military matter and should be left to the Joint Chiefs and other experts to resolve.

While acknowledging that Robertson's viewers had most likely responded in large numbers, I told Weisskopf that in my view most of the calls, telegrams, and letters pouring down on Washington came from retired and active military personnel and their dependents. Indeed, veterans' groups vigorously opposed the Clinton proposal. But it seemed clear that Weisskopf had already written his lead: Pat Robertson and Jerry Falwell had whipped up their supporters to go to the phones, and they were the bogeymen. After I tried to warn him off an inaccurate story, he abruptly ended the interview. I prepared for the worst.

The following day Weisskopf's piece ran on page one of the *Washington Post*. It reported that the tidal wave of phone calls was the work of religious media outlets and labeled the "followers" of religious broadcasters like Robertson "poor, uneducated, and easy to command."[8]

When the newspaper story churned through my fax machine that morning, I knew immediately that we had a major victory. Weisskopf had overplayed his hand. Our governmental affairs office in Washington coordinated with other conservative groups to tie up the *Washington Post* fax machines with copies of their college diplomas and IRS tax returns—solid evidence that they were both well educated and upper-middle class. Meanwhile, Robertson went back on the air, this time flashing the *Post* comment on the screen, and once again produced a torrent of phone calls. I later spoke to a *Post* reporter who told me that the poor woman in charge of reader comments was buried for days. No other episode from the early Clinton administration so heartened and awakened our supporters. We printed up "Poor, uneducated and easy to command" buttons that soon showed up on lapels all over Capitol Hill.

But unlike the religious right of the early 1980s, we knew that we could not build a social movement around disdain for the media or on "hot button" single issues. We knew we needed a positive agenda of our own. As Clinton took office, we still lacked a comprehensive legislative program.

Our legislative staff argued that we needed an issue that was optimistic and broad based, not stereotypical. The problem was not a paucity of issues, but too many: abortion, gays in the military, welfare reform, health care, and deficit reduction. In addition, there was the stream of controversial nominees put forward by the Clinton administration: Lani Guinier as assistant attorney general for civil rights: Roberta Achtenberg as assistant secretary of Housing and Urban Development; and Joycelyn Elders for the office of Surgeon General. Everyone expected us to pitch red meat into the shark tank—perhaps by calling for defunding the National Endowment for the Arts. But that would have been predictable. Instead, in an interview with Jim Barnes of the *National Journal,* I announced that our top legislative priority was to lower the tax burden on the family by increasing the standard deduction for children.[9]

Bill Clinton had already retreated from his pledge to provide tax relief for middle-class families with children. By making family tax relief our top priority, we highlighted Clinton's flip-flop and united economic conservatives and social conservatives on an issue of mutual agreement. That agenda was in no way at odds with the concerns of religious conservative voters. In a survey conducted by the Marketing Research Institute in early 1993, we found that evangelical voters listed the economy and jobs as their top issue, followed by taxes and the deficit, crime, and education. Abortion was one of these voters' lowest priorities. This came as a startling revelation to those who assumed that evangelical voters were driven into politics exclusively by the cluster of social issues that included gay rights, abortion, and school prayer. The data simply did not support that assumption. In fact, network exit polls taken on election day in 1992 found that 22 percent of self-identified born-again voters listed abortion as their key reason for voting. That was double the percentage of the entire electorate, making it by far the most strongly pro-life voting bloc in the nation, but it still meant that most religious conservative voters went to the polls motivated by a broad range of issues, a fact ignored by their critics and even overlooked by some pro-family leaders.[10]

In a humorous event that highlighted our purposeful shift in tactics, we held a news conference to release survey data demonstrating the importance of religious conservative voters and pro-family themes to the Republican party. We wanted to make it clear that if the GOP abandoned pro-family issues, its base would suffer a massive erosion of support. I invited former Secretary of Education and drug czar Bill Bennett to join me at the press conference. After presenting the findings amid colorful charts, we opened the floor for questions. Ralph Hallow of the *Washington Times* asked if the Republicans had to run on family values to win back the White House. I responded that the party should run on the issues that voters cared most about, including taxes and the budget. I cited tax relief for families as a good example of an issue that combined the economic and cultural issues. Bennett stepped to the microphone and strongly disagreed. The culture was paramount, he asserted, and taxes and the deficit were meaningless if the culture continued to disintegrate. (I did not disagree, but thought it better for Bennett to say so than me.) The next day, a *Washington Times* headline reported, "Bennett veers right of Christian group." That may not have been entirely accurate, but the shift—the move to the mainstream—was clearly on.

In a series of meetings on Capitol Hill with moderate, pro-choice Republicans like Susan Molinari of New York and Fred Grandy of Iowa, we lobbied for their cosponsorship of our legislation providing tax breaks for families with children. Once they recovered from the shock, most signed on. The campaign began to build momentum. But just as it was picking up steam, we hit a brick wall in the form of Representative John Kasich of Ohio. Kasich, irascible and mercurial, was the ranking Republican on the House Budget Committee; he was a deeply religious man and committed deficit hawk who was wary of a large tax cut because he feared it might cause the federal debt to yawn in future years.

During a meeting in his office punctuated by jangling telephones, buzzing beepers, and aides scurrying in and out by twos, Kasich engaged me in a spirited and friendly shouting match. His desk was strewn with flowcharts and budget projections assembled by the propeller-heads and policy wonks who made a living analyzing the intricacies of the federal budget.

He resisted our effort to include the family tax cut in the alternative Republican budget. "All you want is goodies for your constituency just like everybody else around here!" he barked. (In a later meeting, he turned to Marshall, our Jewish lobbyist, and tongue-in-cheek called us "greedy Christians" for pushing a tax cut.)

"John, you tell that to families that are sending 40 percent of all they earn to the government," I replied. "All I am asking to do is return the standard deduction to the dollar value it had in 1950."

"Fair enough," said Kasich. "I'll have my staff take a look at it. If we provide a pro-family tax cut, can you mobilize the grassroots in support of a balanced budget plan?"

"I believe we can," I answered. "But if all you offer is cutting programs, sacrifices, and fiscal austerity, I think you will lose the debate."

Deficit hawks like Kasich and supply-siders like Dick Armey and Jack Kemp were initially skeptical—the growth-oriented conservatives mostly because the child tax credit did not lower marginal tax rates. But gradually they were persuaded that putting the pro-family movement at the forefront of the budget issue and forcing Clinton on the defensive was a political coup. It also reduced tensions between libertarians and social conservatives in the party. The Republicans had spent forty years in the minority in the House of Representatives. They desperately wanted to build public support for their budget and tax plan, and they knew that the pro-family grassroots could burn fax machines and light up switchboards on Capitol Hill.

Kasich was a brilliant legislator who became a dear friend, demonstrating the old adage that there is no greater zealot than a recent convert. He allied himself with the pro-family movement in the battles that lay ahead, and did more to make family tax relief possible than virtually anyone else in Congress. We were also indebted to Rod Grams, then a representative from Minnesota, Tim Hutchinson of Arkansas, and Frank Wolf of Virginia for raising the issue and forcing it onto the Congressional agenda.

Now that we had an issue, we laid out our new strategy in *Policy Re-*

view, the flagship publication of the Heritage Foundation. "The pro-family movement has limited its effectiveness by concentrating disproportionately on issues such as abortion and homosexuality," I suggested. "These are vital moral issues, and must remain an important part of the message. To win in the ballot box and in the court of public opinion, however, the pro-family movement must speak to the concerns of average voters in the areas of taxes, crime, government waste, health care, and financial security." I suggested that what motivated religious conservative voters was not a desire to "legislate against the sins of others," but their "devotion to their children."[11] To put teeth into the new look, we launched a $100,000 radio and direct-mail campaign into targeted Congressional districts opposing the Clinton budget because it did not include a tax credit for children. The radio advertisements marked the first time a religious conservative group had jumped into the fray on a purely economic issue, though our rationale was based on the need to strengthen the family.[12]

We aired the radio spots primarily on country music and news–talk stations in the districts of Democrats who we believed could be persuaded to bolt from the president. Among them was Marjorie Margolis-Mesvinksy, the tie-breaking vote in the House of Representatives, who traded her support for a "summit" on deficit reduction in her Philadelphia district featuring an appearance by Clinton. Her trade-off failed, as she lost in 1994. In addition to Margolis-Mesvinsky's district, we blanketed a total of twenty districts with the ads.

Business groups and economic conservatives were surprised by our initiative, and happily so. When our representatives walked into meetings on Capitol Hill, business lobbyists from the Citizens for a Sound Economy and the National Federation of Independent Business would hand them target lists of districts where they had placed antitax radio and television spots. Could we help turn out people to town hall meetings? they wondered. Our answer was always in the affirmative, and we participated in the greatest level of cooperation between economic and social conservatives in the history of the conservative movement—validating what had been an untested theory; that these two wings of the party could work together.

Liberal Democrats seethed with anger. "As someone who has studied the Holy Scriptures, I am absolutely appalled—this action is an abomination," the Ohio Democrat Ted Strickland thundered. He called evangelicals "modern-day money changers" whose "blasphemous" behavior signaled the "death rattle of Reaganomics."[13] (Strickland was defeated in 1994, in part due to his attacks on religious conservatives.) We responded by passing out draft texts of "one-minutes" (the sixty-second speeches that begin each day in the House of Representatives) to friendly Congressmen, who went to the floor to defend us and fire up supporters who watched the debate unfold on C-Span. "It seems to me they have been caught committing democracy," said Representative Tom DeLay of Texas, the future majority whip of the House. "Mr. Speaker, there are some in this Chamber who believe that Christians, like well-behaved children, should be seen and not heard. . . . Christians will not remain silent. We are here to stay."[14]

There were also a few attacks from the right. Martin Mawyer, a former Moral Majority operative, blasted the Christian Coalition for becoming "a slave to public opinion polls" and trying to "Christianize the Republican party by Republicanizing the Christian right."[15] Randall Terry, former head of Operation Rescue and an activist in the U.S. Taxpayer party, claimed we were driving "droves of Christians" into the Republican party's "big tent," a tent that was "happily housing child-killers and sodomites." He accused pro-family leaders of acquiescing to "the whoremongers of child killing, homosexuality, etc., as long as we get to be near the throne."[16] In a strange twist on Ken Kesey and his Merry Pranksters, Terry boarded a bus in the fall of 1994 and headed out on a multicity tour to oppose our new broader agenda, although his jeremiads read more like the book of Revelation than like *The Electric Kool-Aid Acid Test*. He vowed that God would "spew out their lukewarm agenda as a rebuke and a sign."[17]

I never responded specifically to Terry's charges, choosing to remain silent rather than generate more headlines by my reaction. I later received a call from a Christian Coalition member in Raleigh, North Carolina, who stood up at a Terry-sponsored event and said that he was spreading falsehoods about the organization and called him to task. Terry had become a major force in the pro-life community during the rocket booster phase of Operation Rescue and had catapulted to national prominence when he staged sit-ins at abortion clinics during the Democratic National Convention in Atlanta in 1988. While I felt such civil disobedience was perfectly consistent with the protest tradition of the civil rights and antiwar movements on the left, it was not as effective as legislative action after the Supreme Court allowed for some state restrictions on abortion in decisions rendered in 1989 and 1992. Those court decisions, a kind of escape valve for the steam of the pro-life movement, made Operation Rescue a less visible and effective group. While Operation Rescue is often falsely accused of violence by the media, we must forcefully condemn those who are guilty. To take a life in the name of pro-life is hypocrisy, pure and simple.

The charge that our "casting a wider net" strategy somehow signaled a sellout of the moral agenda was nonsense. We would never retreat from our principled stands in support of religious freedom, the sanctity of innocent human life, and the importance of the marriage-based, two-parent family. To us, those were matters of right and wrong, not issues of political expediency that could be discarded in the face of adverse poll numbers. But we also believed that the principles of our faith covered every area of life, including law, education, taxes, and the economy. The biblical principle of chronic debt leading to financial bondage, for example, led us to favor a balanced budget and lower deficits. Like Jefferson, who called the omission of a balanced budget provision the greatest failure of the Framers, we viewed the runaway deficit as a moral issue. Similarly, we supported family tax relief because we knew that families could spend their own money more effectively than the government.

Nor did we suddenly neglect the social agenda. In fact, some of our most celebrated victories in the early months of the Clinton administration came on the moral issues. When Clinton attempted to repeal the Hyde Amendment, which prohibited the use of tax dollars to pay for abortion under the Medicaid program, we swung into action. Working with the National Right to Life committee and other pro-family groups, we targeted fifty-two members of Congress with radio ads, phone banks, and massive mail drops. We contacted more than 250,000 households in these swing districts by letter or phone. We ran full-page newspaper advertisements under the provocative headline, "Al Gore Was Right." The ad included a statement by Gore during his U.S. Senate tenure that it was wrong to use tax dollars to pay for "the taking of innocent human life." Gore had no comment, but the ad had the desired effect, demonstrating that taxpayer funding of abortion was unpopular even among many Democrats. When the final vote occurred in July 1993, the Hyde Amendment was preserved by an overwhelming margin. Of the fifty-two members targeted by the Christian Coalition, forty-three voted pro-life. *IT WORKED!*

Also in early 1993, we found ourselves embroiled in another controversy that underscored our commitment to local issues and local campaigns—in the most unlikely of places. The New York City school board races were scheduled for May of that year, and our local chapter in Brooklyn held an organizational meeting with a few dozen interested membership prospects in the basement of a Baptist church. The opposition to the so-called Rainbow Curriculum and the subsequent filing of conservative, pro-family candidates for school board all occurred without my knowledge or national coordination. It was a rather spontaneous affair, led mostly by white ethnic Catholics in Brooklyn and conservative pentecostal and evangelical African-American and Latino churches in the Bronx. The truth was that our New York City organization was rather small and embryonic. We could not have pulled off a massive organizational effort in a citywide school board race on our own. But media attacks would soon play a role in giving this spontaneous grassroots protest the impetus for our first inroads into urban politics.

Unbeknownst to our local organizer, a tabloid newspaper had smuggled in a photographer, who took pictures of the meeting with a hidden camera. The following day, an account of the meeting, complete with grainy photos, appeared in the New York *Daily News* under the screaming headline, "In God's Name!" It detailed the "Christian Right's Battle Plan to Seize Control of City." (Liberals "vote in elections." Conservative Christians "seize control.") Ironically, the press coverage had the opposite of the intended effect. Instead of unveiling our "stealth" candidates and defeating them, the media printed full-page versions of our voter guides and helped advertise the pro-family candidates far beyond our small base in New York City.

The result was surprising. Sixty percent of 130 pro-family candidates in New York City won, increasing the number of local school boards with conservative majorities from three to ten out of a total of thirty-two districts. Not all the pro-family candidates were victorious, and some results were mixed. But the New York City contest demonstrated yet again that losing the White House to Bill Clinton was not the death knell of our movement that some had thought.

There were later reversals of previous pro-family school board victories in Vista, California, and Lakeland, Florida. But pro-family candidates were winning far more races than the far left and the teachers unions could monitor. They might win back three seats after spending $100,000 in one city in the North. The same day, another one hundred pro-family candidates were winning in a dozen other states. This was true in Lake County, Florida, where the media flocked to report a handful of defeats in 1994. They were oblivious to the fact that those losses were more than offset by hundreds of pro-family victories statewide. The days when school boards were elected solely by labor unions and liberal pressure groups are over forever, and the pro-family community has leveled the playing field.

The press thrives on conflict, and it routinely highlighted controversies like the one in New York. For that reason, we had the luxury of generally deflecting criticism from our right that our broader agenda represented a retreat from our moral beliefs. People for the American Way, the ACLU, and other radical left organizations trumpeted their predictable charges that our involvement in the budget battle represented a "stealth" attempt to hide our real agenda. Thunder from the right, therefore, served an important function. It demonstrated that our agenda was not so stealthy after all; it positioned us more in the political mainstream and proved that not all religious conservatives spoke with one voice. The pro-family movement was growing and also maturing; a diversity of views on issues and tactics was perfectly healthy and natural.

The media began to take note of this transformation. Suddenly, the "new" look of the pro-family community was almost chic. The *Washington Monthly* credited the movement with having "a fairly sensible cultural vision and a not unreasonable policy agenda that's as neoliberal as it is fundamentalist." A "new pragmatism," *Governing* magazine noted, led conservative Christians to speak to more issues and to reach out beyond their evangelical base "to the theologically different," enabling them to "place candidates in higher office." The budget fight of 1993 thus marked a watershed moment in the maturation of the religious conservative movement. Just as Bill Clinton's denunciation of the violent lyrics of Sister Souljah—and the flap with Jesse Jackson that followed—allowed him to appeal to the middle in 1992, our willingness to address the tax issue and weather a few barbs from friends on the right gained us new admirers and grudging respect even from critics.[18]

Not everyone appreciated our new approach. Democrats were still angry that we had taken a position against the Clinton budget instead of just sticking to moral issues. In September 1993, in a spirit of bipartisanship, I invited David Wilhelm, the chairman of the Democratic National Committee, to address our annual national convention in Washington. I knew extending an invitation to Wilhelm was risky. But I wanted to reach out to the Democrats and give them an opportunity to make a bid for our activists. We did not want to make the mistake of being an exclusively partisan organization, and hoped that the Clinton administration would be smart enough to view the invitation as a chance to extend an olive branch.

Wilhelm eagerly accepted. He was scheduled to open the convention, followed by Haley Barbour, who spoke for the Republicans. I had heard through the grapevine about the Clinton operatives and their celebrated tactic of "counter-scheduling," which meant going to an audience and delivering a message opposite to the one it expected. Clinton had done that brilliantly in the case of Sister Souljah before the Rainbow Coalition, and again when he lectured the congregation of a white church in suburban Detroit on the need for racial reconciliation. Concerned that such a stunt might be in store for us, I contacted one of Wilhelm's press aides and asked if he intended to attack us.

"Oh, no," she assured me. "David would not think of doing that. He is very excited about this speech. He is clearly going to express some differences with you on a few issues, but he wants to build a bridge."

The morning of Wilhelm's speech I was backstage at the Washington Hilton when a member of my staff handed me an advance copy of his remarks. Hurriedly, I flipped through it and saw that we had a big problem. Wilhelm was going to accuse us of claiming that members of Congress who voted for the Clinton tax increase had "taken an un-Christian position." The speech also accused us of "savagely" distorting the records of Democratic members of Congress and of using "scare tactics" where "hatred is preached in place of tolerance." These comments were guaranteed, if not designed, to elicit a negative reaction from the audience. But it was too late to negotiate. Wilhelm was standing offstage waiting to be introduced.

I quickly shook Wilhelm's hand and urged him to back off. He smiled wanly. I stared at the back of the room at the twenty television cameras on risers and gulped; it was going to be a bad news day. Walking to the podium, I offered a quick rebuttal to the attack I knew was coming, and then introduced Wilhelm. At first, his words were greeted warmly. "I am a Christian, and I am a Democrat," he said to a wave of applause. But when he attacked us for opposing Clinton, the reaction turned sour. The bottom dropped out when he claimed that his support for abortion on demand derived from Christian beliefs. People began to boo in disapproval, which we attempted to control with floor whips, who roamed through the crowd with walkie-talkies. I remained on good terms with Wilhelm after the episode. He later joked that it was the high point of his tenure as party chairman. But I always wondered why the Democrats passed up an ideal opportunity to find common ground and seek our support for some of their policies. Though they did not know it, we were still willing to work with them on a child tax credit, an issue that could have helped Clinton politically. Instead, they sent the national chairman of the Democratic party to blast one of the nation's leading Christian organizations, a strategy that did little good for the Democrats the following year at the polls.

Later, Bill Bennett came to speak and recommended that if Wilhelm "has theological advice to dispense, he might begin by sharing it at 1600 Pennsylvania Avenue." The crowd roared its approval. He added that for the chairman of the party that gave us Joycelyn Elders, tax-funded abortion, and gays in the military to lecture the Christian Coalition on morality "took a lot of chutzpah." The audience laughed at the irony of a Catholic blasting a Baptist before an evangelical audience in Yiddish.

If the Democrats attacked us, the Republicans sought us out. One reason was that the pro-family community had become increasingly sophisticated in its voter turnout efforts and remarkably advanced in the use of such new technologies as fax machines and computers. A demonstration of that clout came in early 1994 with the stunning defeat of an education bill that would have greatly restricted the rights of more than a million home schoolers. On February 1, 1994, Representative George Miller, a liberal California Democrat, attached an amendment to a large education bill that required that every teacher in a private, parochial, or home school be certified by the state. Few noticed the seemingly uncontroversial provision in a bill headed for certain passage. On February 14 a parent who educated her children at home learned about the bill and called the staff of Representative Dick Armey of Texas to inquire about the provision and its potential impact. Armey's staff reviewed the statute and concluded that it was indeed a dagger aimed at the heart of every private, parochial, and home school in the nation. Armey attempted to remove the offending provision in the House Education and Labor Committee but was voted down. At that point, his only hope was to generate a massive grassroots protest. Armey's strategists alerted the Home School Legal Defense Fund, a grassroots lobby group based in Virginia, which blitzed its members and supporters by posting an alert on a computerized bulletin board used by hundreds of thousands of home schoolers nationwide.[19]

Within seventy-two hours an estimated total of 200,000 activists had been notified by fax, phone, mail, and computerized bulletin boards. Like a rock thrown into a pond that sends ripples ever wider, these activists in turn notified friends via telephone trees, multiplying the lobbying effort until it became a tidal wave. Few in Washington understood what Bill

Kristol has called "the parallel universe" in which religious conservatives live, where Christian radio and television programs reach more people every day than network newscasts and where pro-family organizations can mobilize the grassroots as effectively as the labor unions and civil rights movement did at their peak. Home-school parents and students, for instance, use personal computers to access lessons and communicate with other home schoolers, constituting a ready-made network of hundreds of thousands of cybercitizens. They lit up the Capitol switchboard like a pinball machine. In some cases, entire Congressional offices simply ceased to function. One representative actually turned on a tape machine that informed callers that he was opposed to the bill and requested that they please stop calling. Representative Miller tried in vain to beat back the deluge by playing a taped message to incoming calls that simply stated, "Mr. Miller fully supports the rights of home schoolers."[20]

Christian media outlets turned up the temperature to a boil. Marlin Maddoux of the USA Radio Network, Jim Dobson of Focus on the Family, and Pat Robertson's *700 Club* program covered the controversy extensively, invited friendly members of Congress on the air to encourage more phone calls, and flashed the Capitol switchboard number at regular intervals. Rush Limbaugh gave out the phone number of Representative Bill Ford, chairman of the House Education and Labor Committee, on his national radio program. Although no one would ever know the total for certain, estimates of the number of phone calls descending on the Capitol reached 1 million in a single week. Typical was Representative Jim Ramstad, Republican of Minnesota, who received more than three thousand calls and petitions, not a single one of which supported the bill.[21] Finally, on February 23 the House Rules Committee waved the white flag, announcing that it would delete the teacher certification rule and rush the Miller amendment to a vote the following day. The *New York Times* called the concession a "bow to the religious right." They failed to grasp the deeper significance of the victory, the innovative fusion of grassroots politics with advanced communications technology.[22]

While Miller denounced the "scare tactics" of religious conservatives, his colleagues moved quickly to quell the controversy. On February 24, by a margin of 424 to 1, the Miller amendment lost. Dick Armey's substitute amendment guaranteeing that no parochial or home school would be subject to federal regulation passed, 374 to 53.

The battle over HR 6 revealed a remarkable evolution in the flowering pro-family movement. Neither Old Right nor New Right, these activists make up the Virtual Right, the electronic grassroots of the future. Rather than walk precincts and lick envelopes, they surf cyberspace and dispatch e-mail with the click of a mouse. The entire "leave us alone" coalition is getting in on the act: pro-lifers, anti-tax groups, conservative Christians, home schoolers, small businessmen, and gun advocates.

What explains their embrace of new technology? Not ultimately the Toffleresque view of high technology as a "third wave" that displaces industrial capitalism, though many find these ideas appealing when filtered through the speeches of Newt Gingrich. Rather, cyberspace represents for them a refreshing deliverance from the scorn of the national media. The Internet and its online bulletin boards and web pages allow conservatives to express and exchange their ideas without passing through the filter of the press. Because millions of religious conservatives either are stay-at-home mothers or operate small businesses out of their homes, the computer, fax, and modem are as much a part of their daily lives as the telephone. The blending of those high-tech tools with politics is a natural evolution. Finally, the information highway gives religious conservatives what they have always lacked: a sense that their movement represents the future, not a frozen snapshot of the past. Some may claim that traditional values and the nuclear family are fossilized relics, but it is hard to argue that its advocates are trying to retrofit American society to the 1950s when their main tools are computers and satellite dishes. The pro-family movement of today owes more of a debt to Buck Rogers than to Elmer Gantry.

Consider the recent passage by the GOP-controlled House of Representatives of a spending bill for the Department of Health and Human Services, a traditional battleground over abortion and other contentious social issues. Religious conservatives sprinkled the bill with pro-life amendments like ornaments on a Christmas tree. The day before a critical vote, Brian Lopina, the Christian Coalition's director of governmental affairs, gathered state and county leaders together for a strategy meeting. He did not rent a Washington hotel ballroom, however. Instead, he issued a fax alert, held a strategy session via conference call, and downlinked a private briefing with the House Republican whip, Tom DeLay, from a room in the U.S. Capitol to 281 satellite locations across the country. DeLay, an expert vote counter, relayed the latest intelligence on wavering votes and fielded phone calls from grassroots activists. The strategy paid off. "It gave us instant access to the people who could make the phones ring in Washington," Lopina noted. Within twenty-four hours, the bill had passed the House with most of the pro-family amendments intact.[23]

Steve Largent, the freshman House Republican from Oklahoma, holds town meetings via satellite to keep in touch with his constituents. When Largent introduced the Parental Rights Act of 1995, pro-family groups like Focus on the Family alerted the grassroots to the legislation. Gary Young, a school board president from Gernet, California, bombarded Representative Sonny Bono's office with faxes and phone calls. Two days later a Bono aide called Young and asked him to please stop calling. Bono would agree to support the bill from his critical perch on the Judiciary Committee.[24] Other conservatives are using the Internet in creative new ways as well. House Majority Leader Dick Armey has opened a web site that allows taxpayers to calculate what their tax bill would be under a flat tax. Another site, established by the anti-tax lobby organization Americans for Tax Reform, is designed to promote tax-free private pension plans by inviting citizens to calculate how much more their retirement fund would be worth if it were funded by contributions to an IRA rather than by Social Security taxes.[25]

Liberals are distraught that conservatives have gained such overwhelming dominance of the new communication technologies. At a recent meeting of progressive organizers in Minneapolis, many complained that conservatives are lapping their liberal counterparts in the "manipulation of the mass media, especially in the newer venues of cable TV and talk radio."[26] In 1992 it was the Clinton campaign that rode the information highway to victory. The Clinton rapid-response team downloaded the *New York Times* news service via Lexis and Nexis and buried the news media in a blizzard of faxes, while twenty-somethings toted laptop computers and campaign operatives burned cellular phones and modems. Now it is the conservatives who hold the upper hand. From the Heritage Foundation's Town Hall site on the Internet featuring a chatterbox of conservative intellectual ferment to National Empowerment Television's cable and satellite populist TV network, which now reaches 11 million households, conservatives are promoting the possibilities of cyberspace with the fervor of a tent revivalist. "We're tin cans and string by comparison," moans Senator Christopher Dodd, chairman of the Democratic National Committee.[27]

Another sign that the Democrats were in serious trouble heading into the 1994 elections came with the defeat of the lobby reform bill. Attempting to capitalize on the Perot message of political reform, Clinton had called for campaign finance and lobby legislation changes in his inaugural address, vowing to "give this Capitol back to the people to whom it belongs." Responding to Clinton's challenge, the U.S. Senate overwhelmingly passed— by the staggering margin of 95 to 4—legislation completely banning most lobbyist-sponsored gifts and entertainment for members of Congress and requiring all lobbyists to disclose their clients and sources of income. The normally fractious House of Representatives passed a similar bill with more than three hundred votes in favor. As a conference committee huddled throughout the summer to reconcile the House and Senate versions, President Clinton prepared for the photo opportunity of the year: a signing ceremony for the most dramatic lobby reform legislation in a generation.[28]

But the Christian Coalition and other grassroots advocacy groups waited in the wings for the moment to pounce on the bill in hopes of defeating it. Their reason was a provision requiring individuals spending more than $5,000 a year lobbying Congress to register and to fill out public-disclosure forms. Free speech advocates worried that the bill would limit the ability of citizens to petition their elected officials. Pastors who preached a sermon urging their parishioners to contact Congress and members of grassroots organizations who contributed to lobbying efforts feared they might be trapped in a dragnet of federal regulation that combined the worst aspects of the Internal Revenue Service and the Environment Protection Agency. Yet those real and very reasonable objections received scant attention—until Newt Gingrich, in the waning days of the 103d Congress, decided to activate the high-tech network of grassroots opposition groups.

In September 1994 I received a call from Gingrich expressing his concerns about the lobby reform bill. He feared that the restrictions on grassroots lobbying could deter conservative Christians from organizing on behalf of their values. Moreover, a provision in the bill gave the president the right to appoint someone to enforce compliance—a "lobby czar," who would serve a five-year term, continuing in office long after Clinton's term had ended. Gingrich speculated that Clinton might appoint a liberal like Joycelyn Elders or Roberta Achtenberg, who could use the post to harass opponents of the administration.[29]

The Christian Coalition had been nervous about the bill from its inception. We had no objection to lobby reform; we believed that the influence-peddling of Congress by special interests and gift-giving lobbyists had to end. But we thought the bill was too draconian with respect to average citizens and grassroots groups, which were not the problem. It was like curing a headache by amputating someone's legs. We were joined by the American Civil Liberties Union, an unlikely ally, which criticized the bill as an assault on free expression and the right of citizens to petition their legislators. With Gingrich and others now joining the fight, the grassroots went into action. We immediately sent a fax alert to more than ten thousand activists, pastors, priests, and radio talk-show hosts warning them of the potential chilling effect of the "grassroots gag rule." A computerized message on the Internet reached tens of thousands more. On his daily news program, the *700 Club*, Pat Robertson described in dark detail the free speech implications of the legislation.

From radio sets nationwide, there was a furnace blast of opposition from conservative talk-show hosts. Rush Limbaugh reeled off a litany of woes deriving from the legislation. He suggested in jest that talk-show hosts who gave out the Capitol switchboard phone number could be required to register as paid lobbyists. Not without reason, he saw the bill as an attempt by the Clinton administration and a liberal Congress to gag a conservative, grassroots opposition that had stymied it on issues from gays in the military to Zoë Baird and the budget. Limbaugh was not alone. Lesser-known talk jockeys held forth from their electronic pulpits, peppering their anti-Washington monologues with the talking points provided via fax and computerized bulletin boards by opposition groups. Marlin Maddoux of the USA Radio network and Jim Dobson of Focus on the Family, which reaches more than a thousand Christian radio stations and a combined weekly audience of 5 million listeners, each took time to cover the bill. In Washington Paul Weyrich and his satellite network, National Empowerment Television, also urged viewers to go to their phones.

Members of Congress found themselves buried under a flurry of phone calls that descended like a night artillery barrage. In a matter of days confusion reigned and support for the bill began to disintegrate. Senator Carl Levin of Michigan, who had shepherded the bill through Congress, became so desperate that he requested equal time on Rush Limbaugh's program to set the record straight, only to be rebutted by Representative Ernest Istook, Republican of Oklahoma, a staunch foe of the bill.[30] When the House voted on October 4, the lobby reform measure, once headed for overwhelming passage, survived a preliminary ballot by the razor-thin margin of only eleven votes.[31]

As the battleground shifted to the Senate, opponents of the bill threatened a filibuster, forcing the use of an arcane Senate rule that required the bill's supporters to win sixty votes. Democrats itching to get out of Washington and campaign for reelection watched helplessly as the debate droned on. Opponents insisted that a requirement to disclose "clients" of a lobbyist could include contributors to grassroots organizations, a horrifying prospect for liberal and conservative organizations alike. Throughout the debate, the influence of talk radio predominated. "I might mention," Senator Don Nickles of Oklahoma said, "my interest in this did not really come up until I heard it on a radio program."[32]

Senator Levin and his Democratic colleagues at first denied the criticisms, denouncing them as "scare tactics" designed to preserve the power of "special interests." But as phone calls and faxes continued to rain down on the Capitol, a preliminary head count showed insufficient votes to break the filibuster. Chastened and angry, Levin and William Cohen of Maine strode to the floor of the Senate and offered to remove all the provisions affecting grassroots lobbying from the bill.[33] By then, hopes of passage were flickering. "At best it's on life support, and the prognosis isn't good," one White House official said.[34]

The concession came too late to salvage lobbying reform. By a margin of 52 to 46, fourteen short of the three-fifths needed to end debate, the bill died an ignoble death. Forty-four senators who had supported the bill earlier crossed over to kill it because of their opposition to restrictions on grassroots lobbying. The retiring Senate majority leader, George Mitchell, with the final hours of his political career slipping away in defeat and disappointment, inveighed against the bill's opponents with uncharacteristic anger. "I come from Maine, where we get a lot of foggy days along the coast, and so when I came to the Senate and saw that it was regularly enveloped in fog, I felt at home," he said. The Republicans, he charged, had put up a "smoke screen" because "they do not want lobbying disclosure and gift reform," and were willing "to do anything to stop" the bill.[35]

What enveloped the Capitol that day was neither fog nor smoke. It was a new marriage of high technology and old-fashioned shoe-leather politics that Mitchell and his colleagues did not understand and were wholly unprepared to combat. For decades, liberals in Washington have set the political agenda for the nation with friendly assistance from major media outlets, particularly the television networks and leading newspapers. (It was no coincidence that the *New York Times* editorialized in support of the lobby reform bill the very week a grassroots rebellion defeated it.)[36] But the days of the liberal media monopoly are drawing to a close. We are entering an era of high-speed fax machines, voice mail, microcomputer networks, computerized bulletin boards, a 500-channel cable universe, satellite television, talk radio, and the Internet and its World Wide Web. This era is not merely dawning; it is already at high noon, transforming our politics and culture with blinding speed.

The rise of cyberdemocracy was one of the main features of the conservative grassroots political movement that emerged after the 1992 elections. Along with a broader agenda and a focus on local issues, cyberdemocracy was the third element in a strategy to make the pro-family movement's presence permanent and lasting. An entirely new media universe now exists, populated by conservative activists and their allies. Surveys confirm this fact. Surfers of the Internet tend to be younger, better educated, more informed, and more conservative than the general population. While party identification is evenly divided among the general population, online activists who patronize computerized bulletin boards lean Republican by a two-to-one margin over Democrats (48 percent to 24 percent).[37]

The fusion between new technology and religious movements is nothing new. The Reformation could not have happened without the printing press. The civil rights movement could never have succeeded without television bringing the brutality of "Bull" Connor's police dogs and fire hoses into the living rooms of millions of Americans. Likewise, the explosion of the information highway is creating an alternative means of communication for the burgeoning pro-family movement.

Newt Gingrich understood the technology and the political movement that had learned to use it so effectively throughout the 103d Congress. That was one reason why, while on a trip to Colorado, I received a phone call from an aide to Representative Dick Armey, who wanted our input on a document being drafted for release in September under the title "The Contract with America." The drafters were consulting with a broad range of outside conservative organizations. After discussions with the board and our legislative staff, we made three recommendations: a sizable tax cut for families with children, school choice, and a comprehensive Hyde Amendment that would permanently ban taxpayer funding of abortion. Every issue enjoyed broad public support and energized religious conservatives. Many other pro-family groups also submitted ideas. Soon, however, word came down from Gingrich that because the document had to be signed by every incumbent Republican member of Congress, abortion and other contentious social issues would have to wait.

I did not agree with that decision. My main interest was in advancing the cultural and social issues to the forefront of the national debate. But

Gingrich wanted the document to appeal explicitly to Perot voters. Gingrich's theory was that if the Republicans ran on the Perot agenda of term limits and political reform they would bring the voters back to the GOP, thereby helping to elect freshman Republicans in swing districts. I told Gingrich and Armey that many in the pro-family community would be willing to be patient on the social agenda for a short time while they passed the Contract—on one important condition: Congress must pass a deep tax cut for families to relieve their crushing tax burden and must turn its attention to social issues after the Contract period ended.

Our proposal was an audacious gambit. We agreed to let the social issues wait for the first hundred days. In exchange, we asked for $125 billion over seven years for American families struggling to make ends meet. Gingrich and the Republican leadership heartily agreed. But a group of moderate Republicans objected to the size of the cut, knowing that it would have to be paid for by budget reductions. The GOP leadership sent a not-so-subtle message: touch the tax cut and the social conservatives would go into revolt. In addition to moderates' objections, conservative backbenchers in the House, led by Representative Ernest Istook, began circulating a petition demanding the inclusion of school prayer in the Contract with America. Outside pressure began to build from some pro-family groups who resented being asked to wait their turn. After the disappointment of the Reagan years, paranoia reigned once again about being patronized during the campaign and left at the altar after the election.

I was content to take the tax cut—the largest in history ever targeted directly at families and children—and move on to the other social issues later. Success on the Contract with America, I believed, would build the political capital necessary to gain passage of other legislative initiatives dealing with abortion and school choice. Moreover, the Contract included many social items: welfare reform, elimination of the marriage penalty, tougher laws against pornography, and a tax credit for adoptions. It was, in fact, an ambitious agenda that included many of our most cherished causes. But I was also sensitive to the fact that if we waited too long after the first hundred days before getting to such issues as abortion and privatizing the National Endowment for the Arts, our legislative agenda would languish on the back burner. Furthermore, I could hardly be in the position of opposing voluntary school prayer, which I strongly favored.

The issue came to a head at a meeting with Gingrich in the U.S. Capitol. Joining us were Dick Armey, Gary Bauer of the Family Research Council, and Paul Weyrich, president of the Free Congress Foundation. Weyrich complained that Gingrich had allowed moderates in the House to drive his legislative agenda.

"You're letting the tail wag the dog," Weyrich said.

"No, that is not true," Gingrich replied, his dark eyes darting around the room to gauge reaction. "The decision not to include social issues at this time was mine, and mine alone. I determined that it would play into the hands of the liberals to lead off with the social issues. I did not want liberal columnists to have a field day for two weeks writing about the religious right and the Republican party. That was my call."

After weeks of long hours and weekends on the road, most of those in the room were exhausted and edgy. Tempers were short. When one person accused Armey, who was in charge of the Contract, of deliberately short-changing social conservatives, he forcefully replied that he and his staff had been working their fingers to the bone.

The meeting ended with Gingrich agreeing to hold a news conference with a group of pastors and rabbis pledging his support for school prayer. But I was worried. A press event right before the election could return us to the atmospherics of the Houston convention. The Democrats were already running their entire campaign against Pat Robertson and the religious conservative movement. Would a pro-prayer powwow before the cameras serve their purpose better than ours? I expressed my concerns to Gingrich's staff as well as to other allies in the pro-family movement. At first the news conference was scheduled for Washington. Then it was moved to Charlotte, North Carolina, among a more hospitable regional press corps. But Gingrich was too busy campaigning for Republican House candidates to attend, so the news conference never took place.

A few weeks later, on Election Day 1994, religious conservative voters turned out in the largest numbers ever recorded in the modern political era. An exit poll conducted by the Luntz Research Corporation found that 33 percent of all voters were religious conservatives and that they voted 70 percent Republican and only 24 percent Democrat. An incredible 40 percent of all the votes Republican candidates received came from evangelicals and their pro-family Catholic allies. On the night of the election, I sat in a hotel room in Washington watching the returns roll in from across the nation. It was past three o'clock in the morning when the final results from California came in and I realized the full breadth of the victory. The Republicans had gained control of Congress for the first time in forty years, and conservative Christians had played a central part in the drama.

I should have been thrilled, but my strongest emotion was a combination of exhaustion and foreboding. Exhaustion because I was running on drained batteries after a hectic year of traveling across the country, and foreboding because the biggest danger facing any movement after an overwhelming victory is misreading the returns and overreaching its grasp. In the days after the 1994 campaign, ebullient talk of "our turn" and "payback time" filled the air. My deepest fear was that the pro-family and conservative community could walk into the booby trap of soaring expectations and negative press coverage before the new Congress had a chance to find its sea legs.

In the space of two years we had gone from the lepers of American politics to become a Cinderella story. *Newsweek* credited the Christian Coalition with being one of the main forces behind the Republican landslide. But I had heard those words before. The press had also blown helium into the Moral Majority after the Reagan victory of 1980, only to turn on its leaders with a vengeance. With that memory in mind, the board of directors and state leadership of the Christian Coalition reminded our grass-roots members, "Tread softly, and be careful." Sometimes the only thing worse than being out of power is to have power and not know what to do with it. We had waited for years to enact our agenda to limit government and strengthen the family. But we also knew that we had to move carefully and wisely so as not to jeopardize the historic gains of 1994.

6

NO MORE STEALTH

The Real Agenda

Shortly after the 1994 elections, *Harper's* magazine brought a group of conservative strategists together to discuss the new political era that had begun with the ushering in of the first Republican Congress in forty years. Excitement and euphoria swelled through conservative ranks. Joining the *Harper's* editors over lunch at La Brasserie, a popular Capitol Hill bistro, were Bill Kristol, the pollster Frank Luntz, the former Bush aide Jim Pinkerton, and conservative journalist David Frum. Luntz, who had been Ross Perot's pollster in 1992, advocated passing the key items in the Contract that appealed to Perot voters. Kristol suggested that the Congress phase in its budget reductions and entitlement reforms gradually rather than attempt to achieve them in one giant leap, thus sparking a fiery liberal counterreaction. Frum called for defunding a wide array of federal programs in one fell swoop, including federal student loans and agricultural subsidies. Pinkerton proposed a new version of the Civilian Conservation Corps to demonstrate that Republicans did not want anyone to starve. It was the New Deal with a conservative twist.

Those diverse viewpoints showed the many options that confronted the new Congress. My own belief, also advocated by Kristol, was that the new Congress and its pro-family allies should proceed with a kind of bold

incrementalism, proposing sweeping reforms and adopting them in gradual steps. It was foolish to suppose that what many were calling a "revolution" would happen overnight. Clinton still held the veto pen and might
even get the line-item veto. Barring a cataclysm on the scale of the Civil
War or the Great Depression, the American people usually prefer political
change—even sweeping and dramatic change—to occur in measured
steps, not frightening leaps. I also agreed with Frum that the new Congress achieve "traditionalist ends through libertarian means." There was,
I believed, a false tension between libertarians and religious conservatives. What most conservative religious folk want is not to use government to impose their values on others, but to shrink and delimit
government so the left can no longer impose its secular values on
churches and families. Libertarians and social conservatives both want
smaller government. By using fiscal policy as social policy—shifting control of education to the local level, ending tax subsidies for abortion, and
transferring certain welfare functions to the civil society—social conservatives could reduce the size of government in such a way as to measurably
advance traditional values.

While certainly not coy about my views, I continued to be pestered by
journalists who wanted to know what our "payback" would be from Newt
Gingrich and Bob Dole, the new leaders of the Republican Congress.
What are your demands? they wanted to know. Reporters and talk-show
hosts asked, "What is it you people *really* want?" Charges of "stealth" and
a "hidden agenda" filled the air. Behind the Contract with America, some
on the far left argued, lay a seething, hate-filled agenda of theocratic au-
thoritarianism. Part of the reason for those questions and charges has been
our public effort during recent years to broaden our agenda, to speak to
economic issues that have a very real impact on the family—issues like
welfare reform, tax relief, and a balanced budget amendment. Some have
suggested that this wider agenda is designed to mask our "true" designs,
but these are issues that resonate strongly with people of faith. That is true
of not only the Christian Coalition but many other pro-family groups.
Phyllis Schlafly recently surveyed the members of her Eagle Forum organi-

zation and found that the top two concerns of her members were the deficit and education.

The broadening of our issues focus, however, has sometimes created the mistaken impression that we are less concerned with the moral issues that many associate with the pro-family movement. Nothing could be farther from the truth. Indeed, our evolution on this point is similar to that of the civil rights movement. Its leaders once focused exclusively on ending segregation. But they found after winning that battle that children still attending failing schools, families still lived in unsafe neighborhoods, and many in the minority community still needed jobs and economic mobility. It was no accident that the rallying cry of the March on Washington in 1963 was for "jobs and freedom." The pro-family movement has likewise learned that restricting abortion and battling homosexuality alone do not help families pay their bills, send their children to college, or save for retirement. When the pro-family movement talks about lower taxes or job security, we are not trying to hide our "true agenda," as our critics insist. We are simply addressing both the moral and the financial pressures on so many families today.

The Christian Coalition has been the object of intense media scrutiny and extensive opposition research conducted by liberal groups over the course of seven years. We have been profiled by every major newspaper and interviewed by the television networks countless times. We and other pro-family groups have been featured on the cover of numerous newsmagazines. And we have been remarkably open and cooperative in our dealings with the media throughout this process. There are a lot of things the Christian Coalition could be accused of, but "stealth" is definitely not one of them. People know who we are, and they know what we are about.

What drives the left crazy is that who we are, what we desire for the nation, and what we aspire to be as a people do not conform to their own twisted stereotype of people of faith. There is an element of antireligious bias in their charge of "stealth." To them, the idea of people who pray daily and believe in a literal interpretation of the Bible banding together as a political movement is frightening. They hurl the term "fundamentalist" as if it were an epithet instead of a description of someone's deeply held spiritual convictions. There is an element of McCarthyism as well. Our critics lift a quotation out of context from a decade-old direct-mail letter or a speech given years ago before an obscure forum, and blow it out of proportion as if it represents the "true" views of an entire social movement.

This does not promote civility or understanding. Does the fact that Jesse Jackson once called New York City "hymietown" make the entire civil rights community anti-Semitic? Of course not. Does the fact that the official newspaper of the National Organization for Women once argued that in order to be considered fully feminist, every woman must be willing to be publicly identified as a lesbian mean that every feminist is for lesbian rights? Obviously not. But similarly intemperate statements by religious conservative leaders are routinely dredged up—often without documentation or sourcing—and recycled *ad nauseam* by radical left organizations whose primary objective is to raise money by scaring people about evangelical Christians.

To a degree, of course, this is part of the normal rough-and-tumble of American politics. Anyone who wishes to be in public life should have to answer for their words and deeds. I do not ask that we be held to a different standard. But it is not too much to ask for balance and a sense of fairness. In 1994 I wrote a book called *Politically Incorrect* that laid out a comprehensive legislative and social agenda for the pro-family movement. It confronted our critics and answered many of their charges, and it was extensively reviewed by publications ranging from the *Wall Street Journal* to the *New York Times Book Review*. Yet citations from that book rarely turn up in the conspiracy tracts and direct-mail fodder of the radical left. Why? For the simple reason that it does not confirm their worst fears or play to their ugly caricature of the faith community.

From the charges of the left, you would think that the average Christian conservative keeps guns in the attic, stores bottled, unfluoridated water in the basement, is a card-carrying member of the militia movement, and devours well-thumbed issues of *Spotlight*, the periodical of the anti-Semitic Liberty Lobby. Even members of the well-educated cultural elite hold to this view. I was once asked by a major publication to write an essay on what the Christian Coalition "ultimately" wanted. "What would you do," the editor asked, "if there was no liberal establishment to stop you? Lay it all out for the whole world to see." I worked diligently on the essay, consulting with our legislative staff and other pro-family leaders, and explained most of what was already known about our agenda, but it also included a few surprises. The essay included a call for balanced budgets, term limits, school choice, lower taxes on the family, laws against abortion and euthanasia, and reforms of the divorce laws so that married couples with children could divorce only if there were such grounds as adultery or abuse. In addition, I called for a constitutional amendment allowing for greater religious freedom, a nationwide ban on state-sponsored gambling, and a transfer of welfare functions to churches, synagogues, and local communities. One-third of the functions and spending of the existing federal government would have been returned to state and nongovernmental organizations. After I submitted the article, the editor wrote back in evident disappointment, "This just isn't radical enough." The essay was never published.

The truth is that no matter what we say, our critics will never be satisfied. Their objections have less to do with our honestly held views and cherished values than with hardball politics. Our ideological foes cannot take us at our word, because to do so would be to confess that they were wrong about us and to concede that most people of faith are reasonable people with a common-sense agenda for the nation. When it comes to the phony charge of a hidden agenda, religious conservatives are in a no-win situation. If they extend an olive branch, they are dismissed as wolves in sheep's clothing. If they use strong language that conforms to the stereotype of evangelicals, they are condemned as bigots. It reminds me of the time I spoke to a liberal Jewish organization and acknowledged the pain that evangelicals had caused them in past disputes, promised to seek reconciliation in the future, and urged that we work together on those issues that united us, such as a safe and secure Israel and quality education for our children. As I shook hands with several people and headed for the door, I heard one man mutter, "I knew he would pander." Had I delivered remarks that confirmed his worst fears, he would have thundered, "See, I told you so." In short, no matter what I said, there was no way to change the minds of those who simply resented our involvement in the political process.

There is also an element of class antagonism in the distrust many in the dominant culture feel toward religious folk. A recent Gallup poll asked people who they would least like to have as a next-door neighbor. Less than 5 percent said a Catholic or a Jew; 30 percent said they did not want to live next door to a fundamentalist. This negative characterization of evangelicals is based on an outdated interpretation of populist political movements as necessarily made up of racists, ex-Klansmen, boobs, hayseeds, trailer trash, and anti-Semites. I have heard sneering remarks at political gatherings directed at religious conservatives that express disgust about the "Graco stroller set," women in cotton print dresses, and the "Wal-mart crowd." One gets the sneaking suspicion that if those religious folk shopped at Neiman-Marcus instead of Sears they would not encounter the same disfavor from the chattering class. The concentration of most opinion leaders and cultural trendsetters in bohemian grove and high-income urban neighborhoods like the Upper West Side of Manhattan or the Georgetown section of Washington makes the suburban life of middle-class families in the heartland of America seem remote and almost alien.

Surveys show that religious conservatives are not the boobs some think they are. A survey conducted for the Christian Coalition in 1993 found that the average committed Christian who attends church regularly is a forty-year-old woman who has attended college, is married with children, and whose household income of $40,000 is one-third above the national average. Half of these women under the age of sixty-five work outside the home. Our members are mostly middle class and are employed in managerial occupations; many of them have advanced degrees. One of my favorite comments made about religious folk is that their political agenda will "alienate moderate voters in the suburbs." So pro-choice moderates live in the suburbs. Where do they think evangelicals live—trailer parks? Some of our strongest support can be found in the suburbs and exurbs of the nation's major metropolitan areas: Chicago, Detroit, Orlando,

Los Angeles, Dallas, and Atlanta. Yet the left continues to insist that religious conservatives are "poor, uneducated, and easy to command."

To be sure, we have brought some of those charges on ourselves. We have not always spoken in a way that embraced all of our listeners, have not always sought understanding where there has been enmity, and have not always sought to bring healing where there has been pain. We have sometimes spoken or acted in a manner that did not reflect the grace and humility of Christ. But God is not finished with us yet. We are no different from any other people seeking justice in a world that is wracked and divided. We will sometimes make mistakes in our zeal, but thank goodness we have the heart to speak out for those values that otherwise would have no defender.

If I make an ill-advised remark (and sometimes even when I do not), a quotation attributed to me will appear in liberal publications for a decade, or for as long as the contributions keep flowing. Critics have even gone so far as to equate our pro-family movement with the racist appeals of David Duke or George C. Wallace. But the same critics were silent when I spoke before the Louisiana Republican party convention in 1996, with David Duke sitting in the audience, and said, "To those who have traded the garb of righteousness for the white veil of hatred, to those who have taken the cross of Christ and its theme of redemption and twisted it into the crooked swastika of ethnic bigotry, to those who have taken our message of love for all and turned it into a hate-filled harangue against a few, I say that you do not represent our movement and you do not represent the best and noblest traditions of this party." Don't look for that quotation to turn up in a People for the American Way direct-mail letter any time soon.

Let me address the "stealth" charge head on. Lest there be any confusion, we are as committed as ever to the sanctity of life, the importance of the marriage-based two-parent family, reversing moral decay, stopping the cultural pollution of sexually explicit films and television programs directed at children, and religious freedom for all Americans, including the right to voluntary prayer. On those points we will not compromise, for to retreat would be to deny ourselves and to deny the faith we hold dear. Our message is simple. For thirty years the left has had its chance to social-engineer, to try liberal experiments, to tinker and toy with the government. They have failed. Now it is our turn. Liberal elites have attempted to redefine the family away from the traditional model of a father, a mother, and children, and replace it with "any combination of affectionate human beings living together." From family law to education and government spending, liberalism has undermined (usually unintentionally) some of the most cherished values of the American people, and we need to set that straight. As I have acknowledged in previous chapters, there is much about liberalism that has been good for the nation, particularly in its crusades for civil and human rights that were fired by faith in God. But times change, and with changing times comes a need to try new ideas.

Our political agenda is based on the need to affirm the basic social and religious values upon which the nation was built. Ours is largely a defensive movement. We are not revolutionaries but counterrevolutionaries, seeking to resist the left's agenda and to keep them from imposing their values on our homes, churches, and families. We will do so with a good dose of common sense and traditional values, and with a heavy emphasis on tenacity. My own view is that this agenda will not be realized in one year, one session of Congress, or even one decade. It will take many decades to achieve the restoration of the family and the renewal of our culture.

That is not something Clinton's allies recognized following *his* election. Patricia Ireland of the National Organization for Women held a news conference during the Clinton transition denouncing him for neglecting women in his appointments. This reckless charge—Clinton rebuffed it as "bean counting"—helped produce quota appointments like Zoë Baird and mired the administration in controversy before it was out of the starting gate. Likewise, the pro-abortion lobby demanded that the first executive orders Clinton signed were those reversing Reagan–Bush era pro-life policies. Why not have the first executive order grant waivers for states to experiment with welfare reform? That would have sent the right message: I am a New Democrat, and I want to end welfare as we know it. But

Clinton, trying to balance his factions and preserve his base, caved in to his left-wing allies. At a critical defining moment of his presidency—a time when he needed to appeal to the center of the country—he came off looking ideologically rigid and extremist.

All those warning signs were fresh in my mind when, just days after the 1994 elections, Newt Gingrich dropped a bombshell by telling the *Washington Times* that he planned to hold a vote on a school prayer amendment by early summer. That surprise announcement produced banner headlines. President Clinton, on an overseas diplomatic trip, was asked about the school prayer issue at a stopover in Malaysia. Stumbling with his words, Clinton expressed a willingness to support a constitutional amendment allowing for student-initiated prayer if it were properly worded. Whether he was suffering from jet lag or was still staggered by the midterm election returns was unclear. But Clinton's answer provoked a violent revolt on his left. I was on a much-needed vacation after the election and turned on the television to find the late Art Kropp, my frequent debate partner from People for the American Way, screaming on CNN about Clinton's betrayal.

I knew instinctively that we were in trouble. I called my office in Virginia, and my secretary read from a stack of phone messages from the press. Every major media outlet in the country wanted our reaction to the brewing school prayer controversy. I had hoped to take some time off to collect my thoughts and begin the important work of developing a legislative agenda. In politics, picking the time and the place of a fight is the most important factor in winning. We were not yet ready to do battle. If we were not going to repeat the errors that plagued the left during the early days of the Clinton administration, I knew we had to turn down the heat, and fast.

I called Catherine Manegold of the *New York Times* to give her a reaction to Gingrich's statement. The media were already reporting that the "real" agenda of the Republicans had been exposed. I disagreed.

"I am not sure that now is the best time to raise the school prayer issue," I told her. "We are far more interested in religious freedom and the right of persons to express their religious beliefs free from discrimination." I also pointed out that the pro-family movement was united in opposing any amendment that allowed a teacher or principal to lead a prayer or to compel students to participate.

The next day, the *New York Times* carried a front-page article reporting that many religious conservatives were less than enthusiastic about a vote on school prayer. Beverly LaHaye of Concerned Women for America expressed similar reservations. Though we would revisit the issue later on our own terms—emphasizing religious freedom—we had dodged a bullet. A few days later I sparred with Kropp on *Face the Nation* and played down the controversy, pointing out that President Clinton's views were not all that different from ours. That caused Kropp to squirm in his seat. He had hoped to pick a fight with the dreaded "religious right" and instead found himself in a shooting match with Clinton. I stressed that we were less interested in mandated school prayer than we were in prohibiting religious discrimination.

Later Gingrich and I spoke on the phone. He explained quite persuasively that he was simply trying to send a strong signal that he had not forgotten the role of religious conservatives in the 1994 landslide. He was not going to be co-opted by Washington, and he would keep his word to raise these vital moral issues, he promised. (This addressed the fears of the pro-family movement, which worried that it would repeat the disappointments of the Reagan era, when it had been asked to wait their turn quietly—a turn that never really came.) I thanked Newt for his commitment but told him that most of the leaders I had talked to in the pro-family movement wanted to wait until we had the language for a constitutional amendment ironed out before launching a full-fledged campaign for its ratification. Newt agreed, and he asked me to keep him posted on our progress.

Not only did we seek to avoid divisive tactics, but we pledged to be team players. In a speech before the Economic Club of Detroit in January 1995, I announced a $1 million grassroots and media campaign to support passage of the Contract with America. For the first hundred days, the pro-family community activated phone banks, broadcast cable and satellite television programs, and dropped millions of pieces of direct mail, all in support of term limits, a balanced budget, welfare reform, and tax relief for families.[1] James Carville groused to the *Wall Street Journal* that we were "selling out" our own membership. How so? By working for welfare reform and the largest family tax cut in modern times? Carville's complaint revealed that the liberals were extremely frustrated that we did not present an easy target.

Our objective was to win a big victory on the Contract with America, thereby building up political capital that we could later spend on the social issues. We knew that after the first hundred days were over we would have the opportunity to turn to many of the moral concerns that preoccupied so many millions of Americans. The strategy worked. Bolstered by our grassroots efforts and those of business and taxpayer groups, the Contract with America sailed through the House of Representatives in less than a hundred days. The Republicans won all but a handful of roll call votes during the Contract period.

It was the most significant flurry of legislative activity since Franklin D. Roosevelt swept into power in 1933, and the pro-family movement had played a critical part in its success. Representative John Boehner of Ohio chaired a weekly meeting of the leadership's kitchen cabinet, in which the Christian Coalition joined with lobbyists from the National Restaurant Association, the National Federation of Independent Business, and the Chamber of Commerce. We plotted legislative strategy and ran through vote counts on each item in the Contract. Brian Lopina, our chief lobbyist, had earlier worked for Citizens for a Sound Economy, a pro-business lobby organization, so he already had extensive contacts in that community. Of the $354 billion tax cut included in the Contract, the tax credit for children amounted to approximately $155 billion. It was the largest single item in the tax cut. In addition, there were tax credits for adoption, elimination of the marriage penalty, and other pro-family provisions. The business community was concerned mostly with capital gains and estate tax relief. Together, we agreed to remain united on the entire tax cut so that we were not divided from each other and left fighting over a shrinking pot of money.

But hanging tough on the tax cut proved difficult. One week before the Senate Finance Committee took up the issue, we learned we were in danger of losing the final three years of the $500 tax credit for children. There was also a discussion of lowering the income or age of those eligible to the point where millions of families would receive no tax relief. Several Senators called to warn us that a draft bill was circulating and that if we did not act quickly, we were going to get rolled. Our Washington office sent a strongly worded letter to members of the Finance Committee promising to oppose the bill on final passage if the tax cut was mangled in committee. Senator Don Nickles of Oklahoma, who had introduced his own family tax relief bill, worked diligently to save the day. As a supporter of Bob Dole's presidential campaign, a member of the powerful Finance Committee, and part of the Republican leadership team in the Senate, Nickles was perfectly positioned to ensure that the child tax credit stayed in the bill. We also contacted Bob Dole and Pete Domenici, chairman of the budget committee, and urged them to keep an eye on the process. Bob Packwood had resigned three weeks earlier, and the committee was in turmoil. Phil Gramm, Dole's chief antagonist in the presidential race, was named to the Finance Committee shortly before it took up the tax bill, and he worked hard on our behalf. With the presidential primaries just around the corner, both Dole and Gramm wanted to be the hero and save the tax cut. Although the income cap was lowered slightly, we won a permanent tax cut for families that passed the Senate on a largely party-line vote.

Yet for all this success, the nagging question lingered: now that we had our place at the table, what cultural agenda would we present to the new Congress? I knew that the grassroots were getting restless. They needed something to sink their teeth into on the social issues. In January 1995 we had mailed nearly a million letters to our supporters asking them which cultural issues they wanted to see Congress address. In addition, we commissioned a survey by Frank Luntz to determine the issues that were most important to the general public. We found remarkably strong support for most of our positions, averaging between 60 and 90 percent. Next we had to decide how to present our legislative proposals. Our staff and board of directors kicked around ideas ranging from a Capitol Hill rally to an advance story leaked to a single major newspaper. The latter idea was rejected because we felt it could generate resentment from those reporters who did not receive advance notice. To get our message across without becoming too large a target for the left, we decided to roll out the pro-family agenda at a Sperling breakfast or some other low-key press opportunity.

After we had completed the survey of our members and the public, I called Pat Robertson to run through the items in the proposed Contract with the American Family, including returning control of education to the local level, privatizing federal funding of the arts, and encouraging private charity. He strongly approved of every item on the agenda.

"Pat," I said, "we want to see if we can get the ball moving without becoming a major target. What do you think of a small breakfast of major print reporters where we lay out the legislation?"

"Well," he replied, "if you want to energize the troops at the grassroots, you have to blow a trumpet from the mountaintop. You can't move the army into battle with a whimper. I think you should fly in all fifty state leaders of the Christian Coalition and formally launch a campaign for the Contract."

That was a terrific idea, and we began making plans for a large-scale news conference. But first we had to prepare a document. Some of the issues were simple enough: a religious freedom amendment, ending taxpayer funding of abortion, family tax relief, and ending the tax funding of pornography through the National Endowment for the Arts. The religious freedom amendment addressed the issue most important to many religious conservatives: the creation of what Stephen L. Carter has called a "culture of disbelief." We believed that a seven-year-old having his Valentine torn up by a teacher because it was written to God, a fifteen-year-old receiving a failing grade for writing an essay about the life of Christ, and the Ten Commandments being torn down from courthouses was an intolerant attempt to marginalize the role of faith in our public life.[2] To us, this issue was much broader than school prayer, although we supported student-initiated, student-led prayer in noncompulsory settings. We believed that the First Amendment rights of people of faith were at stake, and that the entire culture had suffered from the treating of religious expression as a danger to be censored and silenced.

Beyond the long-standing causes of the pro-family movement, filling out the list was more problematic. We had decided to include ten items to emulate the model of the original Contract with America. To complete the agenda, we called members of Congress and staff and solicited the views of other pro-family groups. All those sources provided the rest of the issues. I asked Susan Muskett, a Roman Catholic and a former Equal Employment Opportunity Commission lawyer, to draft the manifesto, because she was a capable polemicist who relied on facts and natural law principles to advance her arguments. Susan farmed out chapters to some of the most respected experts in Washington on the various issues. We felt the Contract with the American Family needed to be a serious document that spoke not only to our membership but to the entire political community. Susan and other writers did an excellent job, and I knew the minute I saw the draft that we had a winner.

After months of planning, we unveiled our Contract with the American Family at a ceremony on May 17, 1995, held in the Mansfield Room of the Capitol building and attended by dozens of lawmakers, including Speaker Gingrich and Senate majority whip Trent Lott. The state chairs of the Christian Coalition from around the nation gathered for a private meeting with Senator Bob Dole. The room was filled to overflowing, with members of the press corps spilling out into the hallways and some members of Congress unable to elbow their way to the front of the crowd. At one point, a reporter with one of the wire services banged on the back door of the room and demanded to be let in—there was no way to get in through the main entrance. We took out advertisements in the *Washington Post* and *USA Today* announcing the Contract and its provisions. Among the more prominent items: religious liberty, returning control of education to the local level, restricting pornography on the Internet, a school choice bill targeting vouchers to inner-city youth, a Mothers' and Homemakers' Rights Act that allowed stay-at-home mothers to invest in a retirement plan tax-free, a requirement that prison inmates work and attend literacy classes, and a ban on partial-birth abortions.

"These provisions are the ten suggestions, not the Ten Commandments," I stated. "This is not a Christian agenda. It is not a Republican agenda. It is not a special interest agenda. It is a pro-family agenda" supported by the majority of the American people.[3] Recognizing that repeating the legislative blizzard of the Contract with America was virtually impossible, we placed no deadline on the enactment of the ten clauses in our Contract. Indeed, our Contract was specifically designed to take more than one session of Congress to enact. We felt that if the entire agenda were enacted before the 1996 elections, it would be difficult to spur our supporters to the polls. We wanted not a lightning-fast victory, but a measured and gradual passage of key provisions that built momentum over a period of years.

Reaction from the media to our proposals was relatively muted. "If you're ready to dismiss" the Contract with the American Family as "extremist nonsense," E. J. Dionne concluded in the *Washington Post*, "you are making a big mistake. This is a serious, if slick, document." The CNN analyst William Schneider called it "hardly a radical agenda." Cokie Roberts of ABC News said, "They've played this very smart. They have not come on strong in a way that scared people." This, of course, drove the left wild. Many of them had built entire careers around trying to scare the American people with our agenda, and they now found themselves like a farmer at a cockfight with no bird to bet on. "The Christian Coalition has not only arrived at the table. They're carving up the turkey," Barry Lynn of Americans United for the Separation of Church and State seethed.[4] Senator Arlen Specter, running for the Republican presidential nomination as the sole candidate blasting religious conservatives, saw a campaign issue slip away. During a joint appearance on *Good Morning America* the day we released the Contract, he denounced the document as "subterfuge." After the segment ended, I heard the disembodied voice of Specter, who was sitting in a separate studio, blaring in my ear: "Why won't you debate me? Why won't you debate me?" I knew then that our strategy was working. Later, shortly before he dropped out of the presidential race, Specter and I held a cordial private meeting and agreed to bury the hatchet, though we continue to disagree on issues like abortion.

Some in the press corps were beside themselves that we had presented such a reasonable proposal. They turned up the heat on charges that we were engaged in "stealth" and "subterranean tactics." The *Washington Monthly*, for example, described the Christian Coalition as "an organizational machine reminiscent of Mao Tse-tung that aims to build enough clout to swing any election in the nation."[5] Not to be outdone, a *Washington Post* reporter compared pro-family citizens with "communists and other subversive organizations with ideololgical mandates: agitation to stir up public discord, infiltration of public institutions, even the use of misleadingly-named front organizations."[6] Some in the media had licked their chops awaiting the unveiling of our Contract. Now their disappointment was palpable.

Allies on the right expressed different concerns. A handful of conservatives characterized our Contract as "timid" and "too modest." "It sets the hurdle too low," Pat Buchanan remarked. "The Coalition has given away any boldness in a search for popularity and consensus." One pro-family leader expressed disappointment that there was no mention of opposition to "legislation favorable to homosexuality."[7] The reason we included no proposal dealing with homosexuality (apart from school curricula) was because, apart from a gay rights bill introduced by Ted Kennedy that had no chance of even coming to a vote, there was no major legislation pending before Congress focused on the issue. Judy Brown, president of the American Life League, blasted the pro-life provision as too gradualist, similar to pledging to "close one-third of the Nazi concentration camps." But many of our friends on the right were enthusiastic. We welcomed the support of other pro-family groups and received strong endorsements from the National Right to Life Committee, the American Family Association, and many other organizations.

The truth was that our agenda was bold and ambitious. It included a religious freedom constitutional amendment, the first national school voucher program in American history, the most sweeping antipornography legislation in a decade, the first ban on an abortion procedure since *Roe v. Wade*, the abolition of a federal Cabinet department, and the privatization of $500 million in government expenditures. When I heard my conservative friends say that was too "modest," I felt like replying, "You try passing this program through Congress!" The Contract with the American Family was a reasonable, commonsense document because the pro-family movement is a mainstream political movement. Those on both left and right who were disappointed that the document was not more extreme had failed to grasp that simple fact. Having been involved in the political process for nearly two decades, religious conservatives now understand the difference between what is desirable and what is possible, and with only a slim pro-family margin in the House and a pro-choice majority in the Senate, we had to seek legislation that was viable and had a chance of passage. Yet we also included many of the more sweeping and bold initiatives of the pro-family cause.

Nevertheless, attacks from a few voices on the right further advanced our goal of "surfing the mainstream." Besides, few found the notion that the Christian Coalition was "timid" very credible, especially when pro-abortion groups on the left exploded in outrage. Planned Parenthood launched a broadside against our legislative agenda. Kate Michelman of the National Abortion Rights Action League called our reasonable language "code words" for "using the iron fist of government" to put "women at risk every step of the way."[8]

I didn't exactly assuage those concerns with an address to the Conservative Political Action Conference in February 1995, in which I sent a strong signal that the agenda of conservative Christians should not be taken for granted. The previous day Dan Quayle had stunned the political community by dropping out of the presidential race. I had spoken with Quayle several times in the previous few weeks. In spite of a recent hospitalization for a blood clot, he had assured me that he was perfectly fit and fully expected to run. I knew that he would immediately receive a large chunk of pro-family voters, and probably one-quarter to one-third of the likely Republican primary voters. Bill Bennett had also decided not to seek the nomination, despite the huge following he had developed with his runaway bestseller, *The Book of Virtues*. Privately, I was concerned about the shape of the emerging Republican presidential field. For the first time since

1980 there would be no single pro-family champion, though many aspired to that role.

Without a horse to ride, there was a danger that evangelical voters would be ignored and their issues pushed aside by purely economic concerns. I decided to send a message that those issues were still important. "Pro-family voters, one-third of the electorate," I stated, "will not support a party that retreats from its noble and historic defense of traditional values and which has a national ticket or a platform that does not share Ronald Reagan's belief in the sanctity of human life."

As I stepped off the podium, a tight knot of reporters and photographers gathered like lightning bugs, and I realized that my remarks had touched a raw nerve. Haley Barbour was backstage in the green room, waiting to go on for his own speech. I quickly darted to his side to warn him in case he got questions from the press.

"Haley," I said. "I really didn't intend to ambush you."

"That's all right," Haley said in his trademark Mississippi drawl. "I'll just give the same answer I always do. You don't speak for the Republican party, and I don't speak for you."

When I stepped back outside, the journalists were waiting, pens poised over steno pads and tape recorders stuck in the air. "Were you trying to write Christie Todd Whitman or Pete Wilson off the ticket?" asked Tom Edsall of the *Washington Post*.

"No," I replied. "I am not trying to single out a particular individual. I am simply saying that a sign of retreat on the platform or ticket could lessen the enthusiastic support of pro-family voters. I'll let my statement speak for itself."

I was not about to be drawn into a debate about personalities. We had endorsed no one for the presidential nomination; our posture on the vice presidential pick would be the same. But I worried that I had inadvertently started a firestorm. I called Pat Robertson and several members of our board, and they reassured me that it was important for us to stand tall on the pro-life agenda. Over the next few days our office received a deluge of supportive faxes and phone calls from the grassroots.

I needed that support the next morning. I was in Nashville promoting the book version of the Contract with America and was interviewed by Katie Couric of the *Today* show via satellite. In repeated questioning, she asked if I was imposing a "litmus test" on the Republican party. No, I replied. But I did suggest that taxes, term limits, and the pro-family agenda were a "three-legged stool" on which a conservative majority rested. "If you kick one leg out from under that stool, the whole Republican majority collapses," I said.

Couric was clearly not happy with my answers. When the interview ended, I was glad it was over and reached down to remove the microphone.

"We're coming back to you," barked the producer into my ear. "Don't get up." They were holding me for another segment.

Katie, who has a charming television presence but is a tough and skilled interviewer, zeroed in again. We talked for several more minutes, and I stuck to my guns. Our purpose was not to dictate terms to the nominee of the party, but to lay out broad principles for uniting the entire conservative coalition. Without this coalition, which included economic as well as social conservatives, the Republican party cannot win at the ballot box. And without the pro-family community, the most energetic and fastest-growing element in the new politics of the 1990s, the Republican party would, in my view, return to the minority status it languished in for most of the post–World War II period.

Walking that tightrope proved difficult. Officially, we remained a non-partisan movement and worked closely with the conservative Democrats in the House who were known as "blue dogs." With Quayle and Bennett sitting on the sidelines, there was no single "Christian-backed" candidate for the presidency in the mold of Pat Robertson in 1988, so pro-family activists had spread themselves across the map. Many supported Buchanan and Alan Keyes, but an almost equal number gravitated to Phil Gramm or Bob Dole, the acknowledged front-runner. As one pastor in Iowa joked, in previous years "we ran against the system. Now we are the system, or at least functionally part of it."[9] That meant adopting a strategy of staying above the fray in terms of endorsing candidates, while at the same time encouraging religious conservatives to enter the process to advance a general set of shared values. My speech to the CPAC dramatized the juggling act that we would have to manage through the 1996 elections.

The response to my abortion speech showed how far we had come. In the space of just two years, the pro-family community and the Christian Coalition had gone from being seen as the "sponsors of hate" in Houston to being one of the most important and respected voting constituencies in the electorate. But there were dangers associated with such a profile. We did not want to end up as Jesse Jackson had in the Democratic party, taken for granted by party leaders and having to threaten to run as an independent as the only way to exercise his waning influence. To avoid a purely partisan cast, we therefore worked hard to reach out to traditionally Democratic and liberal constituencies.

One of the best opportunities for such outreach came in April 1995, when the Anti-Defamation League of B'nai B'rith invited me to address its annual leadership conference in Washington. There has actually been much greater friendship and sympathy between evangelical Christians and the Jewish community in the United States than is often realized. One reason for that is the historic devotion of evangelicals to the State of Israel. But there are other common values as well: strong families (Jews have the lowest divorce rate in the nation), education that transmits religious values, and opposition to antireligious bigotry. Jerry Falwell made a pro-Israel stance one of the linchpins of the Moral Majority, and other religious conservative figures like Ed McAteer and Pat Boone had devoted much of their public careers to promoting aid to Israel and raising funds for Jewish emigration from the Soviet Union. Pat Robertson had also long enjoyed a strong relationship with Jews of many ideological stripes. In the mid-1980s, when the late Nathan Perlmutter served as the executive director of the Anti-Defamation League, Robertson flew to New York to address its national board, a meeting that came to a close with the participants joining hands around a conference table to pray together and pledge their mutual friendship. On this basis, we looked forward to establishing a long-term relationship with the ADL on issues of mutual concern.

That was why it came as such a shock to us when the ADL released a scathing report in the summer of 1994 bearing the ominous title, *The Religious Right: The Assault on Tolerance and Pluralism in America*. The report alleged that the religious conservative movement advanced a hate-filled political agenda with anti-Semitic overtones. We responded rapidly by issuing our own report detailing the factual inaccuracies and inconsistencies contained in the ADL report, including several statements attributed to Pat Robertson that he had never made. Among them were the claims that Robertson had said at a Christian Broadcasting Network prayer session that Jews were "spiritually deaf and spiritually blind" (a falsehood) and that he had never denounced David Duke when the latter ran for governor of Louisiana. (In fact, Robertson had denounced Duke on national television just days before the election.) Those were just a few of the most glaring factual errors. "The ADL," our own report concluded, "has displayed neither tolerance nor respect. Instead, it has engaged in a partisan campaign of innuendo, half-truths, and outright falsehoods."

Abraham Foxman, the executive director of the ADL, apologized for the errors but stood by the remainder of the report. The episode strained Christian–Jewish relations and led to a series of internal squabbles that plunged the ADL's national leadership into controversy and internal strife. A regional chairman of the ADL in Houston resigned in protest. National ADL vice chairman Rudy Boschwitz protested that the report was "inaccurate," "ill-founded," and "outrageous," and would "do more harm than good." A group of Jews led by Midge Decter addressed an open rebuke to the ADL in a full-page advertisement in the *New York Times*. The columnist Mona Charen accused the organization of committing an act of "defamation" against evangelical Christians and engaging in "character assassination and name calling."[10]

Although we won the skirmish, the battle was quickly joined again. Shortly after the 1994 elections Michael Lind, a former neoconservative writer and wayward protégé of William F. Buckley, penned a lengthy analysis of Pat Robertson's 1991 book *The New World Order* in the *New York Review of Books*.[11] The article quoted several passages from the book out of context and alleged that Robertson had relied in his research and analysis on several obscure authors with anti-Semitic backgrounds. Lind parroted numerous charges made by the ADL and added a few of his own.[12] The article seemed to be a politically motivated effort to embarrass Robertson as a new conservative Republican Congress took power, providing grist for the mills of liberal columnists, many of whom had reacted to the 1994 election results with a mixture of concern and hysteria. There was also much in Lind's attack that assumed our movement bore the same stereotypically paranoid, conspiracy-sniffing features of the old Populist movement, Gerald P. Nye, the America First movement of the 1930s, the John Birch Society, and the Liberty Lobby. The specter of bigoted hillbillies and anti-Semitic rednecks rising from the swamps and backwoods to bring back a new Dark Age in American politics, with smooth spokesmen like me or Robertson serving as front men, was a classic paranoid fear of the liberal mind.

I know Pat Robertson as well as anyone can on a professional basis. He is one of the dearest and most reliable friends of Israel and the Jewish people to emerge from the evangelical community in the United States in this century. To impute an anti-Semitic viewpoint to him is absurd and irresponsible. *The New World Order*, written against the backdrop of the Persian Gulf war, contended that United Nations–directed military operations could jeopardize American national security interests. The premise of the book was summed up well by Senator Bob Dole in his announcement speech for the presidency in 1995: "American foreign policy will be determined by us, not the United Nations." This warning was vindicated by the bloody quagmires of Somalia and Bosnia, where U.S. military forces suffered casualties and American diplomats were impotent to stop the bloodshed. The book was strongly pro-Jewish and pro-Israel. "Rest assured," Robertson predicted, "the next objective of the presently constituted new world order, under the present United Nations, will be to make Israel its target. The precedent has been set by the action against Iraq."[13]

If Robertson is an anti-Semite, he is the most bizarre and cynical anti-

Semite ever known to man, one who has donated six-figure sums to Jewish charities, denounced prophets of hate like Duke and Louis Farrakhan with courageous words of warning on his television program, and lobbied Congress against weapons sales to Arab states like the committed Zionist he is. I accompanied Pat during a private tour of the U.S. Holocaust Museum in 1994, before the ADL report was issued. At the end of the museum tour there is a multimedia presentation in which survivors of the Holocaust describe their rescue from the Nazi concentration camps by American GIs. It is a deeply moving presentation. Pat wept openly during that visit, and we said very little on the ride back to the airport. For this reason, I was deeply angered by the attack on us by the ADL and the liberal columnists. Nevertheless, we had learned the hard way that the only way to refute such charges was to respond with lightning speed.

I was in New York when Gustav Niebuhr of the *New York Times* called to request our response to the latest allegations. In a conference call with Robertson and his press aide, Gene Kapp, we walked through a statement that Robertson had written himself. I suggested moving one paragraph around, but it was published largely as he wrote it. In an exclusive statement issued to the *New York Times,* Robertson pledged to "condemn and repudiate in the strongest terms those who would use code words as a cover for anti-Semitism." He offered "sincere regrets" if anything in his book offended "my Jewish colleagues who I consider to be dear friends and allies."[14] The dispute, Robertson asserted, was "not about religion, but about politics," a fact underscored by his having "repudiated anti-Semitism repeatedly and in the strongest of terms." He vowed to use all his influence to ensure that "Jews are never again the victims of hatred and discrimination."[15]

Those strong statements brought conservative allies to his defense. William F. Buckley, observing that one is more likely to find a "duck-billed platypus" than a "pro-Israel anti-Semite," wrote that Robertson had been "conclusively exonerated." Norman Podhoretz, the former editor of *Commentary* and an influential voice among Jewish neoconservatives, denounced comparisons of Robertson to Louis Farrakhan as "intellectually absurd and morally outrageous." Podhoretz noted that Robertson had contributed to the United Jewish Appeal, "donated huge sums of money to Jewish causes and organizations," assisted in resettling Russian Jews in Israel, and spoke with "the greatest respect of the faith of 'the God of Jacob.'"[16] The whole flap reeked of politics. But we had learned in 1992 that a lie unanswered becomes the truth in today's adversarial political culture, where personal attacks and seven-second sound bites predominate and news cycles move in hours, not days.

In this strained atmosphere I stepped before the national leadership of the Anti-Defamation League on April 3, 1995. My goal was to acknowledge past insensitivities to the legitimate concerns of the Jewish community while urging common ground in opposing religious bigotry in all its ugly forms—including when it was directed at evangelical Christians. I sought to bring healing and reconciliation, not to stoke the fires of suspicion and distrust further. Because I knew the speech promised to be controversial, I faxed a draft to Pat Robertson, who approved both the tone and the content. I acknowledged in the address that "religious conservatives have at times been insensitive," particularly in their call for a "Christian nation," to the "horrors experienced by the Jewish people. I called for an America "that is not officially Christian, Jewish, or Muslim," where "the separation of church and state is complete and inviolable." I urged Jews and Christians to unite on such common concerns as education and stronger families to achieve "moral stability and a sense of community based on shared values."[17]

Those were new statements coming from the head of one of the nation's leading religious conservative organizations, and as I expected, protest exploded from the extremes at both the left and the right of the political spectrum. Frank Rich, former theater critic for the *New York Times*, dismissively snarled, "Add five words ('Today I am a man'), and Mr. Reed's oration would be a credit to any bar mitzvah." Having grown up in Miami and attended many bar mitzvahs as a young man, I considered that a compliment. From the right, Samuel Francis of the *Washington Times* attacked the speech as an "act of groveling" in which "Mr Reed . . . crawled on his belly" in order to "jump through the hoops the ADL's ringmasters have built for him."[18]

None of those charges bothered us. Sooner or later, we believed, liberals in the Jewish community and conservative evangelicals had to sit down and talk through their differences. America is not Bosnia. We must live and work together, in love and understanding, in tolerance and mutual respect, despite our religious and ethnic differences. But someone had to take the first step and extend an olive branch. That was not "groveling," as our critics charged. It was responsible leadership.

We did not mind dodging bullets from the far left and right because it placed us right where we belonged: in the mainstream of the debate. It also kept our critics off balance and prevented us from being pigeonholed as a fringe movement, as some had attempted to do for years. Beyond the politics of the issue, our outreach to the Jewish community represented a turning point in relations between evangelicals and Jews. Following the ADL speech, invitations to appear before other Jewish organizations poured into our offices. Rabbi Yechiel Eckstein of Chicago assembled an annual meeting of evangelical and Jewish leaders to air differences and promote an ongoing dialogue. I also flew to New York City and met privately with the board of the American Jewish Congress for a remarkably cordial and frank discussion. We discussed the recent ADL report, with which many of them had also disagreed, and promised to keep open a line of communication. Speeches before the American Jewish Committee and the American Israeli Political Action Committee continued the dialogue. The Christian Coalition sent a letter to Senator Bob Dole and Speaker Newt Gingrich urging them to move the U.S. embassy in Israel from Tel Aviv to Jerusalem, publishing the letters as full-page advertisements in Jewish newspapers. While real and deep differences between our respective communities remained, we began to find common ground that united Christians and Jews.[19]

The challenges to the dialogue did not abate. In late 1995 I gave a speech to a Jewish group in New Jersey where a member of the organization compared me to Louis Farrakhan (whom I had publicly denounced on countless occasions) and warned that the views I would share "were not the true agenda of the real Christian Coalition." Such hyperbole is typical of what many Christians encounter as we seek to bring our faith into the public square. Nevertheless, I felt it would be a mistake to allow extremists on either side of the issue to derail our continuing efforts at Jewish–Christian dialogue.

On the appointed evening, a snowfall blanketed New York City, and the traffic into suburban New Jersey resembled a parking lot. By the time my taxi finally arrived, I barely had time to make it to the hall. Passing a crowd of picketers and protesters huddled against the cold wind, I entered the hall to share a simple truth: I began my political career as the executive director of the College Republicans during the term of the first (and only) Jewish chairman in its history; I am a lifetime member of the Yad va-Shem memorial, a member of the U.S. Holocaust Museum, and recently contributed to repair a local synagogue in my home town that was vandalized with anti-Semitic scrawlings. Some were trying to associate our call for school choice, balanced budgets, tax relief for families, and protecting human life with the anti-Semitism of Farrakhan or Hitler. In response, I thought of the words of Senate counsel Joseph Welch to Joseph McCarthy during the Army–McCarthy hearings, "Sir, have you no shame?"

My main interest was not to win converts but to promote understanding. I knew the Jewish community was overwhelmingly liberal and Democratic. There were genuine and deep generational and historical reasons for those political affiliations. But I wanted to build a dialogue based on mutual respect and cooperation. Quoting the late Israeli Prime Minister Yitzhak Rabin, I urged, "We like you are people—people who want to build a home. To plant a tree. To love—live side by side with you. In dignity. In empathy. As human beings. As free men." I added that if Arabs and Jews in Israel could find common ground, then so could Jews and Christians in the United States.

Afterward I was approached at the stage by people expressing their appreciation. One Orthodox Jew came over wearing a yarmulke, a flowing beard, and a look of profound consternation. "Why do you keep apologizing for the Christian nation idea?" he demanded. "If we had more Christians like you and your colleagues in government, America would be a better place to live." I laughed and thanked him for the vote of confidence.

Another elderly man grabbed my hand, pulling me close, and said in a half-whisper, "Don't be discouraged. You have a lot more friends here than you realize."

Those quiet voices would build in the months ahead. In the back of my mind, I considered the possibility of launching a Jewish Coalition as a sister organization in future years. The days of Jewish–Christian enmity, I believe, are fading. First, in purely generational terms, Jews under the age of forty are far more conservative and observant in their faith than their parents. The pendulum is swinging back to the right, particularly among the still small but growing Orthodox Jewish community. As intermarriage and assimilation reduce the size and political power of the traditional liberal Jewish constituency, there will be new opportunities for cooperation among like-minded Christians and Jews, and not just on tried-and-true causes like support for Israel. School choice, for example, is an issue that now has a large following among conservative and religious Jews.

In spite of our previous clashes, Abe Foxman and I developed a very cordial and professional working relationship, trying to cooperate in fighting bigotry when we could and ensuring that disagreements were expressed in a civil way. When I came under attack prior to the New Jersey speech, Abe wrote a kind letter saying that I had "no history of anti-Semitism or racism." He urged that "Mr. Reed should be welcomed and his ideas heard" so that "we can continue the harder task of forthright but respectful discourse—exchanging ideas, not epithets."[20] We still had our differences, of course, but the debate was no longer poisoned by a lack of trust or the presence of harsh animosity. That was a hopeful sign.

We also began to build a strong relationship with the Roman Catholic community, another important traditionally Democratic constituency. For decades, Roman Catholics whose forebears first came to the United States in the Irish immigration of the 1840s were a critical part of the New Deal coalition. They grew up in blue-collar households in the

Northeast and Midwestern parts of the country where portraits of two men hung over the mantel in the living room: Jesus Christ and Franklin Delano Roosevelt. Many of those voters associated the Democratic party with the party of immigration, hope, and opportunity; a fair break for the working man; and their own religious values. Those immigrants experienced the harsh bigotry of Protestants upon their arrival, sparking anti-Catholic riots in cities like Philadelphia and causing the brahmins of Boston to hang signs that read, "No Irish need apply." Outside of the experience of slaves who came in chains from Africa, no immigrant group felt a greater sense of rejection and alienation upon their arrival in America than Irish Catholics. When the Republican party formed in the 1850s, many former members of the anti-Catholic and anti-immigrant Know Nothing party drifted to the GOP, ensuring that the Democratic voting patterns of Catholics would deepen during the nineteenth century. The temperance movement also widened the cleavage between evangelicals and Catholics. Most Protestants were "dry" and lived in rural areas in the South and Midwest; most Catholics were "wet" and lived in urban areas dominated by the big-city Democratic machines.

As I noted in Chapter 3, the marriage between the Catholic vote and the Democratic party reached its critical turning point in 1928, when Al Smith ran as the party's presidential nominee and racked up huge vote totals in the Catholic neighborhoods of New York, Boston, and Chicago. To be sure, Smith lost the election by a wide margin. But that defeat masked a more important development occurring underneath: the rise of the Catholic vote as the cornerstone of a new Democratic majority. Until the emergence of the evangelical vote and the Moral Majority in the 1980s, that was the most important religio-cultural political development in American history. The historic antipathy between Catholics and Protestants simmered just beneath the surface, exploding to the forefront in periodic outbursts, as when John F. Kennedy ran for president in 1960 and some prominent evangelical figures questioned his commitment to the separation of church and state. (How ironic that is, given the current state of affairs!)

But in recent years, as the Democratic party became the party of abortion on demand and gay rights, Catholic voters have drifted away from the party of their past. Richard Nixon won the Catholic vote in 1968 over Hubert H. Humphrey, and every president since has won a plurality or a majority of that constituency. In 1994 Roman Catholics voted Republican in an off-year election for the first time since the first Irish Catholics landed on these shores more than a century and a half ago. Among Catholics who attend mass four times or more a month, the margin was striking: 56 percent Republican to 44 percent Democrat. Clearly, an attitudinal shift is occurring among Roman Catholics. A survey conducted by the Catholic Campaign for America in 1995 found that American Catholics not only are pro-life and favor school choice for private and parochial schools, but also support welfare reform and other pro-family initiatives.

The Catholic community has had a special place in the pro-family movement since the *Roe* v. *Wade* decision legalizing abortion. While most evangelicals were slow to respond following the Supreme Court ruling, the National Conference of Catholic Bishops testified before Congressional committees and lobbied hard for a constitutional amendment protecting the unborn. At the 1980 Republican party convention, Roman Catholic activists played a more prominent role in the adoption of the party's pro-life platform plank than did many evangelicals, who were only just beginning to make their first forays into electoral politics. But over time, rubbing shoulders and linking arms across denominational barriers gave the religious conservative movement a remarkably ecumenical texture. Jerry Falwell estimated that nearly one-third of the Moral Majority's members were Roman Catholics. A survey of the rank and file of the Christian Coalition in 1995 revealed a similarly strong presence of Catholic supporters, around 16 percent of total membership.

We also broke new ground by including a large number of Roman Catholics in key leadership positions. The executive director of Pat Robertson's legal arm, the American Center for Law and Justice, is Keith Fournier, a prominent attorney and Catholic lay organizer. Roman Catholic leaders among the state affiliates of the Christian Coalition can be found not only in states with large Catholic populations like Illinois,

Connecticut, and Michigan, but also in Southern states like Tennessee. The top three lobbyists for the Christian Coalition on Capitol Hill are all Roman Catholic. (Their top assistant is Jewish.) I often joke when I speak before Catholic audiences that if anyone has the resume of a token evangelical I can hire for our staff, please fax it to me. Jesting aside, however, the growth of Catholic involvement in traditionally evangelical groups like the Christian Coalition is a major development in the pro-family movement, expanding its base and broadening its appeal to nontraditional allies.

But the friendship between Catholics and evangelicals is not about political expediency alone. It runs much deeper. After centuries of distrust and theological disagreements, Catholics and Protestants are beginning to reflect on what unites them rather than what divides them. The reason is simple. In a nation where one out of every three pregnancies ends in abortion, where the only safe and successful schools in the inner city are usually connected to the Catholic church, and where our common faith and the values associated with it are under unprecedented attack, we can no longer afford to be divided. The darkness is too pervasive and the social pathologies afflicting our nation too severe to allow people of faith to fight one another. That was demonstrated in 1994, when a group of Catholic and evangelical leaders signed a manifesto pledging to cooperate on issues of mutual concern and to focus their missionary efforts abroad on the unchurched rather than converting members of each other's flocks.

Our leadership had discussed for years the possibility of formalizing our bridge-building efforts in the Catholic community. The perfect opportunity presented itself in October 1995, when John Paul II came to the United States for a papal visit. Pat Robertson, along with several other Protestant leaders, was invited to meet with the Pope at the private residence of Cardinal John O'Connor. The following week we formally launched the Catholic Alliance, a division of the Christian Coalition designed to extend our cooperation with like-minded lay Catholics, headed by Maureen Roselli, a former aide to David Gergen at *U.S. News* and a consultant to the National Right to Life Committee. We assembled an informal advisory group of respected Catholic thinkers that included the lay theologian Michael Novak, George Weigel of the Ethics and Public Policy Center, Keith Fournier, Pat Fagan of the Heritage Foundation, and Father Robert Sirico, president of the Michigan-based Acton Institute. We also prepared a recruitment package for pro-family Catholics, which we soon mailed to more than a million households, with astounding results.

There was predictable opposition from liberal Catholic voices. One bishop declared that Catholic Alliance voter guides would not be allowed in his diocese. A liberal organizer grumbled, "Catholics don't need a political home. They already have one. It's called the Catholic church." But this opposition only showed how effective the emerging Catholic-evangelical alliance was as a new force in American politics. Nor were we universally opposed. Roselli met with Bishop McHugh, the head of the pro-life office of the American Catholic bishops, and pledged to cooperate closely in opposing abortion, euthanasia, and physician-assisted suicide. We agreed to respect the authority of the bishops and assiduously avoid appearing to speak for the Church. I also held a cordial meeting with Bishop Pilla, the president of the U.S. Catholic Bishops' Conference, to reassure him of our nonpartisan goals and desire for genuine dialogue. We also met in New York with Cardinal O'Connor, with whom we had built a warm friendship over the years, and we were warmly received and greatly encouraged.

In December 1995 we held the first meeting of the Catholic Alliance in the city of Boston. The gathering was rich in irony. We met in the city where the first Irish had arrived in the New World, the city where Catholic immigrants first gained political power, the city that gave us the Kennedy family dynasty. In that same city, against the backdrop of that remarkable history, we were setting out to build a bold new Roman Catholic presence in American politics. More than five hundred activists from across the Northeast packed into the hotel's ballroom; many had driven all night and braved a blinding snowstorm to attend. One of our featured speakers was Representative Henry Hyde of Illinois, a man so sweet, so gentle, and so genuine in his faith that I have sometimes wondered if he was not an angel in a blue suit roaming the halls of Congress. After Hyde finished, we pumped hands and exchanged a big bear hug as he headed to the airport.

As I walked into the ballroom, I could feel the electricity shooting through the room. "What a breakthrough this represents for the pro-family movement," I thought to myself.

As I walked on stage, the room exploded in applause and cheering. The press hardly knew what to make of it all. "If Catholics and evangelicals can unite, there is no person who cannot run for any office in any city or any state in America that cannot be elected. There is no bill that cannot be passed in either house of Congress or any state legislative chamber in America." I discussed the past theological differences that had kept us divided and stressed the importance of working together to become a force for mercy and justice in a culture where the tender values of faith and life are all too often trampled underfoot. Training seminars continued throughout the day, featuring a nuts-and-bolts presentation on how to build a precinct organization, similar to the curriculum we had been teaching evangelicals for years. Upstairs, the liberal Interfaith Alliance held a news conference condemning our Catholic coalition efforts. Few members of the media attended. They might as well have been standing on the beach and yelling "Stop!" to the advancing tide. The Catholic–evangelical presence in American politics is becoming a fact of life. Our goal is to recruit 250,000 more Catholics into our ranks by election day, 1996, and more than 2 million by the end of the decade.

A few weeks later we held a series of focus groups of ethnic Catholic voters in suburban Chicago. They had voted Republican for Congress in 1994, but many had supported Clinton or Perot in 1992. How could we reach these voters? We knew that if Irish, Italian, and Polish Catholic voters forsook the liberal agenda and worked more closely with their evangelical allies, we could build upon our earlier success. When Frank Luntz, the focus group moderator, asked what the most important issue facing the country was, no one mentioned education, crime, or the budget deficit. Only one mentioned jobs. Their number one answer: a decline in morality. The symptoms of moral decay tumbled from their lips: punk kids dealing drugs in school, violence on television, criminals being let out on the street, and Hollywood's unholy harvest of violent and sexually explicit films. There was anger about the way the media and the dominant culture treated Christians and family values. "You're now treated like a bad guy if you're a Christian," said one Irish Catholic male in his mid-fifties.

The focus groups revealed that ethnic Catholic swing voters felt the same estrangement as evangelicals from the aggressive secularism of the broader culture for its negative portrayal of religious people. They singled out three main proposals: welfare reform, a religious freedom constitutional amendment, and curbs on sex and violence in films and on television. Meanwhile, the Catholic Alliance began to build a grassroots network, appointing Catholic coordinators in all fifty states, around those themes. We also began the important work of meeting with sympathetic members of the American bishops' conference, not asking for their endorsement so much as explaining our true goals. We assured them that we did not wish to speak for the Roman Catholic church or to usurp the authority of the bishops, which we respected. But we believed that the social teaching of the church had encouraged many Catholic lay people to get involved in the broader society. The Catholic Alliance was giving them a way to make a difference.

In the summer of 1995 the Christian Coalition held a conference on racial reconciliation in Dallas, attended by more than a hundred African-American pastors and community organizers from twenty-four states. Among those who spoke were Starr Parker, a former welfare mother and conservative activist; the Boston radio talk-show host and minister Earl Jackson, and Representative J. C. Watts of Oklahoma. We prayed, held hands, wept, and devoted ourselves to working together on the issues that united us. A few were drifting to the Republican party, but most remained staunch Democrats.

When it came my turn to speak, I did not mince words. "As a pro-family movement, we need to go back and do our first works over," I said. "The white evangelical community was not only on the sidelines, but on the wrong side of the most central struggle for social justice in this century: the struggle for civil rights and a color-blind society. We allowed our black brothers and sisters to be held in bondage and treated as second-class citizens for four centuries, and we quoted Scripture to justify it." I asserted that until the pro-family community repented of that sin and made racial reconciliation a priority, it would never gain the morally compelling voice it desired in American public life. Everyone in the room stood and applauded, and throughout the weekend there was much praying, weeping, and hugging.

Those and other acts of racial bridge-building are a unique feature of the new pro-family movement that distinguishes it from the old religious right or its racist predecessors in the segregationist South. Commentators have by and large completely missed this fact. Most journalists who attended the Christian Coalition Road to Victory conference in Washington in September 1995 reported on the presence of all the leading Republican presidential candidates. Only a few accounts noted the remarkable presence of more than two hundred African-American and Latino pro-family activists from across the country. This multiracial presence is small but growing. In 1995 the Southern Baptist Convention passed a resolution at its annual meeting condemning racism and repenting of its involvement in the support of slavery and Jim Crow. The Promisekeepers movement, now more than a million strong, is a ministry that encourages men to be better husbands and fathers through a return to the teachings of the Christian faith. It has made racial reconciliation one of the seven "promises" that its members have vowed to keep.

At the Christian Coalition we have seen the power of the emerging Rainbow Coalition on the right in startling ways. In 1993 African-American churches distributed our nonpartisan voter guides and contributed to the pro-family victories in the New York City school board races. In 1994 we identified tens of thousands of African-American Christians and turned them out to the polls in a Democratic primary (that's right—a Democratic primary) in Houston between Ken Bentsen and Beverly Clark, a black pro-lifer and former member of the Houston city council. Clark forced a runoff; though she lost her bid for Congress, her campaign demonstrated that the color barrier is being broken across the country.

We also saw the power of the black church vividly demonstrated in 1995 when we were engaged in an apparently hopeless battle to defeat riverboat gambling in the Virginia General Assembly. Because many of the casinos on water would have been located in our headquarters region of Hampton Roads, we viewed a defeat as an enormous symbolic setback. If we could not resist the gambling industry in our own backyard, how could we lead a national crusade against it? From the perspective of the pro-family movement, gambling was a nationwide scourge that had to be stopped. The casino companies had hired more than forty lobbyists and were estimated to be spending $2 million to try to ram the riverboat gambling bill through the legislature. Because the Republicans were in the minority, our only hope to defeat the bill lay with Democratic members of the assembly. There was only one constituency the Democrats truly feared: the African-American community.

Just days before a critical House of Delegates panel prepared to consider the bill, we were contacted by a group of black pastors who proposed a bus cavalcade to the state Capitol in Richmond. We offered to lend our phone banks and provide logistical assistance to the effort. The result was a huge rally on the Capitol steps in which African-American pastors pledged to help defeat any member of the legislature who voted to bring gambling into their communities. Because the chief sponsor of the casino bill was a black member of the State House from Norfolk, the rally was particularly effective, causing many other Democrats to urge that the bill never get to the floor. In the end, the House committee never even voted. The pro-family community, working with black and white churches together, had defeated a massive lobbying effort by the gambling industry without firing a single shot.

Nor was that our only victory. In Michigan our state affiliate gathered more than seventy thousand petitions opposing riverboat gambling. As the campaign began to pick up steam, Governor John Engler also announced his opposition. The effort by the gambling interests to build riverboat casinos in Detroit fizzled.

The wholesale destruction of people and families by legalized gambling has led Representative Frank Wolf, a conservative Republican from Virginia, to introduce legislation to study its spread as the first step to controlling it. "When I hear stories of mothers dragging their young children into casinos to plead with dealers to turn their husbands away from the tables, I get concerned," Wolf says.[21]

As recently as a decade ago, only a few states had legalized some form of gambling. Today there are only a handful of states that do not. In 1995, there were thirty-seven state lotteries and casinos in twenty-three states; by the turn of the century, 95 percent of all Americans can expect to live within a three- to four-hour drive of a casino.[22] Lotteries and casinos lure state governments with the appeal of easy money and employment, but staggering social costs overwhelm the economic benefits. Alcoholism, theft, organized crime, suicide, divorce, and unemployment follow gambling wherever it appears. The burden falls heaviest on the poor. Gambling entraps those who are least able to afford it. One study found that persons in the lowest income group spend *four times* as much on gambling as those in the highest income category. Gambling rates are next highest among unskilled laborers, African-Americans, Hispanics, and other minorities.

Organized crime and gambling have gone hand in hand since the days of Al Capone and Bugsy Siegel. Consider the experience of Atlantic City, New Jersey. The city legalized gambling in 1978. City leaders promised that the casinos and hotels would revitalize the community and create thousands of jobs. But at what cost? Within three years, its per capita crime rate went from fiftieth in the nation to first. Over the long haul, the crime rate rose a horrifying 230 percent from 1977 to 1990.[23] The toll in human misery is staggering: William Safire has described state-sponsored gambling as "a $40-billion-a-year cancer ravaging society, corrupting public officials and becoming the fastest growing teen-age addiction."[24] The emergence of a multiracial movement to oppose gambling offers the greatest hope of stemming its tide. In 1996 the Christian Coalition joined with the National Council of Churches, the Presbyterian Church, and the United Methodist Church in opening a fully staffed lobbying operation in Washington to lobby against legalized gambling. It was one more example that our movement is not always as "right-wing Republican" or partisan as our critics would have the public believe.

Our efforts to broaden our base and our agenda did not end with the pro-family landslide of 1994. If anything, that experience only served to validate our belief that we were doing the right thing. Part of that recognition is the realization that the Christian Coalition is far from the only group reenergizing and re-creating American politics. That is why, in addition to our outreach efforts to Catholics, Jews, and the minority community, our relationship with Perot voters is so important.

Perot voters are the mirror image of religious conservatives. The Perot vote is overwhelmingly male (60 percent), while the religious conservative vote is heavily female (62 percent). Perot voters are generally less affluent, while religious conservative voters have an average household income of $45,000 a year. While Perot voters are younger, the median age of pro-family supporters is forty-four, slightly older than the national average. While religious conservatives are frequent church attenders and are concerned primarily with moral issues, Perot supporters are secular, attend church infrequently, and care little about abortion or school prayer. Their blood boils over issues of economic security like NAFTA or over process issues like term limits and campaign finance reform. When the Perot and religious conservative constituencies back the same candidates—as they did in 1994—the result is a tidal wave of historic proportions. This, more than anything, explained my willingness to support the Contract with America and to give the Perot constituency its day in the sun before our agenda took center stage.

I first met Ross Perot in the summer of 1994 in Washington at a private meeting of pro-family leaders organized by Representative Ernest Istook of Oklahoma. The purpose was to determine whether there might be areas of cooperation between United We Stand and the pro-family movement. Perot seemed curious and intrigued by the strength and size of the religious conservative community.

"Do you realize," he said, "that there are one hundred million people in church every Sunday? Most of those folks are hard-working, patriotic Americans." He also commented on the importance of organizing the small business community, another key to the future of American politics.

"Mr. Perot," Gary Bauer of the Family Research Council said, "it is impossible for us to sit down together without raising the question that is on everyone's mind. Are you planning to run for the presidency again in 1996?"

"I hope not," Perot responded cryptically. "I've said before that running for president is like having brain surgery without anesthesia. I hope the two political parties will get their act together."

A few days later I received a handwritten note from Perot and a copy of the Congressional Bible, an edition of the Scriptures commissioned by the U.S. Congress shortly after the founding of the nation, the only Bible ever officially printed by the federal government. The next time I heard from Perot was after I debated Jesse Jackson on *Larry King Live*. Jackson, in a speech in New York, had compared the Christian Coalition to the Nazi party in Germany in the 1930s, and we had called him to task. Jackson and I spoke cordially off camera, but our on-air sparring sent sparks flying.

"Are you a preacher?" Perot asked in his Texarkana twang when I picked up the phone.

"No, Ross, I'm not."

"Well, you ought to be a preacher. Or maybe a diplomat. I don't know how you handled those personal attacks without appearing mean-spirited or angry. You ought to work for the State Department."

I laughed and thanked him, and we continued to talk on the phone occasionally, agreeing that eventually we should meet privately to discuss our mutual interests. There was no discussion of a Perot–Christian alliance or of support for given candidates. But we both agreed that our respective supporters were engaged in rewriting the script of American politics, creating a kind of "post-partisan" electoral environment in which almost anything could happen—and often did. For that reason, we needed to be able to have a good relationship.

I flew to Dallas in July 1995, and Perot escorted me to a simple conference room with red leather chairs and floor-to-ceiling glass windows offering a panoramic view of the city. Original Norman Rockwell paintings graced the walls, along with portraits of Perot's wife, Margot, and their daughters, framed business citations and awards, and an original copy of the first public stock offering for Electronic Data Systems, the company that made Perot a billionaire, which dated from 1967. It is easy to forget that prior to his entrance into presidential politics Perot was one of the most remarkable business success stories of his time.

In private, Perot is a genial host, courteous and self-effacing. Contrary to his public image, I found him to be a no-nonsense pol who bears the scars of a bruising presidential campaign, two failed campaigns against NAFTA and GATT, and the scorn of the national media. But he is no Boss Tweed. He speaks the language of his supporters, idealistic and homespun, yet plainspoken and blunt.

"I'm hesitant about Dole," he said as we reviewed the 1996 presidential race. "His age will be an issue. I met with Reagan in his second term and saw first hand the effects of his age. He literally read from cards during our meeting. Dole will be seventy-three years old if he becomes president, even older than Reagan when he took office."

He spoke highly of Gramm and expressed admiration for Pat Buchanan's courage and convictions. Perot seemed to hint that if the Republicans moved forward on lobbying reform and campaign finance reform, and could begin to bring the budget into balance, he would be generally supportive. If Bob Dole were the Republican presidential nominee and he picked a relatively young, capable vice president, Perot suggested that he himself would be unlikely to run for president in 1996, though he did not rule out any options. He did not have a high opinion of Bill Clinton. At one point he asked me if I thought a challenge to Clinton in the Democratic primaries could succeed. I gave him my best read: no incumbent president who had sought his party's nomination in the twentieth century had ever been defeated.

Perot jokingly called himself the "white albino monkey" of American politics. "When people get tired of seeing the lion and the giraffe," he quipped, "they bring in the white albino monkey so people will go to the zoo. That's me."

We parted company agreeing to stay in touch. He invited me to send a Christian Coalition representative to attend the coming national conference of United We Stand, an offer I accepted. We saw that our constituents shared many of the same goals: balanced budgets, lower taxes, choice in education, term limits, and political reform. If they could join forces, there would be no legislation that they advocated that could not pass in Congress or the state legislatures and no candidate they could not elect at any level of government. It is unlikely that the pro-family movement and the Perot movement can ever become one, but our agendas are not as far apart as is commonly believed, and the future lies much more in our collective efforts than in the traditional two-party system.

Later, when Perot formed his Reform party, he called to assure me that his main purpose was to force the Democrats and Republicans to clean up their act. Knowing that the Perot voters and pro-family voters had supported many of the same Congressional candidates in 1994, he made it clear he had no intention of fielding candidates for the House or Senate.

"What is the endgame, Ross?" I asked.

"Well, only time will tell," he answered. "If the Republicans nominate another George Washington, we won't need a candidate of our own. But if we can raise a lot of money, say $50 to $100 million, and get on the ballot in all fifty states, we could offer our spot to many distinguished Americans who might not otherwise be willing to go through the exercise of having to raise money themselves."

Well, I thought, requiring another George Washington as a condition of not running seemed to be setting the bar rather high. Which "distinguished Americans" was Perot referring to? He had spoken highly of Democrats like Senator Bill Bradley of New Jersey, House minority leader Dick Gephardt, and Senator Sam Nunn, but they were unwilling to run as independents. I privately viewed the Reform party as a political dead end unless Perot himself ran. I had told Ross earlier that the best way to influence the direction of the country was the way we had chosen: eschew the presidential candidate route and focus on building a permanent grassroots army that would force politicians to pay heed to their agenda.

I cannot predict what Perot will do in 1996 or beyond. For now, he seems intent on pursuing another ill-advised and futile run for the presidency. But I do know this: His constituency will be an important part of the political scene for at least the next decade. The issues he ran on and the voters he mobilized cannot be ignored by the two political parties or they will pay dearly at the ballot box, as George Bush did in 1992, and as the Democrats did in 1994, when Perot voters cast 66 percent of their ballots for Republican Congressional candidates. Whatever one thinks of Ross Perot, there is a free-floating constituency amounting to one-third of the electorate that is tired of politics as usual and is ready to shake up the system. They represent a secular analog to the pro-family movement in their willingness to challenge the political establishment as a grassroots, "outsider" force.

Our reason for pursuing the grassroots, nonpresidential strategy I had recommended to Perot was not rooted in theory. It was based on a proven track record of success. Hundreds of state legislators and school board members were climbing the ladder of the political system, taking their knocks, occasionally missing a rung, but always moving upward. We were finding that a friendly Congress was far more suitable to advancing our agenda than a friendly president.

Throughout 1995 our Contract with the American Family moved slowly but surely through Congress. One of our most important victories was the passage of a partial-birth abortion bill banning a controversial procedure used in late-term abortions. This legislation, drafted by the National Right to Life Committee and included in our contract, passed the House with the votes of liberals like Dick Gephardt, David Bonior, and Patrick Kennedy, the nephew of Ted Kennedy. The Clinton administration was in a quandary. If it opposed the bill, it would expose the president's talk about making abortion "rare" as an empty letter. But by supporting it, the White House risked a blowup with the pro-abortion lobby, to which the president is closely tied. In the end Clinton vowed to veto the bill, a politically explosive move that will surely lead to a huge turnout of evangelical voters and an erosion of his support among Roman Catholics.

Another important success came with the passage of restrictions on pornography available on the Internet. The cyberporn victory offers an insider's look at how religious conservatives have turned their grassroots punch into inside-the-Beltway clout.

Few observers gave our plan to restrict hardcore and child pornography on computer bulletin boards much chance of passage. In June 1995 the Senate took up the massive telecommunications bill, the most sweeping revision of communications law in the United States in a generation. Nebraska's Democratic senator J. James Exon, a crusty World War II veteran and partisan curmudgeon who had announced his retirement from the Senate, strode to the floor to offer an amendment banning pornography on the Internet. Exon had been stoked to a white-hot temper by his staff, who had assembled what would become known infamously as the "blue book." The book, a manual wrapped in an unassuming powder-blue cover, contained graphic photographs pulled from sexually explicit bulletin boards on the Internet. Among the depictions: bestiality, sadomasochism, child molestation, and torture.

Exon swaggered across the floor, flashing the pages of the blue book to horrified colleagues. Democrats and Republicans alike were aghast. Most of them did not even know what the World Wide Web was, and they were astonished to learn that such indecent material was available to any child on a computer with a few clicks of a mouse. Within minutes, opposition to the Exon amendment melted away. Stalwart liberals like Christopher Dodd, Barbara Mikulski, and Diane Feinstein voted for it. The cyberporn provision passed overwhelmingly and became part of the mammoth telecommunications bill. That evening, I appeared on *Nightline* to debate an opponent to the bill and confidently predicted victory. We were on our way.

In the House of Representatives, however, matters were more complicated. A few days after the Senate action, Speaker Newt Gingrich had announced his opposition to the cyberporn restrictions in an interview on National Empowerment Television, the conservative cable and satellite network. The media played up his objections to the bill, making our job more difficult. I did not want to confront Gingrich, a good friend and ally, directly. Yet we had to figure out a way out of the bind. There was no companion House legislation that could be attached to the telecom bill, as in the Senate. After weeks of vigorous lobbying of those on the committee considering the bill, we had come up dry.

Finally, help arrived in the unlikely form of an amendment by Edward Markey, a Democrat from Massachusetts. Markey wanted to require manufacturers to install a "v-chip" in television sets so parents could screen out violent programming. Backed by President Clinton, the bill enjoyed broad bipartisan support, although predictably the television networks fiercely opposed Markey's amendment as an act of censorship.

A few days before the bill was scheduled to reach the House floor, I received a phone call from a lobbyist for one of the major television networks. Would I be willing to help defeat the v-chip? No, I would not, I replied. The Christian Coalition was already on record in support of technology to help parents protect their children from violent or sexually explicit programs. I warned him that I thought the momentum in the Congress toward doing something about the coarseness of television programming was snowballing. The networks were offering a fairly tepid plan of their own that would have created a voluntary rating system and industry investment in new technology to permit parents to block out programming on existing television sets. (The "v-chip" could be installed only in new TVs.) Nevertheless, I offered to take a low profile and not to make the v-chip our top priority in the battle—if the cyberporn provision were included in the bill. The network executive said he would see what he could do.

By now the House Republican leadership was anxious to defeat the v-chip, which they believed would hand Clinton a legislative victory that would allow him to portray himself in the coming campaign as a champion of family values. Our private head count in the House showed that the v-chip was likely to pass no matter what we did, but we were willing not to play a prominent role in its passage if that meant saving the cyberporn bill. In the end, that was not much of a concession, since the v-chip passed easily.

NO MORE STEALTH

In a meeting in the Capitol late one night, I huddled with Jack Fields, the chairman of the subcommittee drafting the telecom bill. Also present was Bill Paxon, who would sit on the conference committee, and John Linder of Georgia, the Speaker's personal emissary on the bill. We had been trying to set up the meeting all day, but conflicting schedules gave us only fifteen minutes, right before I was scheduled to appear on *Christian Coalition Live,* our monthly satellite television show, which is broadcast to three hundred downlink locations around the country.

Jammed into a little anteroom just off the House floor, with staff lining the walls, the atmosphere was tense. Regional Bell telephone companies were deluging Capitol Hill with bags of mail and armies of lobbyists trying to defeat the bill. Long-distance carriers like Sprint and MCI were also weighing in with telegrams, phone calls, and computer-generated mail. The Capitol was buried beneath millions of cards and letters. Billions of dollars were at stake. Now the entire package of legislation hinged on a provision dealing with pornography. As I sat on the couch across from several House members, I received signals from Heidi Stirrup, our chief lobbyist on the bill, who nodded her head when things were going well.

Time was short. We got right down to the business at hand. "I cannot oppose the v-chip, but I don't have to actively push it," I said. "We already have too many irons in the fire on this bill anyway. But we need your assurance that our restrictions on pornography on the Internet will find their way into the bill."

"We understand. We also know you can't oppose the v-chip," Fields replied.

"Where does Newt stand?" I asked. The last thing we needed was Gingrich intervening late in the game.

"I don't think he plans on becoming personally involved," Linder said.

Out of the corner of my eye I saw Heidi and Brian Lopina flashing distressed hand signals, letting me know that we had to leave. I quickly glanced at my watch. We had just five minutes before our satellite television show began, and the studio was four blocks away.

"How do we get the cyberporn restrictions into the bill?" I asked.

They explained that Henry Hyde, who chaired the Judiciary Committee, would draft language outlawing cyberporn. It would be offered as part of the "en bloc" or chairman's amendments by Representative Tom Bliley of Virginia, chairman of the Commerce Committee, meaning that we did not have to record a roll call vote in the House—avoiding a confrontation with Gingrich.

I thanked the members for their time, we shook hands, and I bolted for the door. I ran across the Capitol grounds at breakneck speed and jumped into a waiting car, which squealed out of the parking lot and headed for the television studio. We walked in the door thirty seconds before air time, out of breath but content that we had made important progress in passing our cyberporn bill.

But we had not cleared the final hurdle. As a conference committee dragged through the fall, the computer industry launched a well-financed counterassault. Through editorials and position papers, they portrayed our cyberporn amendment as a dagger aimed at the heart of the First Amendment. Newspapers would have to censor editions on the Internet that they distributed freely on paper, the industry charged. *Catcher in the Rye,* critics hysterically argued, would be banned from computers.

That was sheer nonsense, of course. All our amendment did was apply the same federal laws that regulated television and telephones to computers as well. No one can dial a 1-900- phone-sex line without presenting a credit card and proof of being over eighteen years of age. Our legislation required the same safety features to ensure that minor children were not exposed to pornography. Adults would continue to have unrestricted access to explicit bulletin boards. No censorship would be allowed. The computer industry knew that, but it wanted much weaker standards and no liability if those standards were violated. This, we argued, was insufficient to protect children. But the charges from the computer industry had an impact. To make matters worse, the pro-family movement was divided. Some pro-family groups opposed our amendment and supported a weaker substitute. Also nominally on the other side was "Enough Is Enough," an antipornography group headed by Dee Jepsen, wife of the former Iowa senator Roger Jepsen, and Donna Rice-Hughes, who had been caught up in the Gary Hart scandal in 1988 and had since become a born-again Christian and pro-family crusader. The media gleefully played up those divisions.

In December 1995 we held a private meeting with Jepsen and Rice to plot strategy. We agreed to unite on whatever emerged from the conference committee. I also put in a call to a vice president for America Online to reassure the industry of my desire to work with that organization in drafting a bill that would be acceptable to both sides.

Having smoothed over differences behind the scenes, we then moved to a final vote. The Senate, backing the Exon amendment, was already locked in to our position, but the House was divided. Rick White, a Republican from Seattle, the home of Microsoft, offered an amendment that would have raised the legal standard for what constitutes pornography and indecent material, tying the hands of federal prosecutors who might try to crack down on pornographers.

Our hard count showed that we would lose to White, but to keep up the pressure we displayed an upbeat face in public. In an interview on CNN, I confidently predicted victory—how, was not altogether clear. Our lobbyists put in calls to members of the conference committee the day prior to the vote, pleading for their help. Ironically enough, we made some of our greatest progress among Democrats.

On December 6 the House conferees met in private session and, as we had feared, the White amendment passed easily. Then, in a surprise move, Representative Bob Goodlatte, a conservative Republican and Christian Coalition ally from Virginia, stunned those in the room by offering an amendment that replaced part of the White provision with stricter indecency language. When it came time to vote on the Goodlatte amendment, three liberal Democrats, including Patricia Schroeder of Colorado, switched their votes. Our amendment passed by a razor-thin 17–16 margin.

The pro-family movement had overcome the opposition of the entire computer industry, the news media, the Speaker of the House, and powerful committee chairs to pass a law that protected children from cyberporn. And we did so with the votes of Chris Dodd, Diane Feinstein, and Pat

Schroeder. President Clinton had threatened to veto the bill for reasons unrelated to our provision, but in a final negotiating session Vice President Gore ironed out compromises on long-distance services that pacified the administration, and Clinton then called for the bill's passage and was expected to sign it. That gave us the first provision of the Contract with the American Family to become law and one of the biggest legislative victories in our history.

The telecommunications bill was a defining moment for conservative Christians. We could have stood on the outside throwing rocks at those in power. But instead we rolled up our sleeves, pulled up a chair, and sat at the table drafting one of the most important pieces of legislation in our lifetime. Far from the wet-behind-the-ears partisan movement our critics describe, the pro-family movement today is demonstrating a level of sophistication and a willingness to work across party lines that would have been unthinkable just a few years ago. The cyberporn bill would never have become law without the votes of liberal Democrats at almost every critical stage. And by working with the computer industry, we crafted a compromise that both sides could live with. It was a classic example of the effectiveness of the grassroots combining with a common-sense accommodation to the gritty realities of life on Capitol Hill.

This episode also demonstrates the strategic relationship between religious conservatives and the Republican party. The two are not one and the same. Indeed, the partnership between the pro-family movement and the GOP is less a romance than a shotgun wedding. Though they might prefer otherwise, the Republicans cannot achieve a majority or govern without the support of pro-family voters. For its part, the pro-family movement would frankly prefer a more bipartisan posture but has so far found the national Democratic party both unwilling and unable (given its domination by liberal special-interest groups) to work with it. Nevertheless, the Christian Coalition continues to have between one-fourth and one-third of its members in the Democratic party. Will white evangelicals go the way of their African-American counterparts, becoming a largely one-party phenomenon? I certainly hope not. But if Democrats continue to attack and demonize conservative Christians, and if Republicans do not abandon the pro-family stands of the Reagan legacy, the overwhelmingly partisan voting patterns among religious conservative voters we saw in 1994 will probably continue.

In the end, any successful reform movement must work within *both* political parties. Where would Martin Luther King have been without Nelson Rockefeller and other Republicans sympathetic to civil rights? The central figure in the passage of the Civil Rights Act of 1964 was Everett Dirksen, the Republican leader in the U.S. Senate. Liberal feminists advanced the Equal Rights Amendment commensurate with their ability to attract support from prominent Republicans like Betty Ford and Mary Dent Crisp. Once the Equal Rights Amendment was dropped from the Republican party platform in 1980, it was only a matter of time before it went down to defeat. Likewise, the religious conservative movement must resist the temptation to identify its fortunes solely with those of the Republican party. Political parties lose power as quickly as they gain it, while social movements have a larger responsibility to advance an agenda that transcends electoral politics. That leads us to consider the new challenges facing the pro-family community as it struggles to make active faith a real factor in American politics.

7

LOOKING AHEAD

In February of 1995, I was in a Holiday Inn on the road after giving a speech when I received a phone call in my room.

"Ralph, it's Dan Quayle. How are you?" came the voice at the other end of the line. Quayle informed me that he was planning to seek the Republican presidential nomination in 1996. As with every other prospective candidate, I told Quayle that, given my position at the Christian Coalition, I could not offer any direct support or a personal endorsement, but I would be able to occasionally offer advice and counsel, as well as provide him with the same access to our grassroots that other candidates enjoyed. What Quayle did not know was that we had recently commissioned a survey of Republican primary voters; it showed that if he sought the nomination, he would receive roughly one-quarter to one-third of the vote, barely trailing front-runner Bob Dole. Had he run, the survey revealed, Quayle would have been the overwhelming favorite of religious conservatives. We braced for what promised to be one of the most raucous primary battles in modern times, a knock-down fight to the finish between pro-family champion Dan Quayle and Bob Dole, the consummate legislative tactician in the United States Senate.

In the course of several conversations in the ensuing weeks, Quayle

236

and I discussed possible political consultants, field staff, fund-raisers, and pollsters. He was sharp and focused, rested and ready, and anxious to jump into the fray. At his invitation, direct mail fund-raiser Ben Hart, who also consulted with the Christian Coalition, flew to Indianapolis to discuss how to build a file of millions of potential pro-family donors and supporters. John McConnell, a speechwriter for Quayle during his vice presidency, left his law practice in Wisconsin and moved to Indiana to begin the work of sorting through resumes and building a field effort.

A few weeks later, I was at the office working the phones and laying out our legislative strategy for the new Republican Congress when a friend called. "Have you heard about Quayle?"

"No, what's up?" I asked.

"He's been hospitalized with a blood clot. Reports are that it is life threatening," my friend replied. I was shocked. After surgery and blood-thinning therapy, Quayle spent several months at home recuperating, and pronounced himself perfectly fit. He later called me at home and vowed that in spite of the temporary setback, he fully intended to run. He spoke movingly about how his bout with illness had confirmed and deepened his faith in God. In spite of news accounts to the contrary, he was in excellent health. But then, in a dramatic turn of events, Quayle announced that he would not seek the presidency. He confided to me that his children were reluctant to undergo another brutalizing national campaign. While I respected his decision, I knew that Quayle's absence would create a vacuum on the cultural right that would inevitably be filled by someone else.

The question was: who? During the ensuing months, many other good people chose not to run. Bill Bennett, Jack Kemp, and Dick Cheney joined Quayle on the sidelines. The entire scenario was strangely reminiscent of the Democratic primaries of 1992 when, one by one, potentially formidable candidates like Sam Nunn, Al Gore, and Mario Cuomo declined to campaign, allowing a Southern small-state governor named Bill Clinton to limp across the finish line for the presidential nomination. This time Republican heavyweights who had waited a lifetime to seek the White House were stepping aside, and the chief beneficiary was Bob Dole.

The media yawned with undisguised boredom at the prospect of the Republican field without some of its most distinguished leaders in the pack. This in part explained the transparent attempt by the press to lure Colin Powell into the race in late 1995. Many howl about the liberal bias of the media, and there is certainly plenty to criticize. But more than anything, the working press needs a good story. In 1992 they had reveled in Gennifer Flowers, Clinton's draft evasion, Ross Perot, and the Houston convention. Compared to that colorful cast of characters, the Republican presidential contest of 1996 seemed dull and listless. Then along came Pat Buchanan.

I had gotten to know Buchanan during frequent appearances on his *Crossfire* television program, where he and I fenced with house liberal Michael Kinsley. He had also occasionally addressed Christian Coalition gatherings, where he and I engaged in the good-natured backstage joking and ribbing that was his trademark. I found him to be likable, funny, and a street fighter in the Nixonian sense. In early 1993 Buchanan invited me to join him for a quiet dinner at La Colline, a restaurant across the street from the U.S. Capitol, where we were joined by his wife Shelley, his sister Bay, and his ever-present press aide, Greg Mueller. It was clear that Buchanan was planning to seek the Republican presidential nomination again, and he was feeling me out to determine our plans.

Was Pat Robertson planning another presidential campaign? he wondered. No, I assured him, Robertson believed he could be far more effective through his television ministry, evangelistic outreaches, and cable television properties than he could as a presidential candidate. I also told Buchanan that we had decided not to back a specific presidential candidate in 1996, since there did not now appear to be a single staunchly pro-family champion on the model of Robertson in 1988.

At one point, Buchanan asked me who I thought would win.

"Hard to say. But it is clearly Dole's to lose. He has three main advantages. He will win Iowa because it borders Kansas. He has an excellent shot in New Hampshire because he will not have recently voted for a tax increase, and in fact he led the fight against Clinton's tax hike in the Senate.

And once he heads South, he can put Elizabeth on a twin-engine plane and parachute her into medium-sized media markets where she can talk about her evangelical faith. That means a strong showing if not a sweep on Super Tuesday."

Buchanan looked at me for a moment, completely silent, his dark eyes piercing through me, sizing up whether I was sharing what I thought would happen or what I hoped would unfold. I stared back, wondering if I had offended him by my honesty. There was a long pause that seemed to last for several minutes.

"No way," Bay finally exclaimed. "We're going to win this thing. We're going to go after the social conservatives in Iowa, and we're strong in New Hampshire. We almost beat Bush up there, and we will beat Dole. After that, his campaign will collapse, the myth of inevitability will be shattered, and we can go all the way to the convention," she said, her hands chopping the air in Pat-like fashion to punctuate her points.

"But in 1992 Pat was a protest candidate against Bush. Half of the vote you got in New Hampshire came from self-identified liberals. Many were voting against Bush," I argued.

Pat nodded.

"People always say that we were the protest candidate. They were for Pat, the voters responded to his message. They will do so again," Bay insisted.

In the middle of the dinner, Haley Barbour, the newly elected chairman of the Republican National Committee, walked over and charmed us all with his Southern "How y'all doin'" drawl. Haley, who had just assumed the helm of a party still reeling from losing the presidency, must have been startled by the sight of the head of the Christian Coalition apparently plotting strategy with Pat Buchanan. After he walked away, someone whispered, "His ears must be burning." We all laughed.

Buchanan seemed both intrigued and disappointed by my analysis of the 1996 campaign. He was running and expected to win. As we got up from the table, he joked, "You just keep working on those school board races and leave the presidency to me."

In the ensuing months, I remained on good terms with Buchanan as well as all the other candidates. I joined Senator Richard Lugar at the same restaurant a few months later, just a few tables over from where I had dined with the Buchanans. Pat Robertson and I had also had dinner with Phil Gramm, who impressed us with a computerized presentation on how many hands he had shaken, how many donors he had recruited, and how much money he planned to raise. I was giving a speech at Princeton University in the summer of 1995 when I was called to a phone to take a call from Gramm, who offered me a position as political director of his campaign. I politely declined, but we remained good friends and occasionally talked on the phone. In the months ahead, I came to admire Phil's tenacity and his commitment to conservative principles, and our friendship deepened.

Later, Gramm invited me to a meeting with Jim Dobson and Gary Bauer to discuss how to build better relations with the pro-family community. When Dobson told Gramm that he was disappointed by his unwillingness to make the moral issues a central theme of his campaign, Gramm waved him off and announced, "I am not running for preacher. I'm running for president. I just don't feel comfortable going around telling other people how to live their lives." The meeting then broke up as Gramm had to depart for a speech at the National Press Club.

As we filed out of Gramm's office and headed down the dark, cavernous halls of the Russell Senate Office building, Dobson turned to me, his cheeks flushed with anger, and exclaimed, "I walked into that meeting fully expecting to support Phil Gramm for president. Now I don't think I would vote for him if he was the last man standing." It was one more break for Bob Dole.

But Dole was more than just lucky. As with all winning campaigns, he made his own breaks. He hired a crackerjack campaign staff, headed by former Kemp operative and Republican National Committee executive director Scott Reed, who did an excellent job conserving financial resources, building a field organization, and reaching out to pro-family voters. Dole also hired top operatives like Maury Messing, Will and Jill Hansen, and to reach the religious conservatives, he recruited Judy Haynes, my former deputy at the Christian Coalition. I had known Scott Reed for years (we both traced our national political roots to the Kemp campaign in 1988), and I knew him to be one of the smartest and most underrated political operatives in the country. Many in the political community worried about Dole's earlier penchant for trying to run his own campaigns and his reluctance to take direction from his staff. Then, one afternoon while I was getting my hair cut, my cellular phone rang. As the hairdresser snipped her stainless steel scissors around the phone that was glued to my ear, Scott told me that he had just accepted the job as Dole's campaign manager. I congratulated him and hung up.

"Dole is halfway to the nomination. Anyone smart enough to hire Scott Reed could go all the way," I said to no one in particular.

Dole allowed Reed to run the operation, avoiding the micromanagement that had plagued him in 1988. Even after he barely survived in Iowa and stumbled in New Hampshire, Dole let his staff do its job. In the all-important South Carolina primary, where Bush had finally defeated both Dole and Robertson in 1988, they made their last stand. With professing evangelical Republican governor David Beasley at his side, Dole stumped the state with newfound stamina and energy. On Thursday, February 29, just two days before the primary, the Christian Coalition held a candidate forum at an Embassy Suites hotel just off the interstate in Columbia, the state capital. Dole had originally planned to send his wife Elizabeth, and then changed his schedule so he could be present to address the crowd. It was a powerful message that he was not going to concede the Christian Coalition vote to Pat Buchanan.

During the candidate forum, Buchanan delivered a stemwinder in defense of the Republican party's pro-life plank, pledging to appoint only pro-life judges to the Supreme Court and to repeal NAFTA and GATT. Many in the crowd supported him, and we made no effort to dissuade them. In fact, we welcomed their involvement. We knew that the activism and energy represented by the Buchanan campaign was a critical part of our broader effort to preserve the pro-family and pro-life stands of the Republican party. As Buchanan whipped the crowd into a cheering and shouting frenzy, Dole breezed into the holding room with his entourage of Governor Beasley, Senator Strom Thurmond, former governor Carroll Campbell, Elizabeth Dole, and several staff members. I shook hands with Dole and he thanked me and Roberta Coombs, our very able state chairperson, for the opportunity to be with our supporters.

"Look at this," he said, holding up copies of our *Congressional Score-card.* "I scored 100 percent in 1993, 1994, and 1995. I'm going to hold these up and show them that I have a record. Rhetoric is easy. A voting record counts."

After Buchanan finished, Beasley went to the podium and delivered an emotional introduction of Dole. As Dole began his remarks, he held up the scorecards, pointing out his long-standing support of pro-family initiatives and causes, and defending the right of conservative Christians to enter the political arena. "For liberal critics, it's an article of faith that people motivated by religion have no place in American politics. Religious faith is something they're willing to overlook as long as we keep it to ourselves," he exclaimed. On abortion he gave no quarter: "I have a flawless record of protecting the unborn, and that's not going to change when I become president of the United States."

About halfway through his speech, Dole discarded his prepared text and spoke from the heart about the wounds he suffered in Italy during World War II. He talked about his excruciating recovery over 39 months in a veterans' hospital, and about the first time during that recovery when he buttoned his shirt and dressed himself, how that had given him hope and persuaded him that he had a future. "I've never given up easily. I've been a fighter all my life," he said.

When the candidate forum ended, I headed for the exit and bumped into several members of the media. They told me they thought Dole had delivered the best speech of the entire campaign. Two days later, Dole won South Carolina 45 to 29 percent over Pat Buchanan, and won the votes of Christian Coalition members—nearly a quarter of the vote—by a margin of twenty-two points. South Carolina was the gateway to the South, and Dole went on to win eight out of eight primaries on Junior Tuesday and nearly every delegate on Super Tuesday, anchored by huge victories in Florida and Texas. In Florida, he won religious conservatives by a margin of 56 to 25 percent. The battle for ideas continued as Pat Buchanan vowed to stay in the race all the way to the San Diego convention, but the contest for the nomination was over. In hindsight, the secret to Bob Dole's comeback from the abyss could be found in that hotel ballroom in Columbia, South Carolina, where he at last emotionally connected with the pro-family activists who are the base of the present-day Republican party.

After South Carolina, many pundits pointed to the religious conservative vote as the key to the final outcome. They credited the Christian Coalition with a "pragmatic" strategy of working within the GOP that had triumphed over the tactics of my good friends Gary Bauer and Pat Buchanan, who showed less concern about holding together the existing coalition. But the reality was not that simplistic. I had never opposed Pat Buchanan and I had never directed our members to support Bob Dole. But my consultations with Pat Robertson, our board of directors, and the grass-roots state leaders persuaded me that our movement was divided. Robertson in particular, having himself run eight years earlier, cautioned that our membership was split and that we should remain on good terms with Dole, while not shackling ourselves to a single candidacy. For that reason, we remained neutral, and our movement was not tied to the success of the candidacy of Pat Buchanan—or anyone else, for that matter. That meant that everyone in the party and the pro-family movement won as long as the coalition that had brought victory in 1994 remained intact.

While I was friendly with Dole, I never attacked Pat Buchanan as some did. When Buchanan was denounced by some as an "extremist," I rejected that label and called such charges the "trappings of demogoguery." These attacks, I said in a speech at the Conservative Political Action Conference, were "the curse words of the establishment and the slurs of the chatter class." When members of the press ambushed me after the speech, they wanted to know if I had intended my remarks as a shot across Dole's bow. "Absolutely not," I insisted. "I would not presume to offer advice to the Dole campaign." This episode was instructive of the delicate dance we performed throughout the primaries, never publicly endorsing Buchanan or any other candidate but also never joining in the unfair attacks against him and his supporters. Our objective was simple: maintain a focus on values and issues so that all of our supporters could reunite in the fall campaign.

For us, Buchanan's candidacy represented an altogether fortuitous opportunity for religious conservatives by virtually ensuring that the ultimate presidential nominee would keep the pro-life plank in the party platform. While his campaign and some in the media trumpeted his trade and economic views, the truth is that Buchanan's greatest appeal was on the moral issues. To those who had hoped to water down the pro-family message or relegate the moral agenda to the sidelines, the Buchanan surge in Iowa and New Hampshire represented a thumping affirmation of the strength of the religious constituency.

But Buchanan also represented a detour of sorts because his campaign recalled the pro-family movement's previous status as the red-headed stepchild of American politics. His choice of the populist metaphor of "peasants with pitchforks" storming the barricades of the "establishment" to describe his supporters belied the tremendous influence that religious conservatives had gained in recent years. No longer greenhorns throwing rocks at the castle, many pro-family activists are now inside the castle. In many states, they operate the machinery of the Republican party and serve with distinction as state party chairs, state executive committee members, and national committeemen and women. To look at some of the key players of 1996 was to see the success of this strategy. Republican governors David Beasley of South Carolina, Steve Merrill of New Hampshire, and Kirk Fordice of Mississippi are all professing Christians and grassroots conservatives who are strongly supported by pro-family voters. These men also supported Bob Dole. So when Pat Buchanan lashed out against the party "establishment," he was attacking people who shared most if not all of his views on the issues. For many religious conservatives, charging the breastworks of the GOP was like training their artillery on their own positions.

Buchanan did not seem to fully understand this fascinating evolution.

LOOKING AHEAD

In a curious way, his appeal to the pro-family vote and his excoriation of the party leadership were incompatible messages. Religious conservatives were no longer "outsiders" in a party where the majority of the House Republican freshmen were committed evangelicals or devout Roman Catholics. Newt Gingrich, the back-bench bomb-thrower of just a decade earlier, was now the Speaker of the House. Trent Lott of Mississippi, a hero of the pro-family movement in the Senate, was one step away from becoming Senate Majority Leader. Nor were pro-family activists itching to start a war with Chamber of Commerce-style Republicans. While they continued to disagree over abortion, they had generally agreed not to oppose the other constituency's primary agenda items.

An increasing number of religious conservatives had concluded that it was strategically unwise to position themselves as a permanent insurgency within the Republican party. If they were seen as the GOP equivalent of the McGovern wing of the Democratic party of the 1970s or the Jesse Jackson wing of the 1980s, dominating party conventions but sending its candidates to crushing defeat at the polls, religious conservatives would not move into the position of permanent and lasting influence that they had sought for so long. In short, if they are to be taken seriously, people of faith must do more than rock the boat and panic the establishment. They must exhibit a seasoned capacity and an enthusiasm for governance, coalition building, and working within a political party that stands on the brink of long-term majority status.

The media knew this well, which explained why their dispatches from Iowa and New Hampshire suggested that the Buchanan brigades were heavily populated by the dreaded "religious right." The coverage lumped religious conservatives and Buchanan together in a way that suggested they were joined at the hip. Exit polls conducted by the television networks, for example, asked voters if they were members of the "religious right" and how they had voted. This flawed polling methodology excluded many mainstream evangelicals and traditionalist Roman Catholics who attended church regularly, had an occasional glass of wine with dinner, and strongly supported pro-life and pro-family candidates, but who would never identify with the media's biased shorthand term, the "religious right." As a result, the networks inaccurately reported that Buchanan had defeated Dole two-to-one among religious conservatives in Iowa, when in fact they had run fairly evenly (Dole 24 percent, Buchanan 23 percent). News accounts solemnly predicted that "rule-or-ruin fundamentalists," whom they routinely denounced as "McGovern Republicans," were impaling candidates like Steve Forbes with single-issue stilettos and pulling the party so far to the right that defeating Clinton in the fall would be nearly impossible.

After this diabolical scenario failed to unfold and Bob Dole won a healthy share of the religious conservative vote in the later primaries, virtually ensuring himself the nomination, these experts were proven wrong. To explain their errors, they spun another conspiracy yarn about Pat Robertson or me allegedly striking a secret deal with Dole in exchange for carving up the spoils after the election. What was the true size of Dole's debt to the leaders of the Christian Coalition? they asked with bated breath. Among the items over which it was suggested we had gained a veto were the vice presidency, Supreme Court appointments, a child tax credit, and a constitutional ban on abortion. Such speculation was as absurd as the earlier conventional wisdom that religious conservatives were a herd of wild boars stampeding to Buchanan. Dole won the support of religious conservatives not because we had secretly directed the minions of our movement to march in lockstep on his behalf, but because he had addressed their issues and shared their values. We were not about to dictate terms to Bob Dole. He had won the nomination in his own right, and we had no intention of making harsh demands like those that the labor unions and the radical left had made of presidential nominees in recent years.

Religious conservatives reached a fork in the road in 1996. They could have identified their message of stronger families and a more children-friendly culture with economic nationalism and protectionism. But to have done so would have taken the pro-family community down the failed road of Bryanism. William Jennings Bryan tried to combine his fundamentalist moral views with an inward-turning, backward-looking economic agenda designed to preserve the agrarian way of life against the onslaught of industrial capitalism. It was a losing struggle against the tide of history. He won his party's presidential nomination three times, more than anyone in history except for Franklin Roosevelt, but each time he took his party over the cliff to defeat. Why? Because Bryan's religious views became confused in the public mind with a vision of the United States as an agricultural republic with a limited role in international affairs. Theodore Roosevelt's more expansive and optimistic view of an industrial nation leading the world into the twentieth century carried the day.

Buchanan's protectionist message has appeal, but it resonates more with the Perot constituency than with pro-family voters. Ross Perot led the fight against ratification of NAFTA, whereas groups like the Christian Coalition have never made trade deals or immigration policy the central part of their agenda. As a purely tactical matter, it would be unwise to marry our pro-family legislative program to the economic views of Dick Gephardt and Ralph Nader. Blue-collar FDR Democrats can be attracted to the Republican party with the magnet of social issues such as abortion and gay rights without further exacerbating the already simmering tensions within the party, whereas drawing them with anti-Wall Street and anti-Big Business rhetoric threatens to alienate the economic conservatives who comprise the other half of the party's base. Pouring the new wine of economic nationalism into the old wineskins of a free trade, pro-business party is a high-risk strategy, and will be far more difficult than grafting in millions of social conservatives, most of whom already share the party's conservative economic views.

This is not to suggest that Buchanan's message of fair trade and an end to what he calls "corporate butchers" has no appeal among religious conservatives. There is a continuum of views in the pro-family community on such issues. Some oppose trade deals with Mexico and other countries, while others support them. In the rust belt and industrial heartland, factories have been shuttered, good jobs and good wages are gone, and once thriving communities have become ghost towns. But 64 percent of religious conservatives can be found in the South and West, where job growth is high and the computer industry and export-driven small businesses thrive. In South Carolina, for example, protectionism failed to move many voters. According to network exit polls, only 7 percent of voters thought trade was the most important issue in the campaign. Half of all voters said trade "creates more jobs than it loses," a less than surprising conclusion in a state where 9 percent of all jobs have been created by subsidiaries of foreign companies. Even in New Hampshire, where Buchanan's message caught fire, only 9 percent of all voters and 11 percent of Buchanan voters listed trade policy as a major factor in their voting behavior.

It is a mistake to identify the pro-family agenda with a particular economic philosophy, whether it is Buchanan's economic nationalism or Jack Kemp's supply-side agenda. One need not be for capital-gains tax cuts and a return to the gold standard to favor the protection of unborn life and religious freedom, and one need not be for repealing NAFTA to be a staunch pro-family supporter. Neither economic agenda is a litmus test of what it means to be a religious conservative.

It is still possible that a "third way" modeled after Ross Perot's Reform party could emerge, combining economic populism with pro-family conservatism. But it is unlikely for two reasons. First, religious conservatives have invested too much blood and treasure in the hard-earned gains they have won in the Republican party since the late 1970s. To simply walk away from that union, which has endured for almost twenty years and produced several electoral landslides, will take more than a family squabble. Second, many religious conservatives are enmeshed in the export-driven economy of the future. From Silicon Valley to North Carolina's Research Triangle to Boston's Route 128, millions of religious entrepreneurs and small businesses are on the cutting age of an information-based post-industrial economy. They are not cowering in fear of the onslaught of a global marketplace; they are embracing that market as the key to their own prosperity and the prosperity of the nation.

In this sense, Buchananism is not synonymous with the pro-family agenda. Buchanan's opposition to aid to Israel is in sharp contrast to the staunchly pro-Israel stance of conservative evangelicals. Jerry Falwell released a statement defending Buchanan's position on Israel, but many other evangelical leaders remained ambivalent about his previous references to Congress as "Israeli-occupied territory." I was asked numerous times during the recent presidential campaign if I thought Pat Buchanan was an anti-Semite. I always said that, in my view, he was not. The gravity and seriousness of that charge, leveled in the same century in which the Holocaust took place, requires a higher standard of proof than the handful of phrases that have appeared in some of Buchanan's columns over the years. He has never uttered anything in my presence that remotely resembled an anti-Semitic remark. But I do think he has at times made statements that could be interpreted as insensitive to the past suffering of Jews, and I would strongly advise him to more aggressively and unequivocally refute the charges against him. I say this not as a critic, but as a friend. If he did so, Buchanan would enjoy even more support among conservative evangelicals, among whom love for the Jewish people and the state of Israel is a defining characteristic.

In the area of economic policy, Buchanan's opposition to foreign trade deals neither contradicts nor is equivalent to pro-family conservatism. One may be a pro-family conservative and at the same time be a monetarist, a protectionist, a supply-sider, or a deficit hawk. While it might be temporarily gratifying to frighten the party establishment into unrestrained panic with insurgent candidacies, pro-family conservatives have now moved into a position of such responsibility and maturity that they can no longer afford the luxury of fulfilling their own self-indulgent designs. They must do more than "send a message" to the elites and party leaders. They must win elections. They must govern. They must pull the levers of government and turn the wheels of the larger society for the good of the nation. Politically, people of faith have come of age. They must act the part.

I do not agree with those who excoriated Buchanan as an "extremist" and accused him of "flirting" with fascism. Without ever endorsing him for president, I have defended him against such charges in numerous public statements and speeches. Buchanan has been a loyal Republican, a rock-ribbed conservative, a top aide in three White Houses, and an articulate defender of Republican principles on television and in his newspaper columns for years. To attempt to write him out of the mainstream of political discourse is unfair to him and his supporters.

An even greater test than Buchanan's candidacy of the newfound prominent role of religious conservatives in American politics was presented by the mass genuflection at the feet of General Colin Powell. A man with a story that seemed to embody the American Dream, Powell in 1995 stood at the beginning of a path that seemed to lead directly to the White House. Powell's eloquence, charisma, personal honor, and rectitude made him tower above his prospective foes, generating more excitement as a non-candidate than anyone had generated as a candidate since Reagan. But the Powell boomlet said a lot more about the nation and the sad state of its politics than it ultimately said about Powell. The American people hungered for a hero, yearned for a moral symbol, and sought a figure who transcended party affiliation, ideology, and race, and who would unite us as a nation again.

Powell was not to be that figure. He represented the mirror image of Buchanan. While Buchanan was unacceptable to the economic conservatives and relied almost entirely on religious folk for his support, Powell appealed to the business wing of the Republican party but made no effort to reach out to the social conservatives who had become so important to the electoral fortunes of the GOP.

From the moment Powell's autobiography was released and the media frenzy over his potential candidacy began, we pursued a strategy of salutary neglect. This strategy was based on several major assumptions. The first and most important was my strong hunch that General Powell would not run. He was enjoying private life after thirty years in government service, had a lucrative career on the speaking circuit, and was spending quality time with his wife and children. By his own account, he lacked the burning desire to be president. This took a great deal of pressure off us, making it easy to be gracious in private and complimentary in public. In politics, it is always better to speak softly and carry a big stick. Because the Christian Coalition planned to distribute 22 million nonpartisan voter guides in the presidential primaries in 1996, I was confident that Powell's liberal social views would receive the full scrutiny of the voters at the appropriate time. We had built formidable field organizations in the early-primary states of of Iowa, New Hampshire, and South Carolina, all well-oiled machines ready to churn out a large pro-family vote. These voters would speak more loudly than us. There was no need for us to chest-thump or saber-rattle for the cameras. While some of my friends urged me to attack Powell, I resisted. I thought Powell was an admirable man of genuine character, despite our issue differences. Besides, I believed it would reflect poorly on the Christian Coalition if its leadership established the unfortunate precedent of attempting to dictate who should seek the Republican nomination for president.

There was another assumption as well. In 1993, shortly after George Bush lost the election, I had accompanied Pat Robertson when he met privately with Colin Powell at the Pentagon. Robertson had urged Powell to seriously consider the possibility of running for president, telling him that he could be another Eisenhower, provided he could unite the party. Implicit was the gentle but unmistakable suggestion that Powell consider carefully his stands on the social issues, so vital in recent years to attracting religious folk to the party.

"But you don't know where I stand," protested Powell.

"You're right," replied Robertson optimistically. "But I would like to find out."

The meeting ended inconclusively, but we felt we had at least begun a dialogue. If Powell wanted the presidency badly enough, and if he stood solid on the pro-life and values agenda, we were open to being helpful. My American Journey, Powell's autobiography, appeared two years later. In it he alluded to numerous individuals who had urged him to seek the presidency, but the meeting with Robertson went unmentioned. That suggested to me either that Powell did not desire to run or that he was not interested in pursuing the support of religious conservative voters. In either case, I thought it unlikely that he would be nominated. Therefore, we chose to keep our powder dry during the hoopla of his book tour.

Our attitude of watch and wait was not adopted by all in the pro-family movement. When I next appeared on *This Week with David Brinkley*, Sam Donaldson peppered me with questions as to whether or not I would support Powell. I declined to take the bait. After the segment ended and I stepped off the set, Sam warned me that I may have been able to get away with that today, but that I would not be able to get away with it forever. Donaldson's prediction came true sooner than I feared. The following week I received a heated letter from Jim Dobson expressing his concern that I was trying to "skirt the great moral issues of the day." He worried that I might have inadvertently conveyed the impression that "politicians who promote abortion can still get our support, and that hypocrisy is a respectable avenue."

Jim's concerns were perfectly legitimate, but in this case misplaced. My tactic of declining to attack Powell was not designed to give him the nomination, but to ensure that he would not seek it. In a counterintuitive way, I believed that if he were sharply attacked, Powell might run. If he received praise on those issues on which we agreed, such as abstinence, he would likely stay out. In the end, this strategy was vindicated, but it required a delicate balancing act to maintain our focus on the long-term goal rather than the short-term political challenge presented by Powell's noncandidacy.

Most of Dobson's wrath was directed at Bill Bennett, whose admiration for Powell had led him to publicly indicate a willingness to support him despite his pro-choice views. I thought the whole debate was rather diversionary. Powell was not a candidate. Why cut ourselves up over someone who was not even running?

Nevertheless, I knew I needed to respond immediately to Dobson's letter, which had already been copied to numerous people and was in the process of being faxed all over Washington. In a forceful reply, I informed Dobson that I had long defended the pro-life plank in the Republican platform and had never equivocated in my defense of innocent human life. "You suggest that I should have attacked Colin Powell more aggressively," I wrote. "That is an honest disagreement. My own view is that he is unlikely to run." Later Jim and I had a pleasant phone conversation in which we ac-

knowledged our tactical differences and agreed to communicate more frequently in the future through private conversations.

As the day of Powell's announcement of his presidential intentions
drew nigh, conservatives grew increasingly nervous about his phantom
candidacy. On November 2, while out of the country on business, I received an urgent call from our Washington office and was told that a group
of conservatives were holding a news conference the following day to announce their fervent opposition to Powell. They wanted me to attend. I declined, sending a copy of previous quotations I had already made on Powell
that had appeared in the media. As a result, we were mentioned in few
news accounts of the press conference, and several reporters noted my
conspicuous absence.

At the news conference, a representative of one conservative group
quoted Powell's statement that he considered himself a "Rockefeller Republican" and drew an astounding parallel between Powell's views and
Rockefeller's reputation as a "conspicuous adulterer." Gary Bauer predicted that the nomination of Powell would cause religious conservatives
to leave the Republican party in droves. Paul Weyrich compared Powell's
military service to the Gilbert and Sullivan character who becomes "ruler
of the Queen's Navy by polishing the brass handles on the big front door."
Republican strategist Bill Kristol called the pow-wow "chest-thumping
childishness by portly conservatives." Most of these leaders were long-time
friends of mine, and our private differences over how to handle Powell
faded once he dropped out of the race.

There was no reason to gloss over the differences between Powell and
the pro-family movement. But the Powell episode was not, in my view, the
proudest moment for the religious conservative community. Powell was
clearly not a person who shared our views on most of the issues, including
the protection of innocent human life. That was a cold, hard political fact.
I had publicly stated on numerous television programs and to countless reporters our public-policy differences with the general. But in expressing
those differences, I believed then (and now) that we should have remained
optimistic and confident that Powell might eventually move closer to our

position. This was certainly the case with Bill Bennett and Jeane Kirk-patrick, former Democrats and liberals who had become more conservative over the years.

We may not have seen the last of Powell, even in 1996. The media has already begun another campaign of speculation like the one accompanying his book tour—this time promoting him as vice president. Those flames were fanned by Dole advisors who announced that they desperately wanted Powell on the ticket as the surest way to defeat Clinton. Powell appeared to close the door on this option at his farewell news conference. When asked about the vice presidency, he replied, "I have ruled it out." Sources close to Powell have told me in no uncertain terms that he remains thoroughly uninterested in being vice president. But that matters little. As soon as Dole wrapped up the Republican presidential contest, a spate of media-generated Dole-Powell stories began to proliferate. Surveys have been conducted by major news outlets purporting to show that selecting Powell—and only Powell—as the presidential nominee's running mate can bring victory to the Republican party.

Powell, for his part, has issued statements to the effect that he continues to have no interest in the position. However, the temptation will be great. Five of the last nine vice presidents have risen to the Oval Office. Nine of the past twelve presidential elections have featured a former vice president as the nominee of one of the two major parties. The office of vice president is to the twentieth century what secretary of state was in the nineteenth century: the surest road to the White House. There will be enormous pressure on Dole to at least extend an offer of the second spot on the ticket to Powell, and an equal amount of pressure on Powell to accept.

Could the Christian Coalition live with Colin Powell on the ticket? Our members would clearly prefer to support a ticket that included a pro-life, pro-family, low-tax, pro-term-limits conservative running mate. But that is a decision they will make on their own. Neither I nor the organization I head will address specific names or hypothetical candidates for vice president. In any case, the issue has been rendered moot by Powell's Sher-manesque declaration that he has no interest in the job. My best guess is that we will all be surprised. Spiro Agnew, Dan Quayle, and Al Gore were all dark horses and unexpected selections who delivered at the ballot box for their parties.

Nevertheless, how the pro-family movement of religious conservatives approaches the second Powell boomlet will have a lot to say about who we are. The way we handle Powell underscores the importance of thinking strategically, not speaking harshly when soft words more than suffice, and asking questions before shooting. It also serves to reinforce my belief that how we say things is frequently more important than what we say. In short, our words are at times as powerful a witness of our faith as our beliefs—for good or for ill.

Thus, if I may put it this way, another lesson of the Powell interlude is the need for a new theology of political activism for religious conservatives. While developing such a theology will require the collective thinking of scholars and intellectuals with minds far more subtle than mine, I would gingerly offer the broad outlines of an answer to the question of why religious people should be involved in the political process. This new political theology is defined by its essential optimism, charitable spirit, understanding of the limits of politics, and appreciation both for man's strength and his moral shortcomings.

As a community of faith, we stand at a crossroads. Down one path lies the fate of many other great religiously-inspired political movements of the past: irrelevance and obscurity. It is a path defined by its spiritual arrogance and by its faulty assumption that the most efficacious way to change the hearts of men and women is through the coercive power of the state. This is the path taken by the prohibitionists, the Social Gospel advocates, the New Dealers, and the architects of the Great Society. It is not the right path for our movement. Fortunately, there is another way. Admittedly, that path is a dim and dangerous one. But at the end of it lies not simply a wider circle of influence and greater political impact, but a changed society and a thoroughly Judeo-Christian culture. How do we get there? What are the road signs?

We begin with a principle of the Social Gospel. Reinhold Niebuhr said,

"The purpose of politics is to establish justice in a fallen world." In attempting to right wrongs and ameliorate social evils, people of faith should use the political system wherever possible and advisable. The state clearly has a role both in executing the will of God and society by punishing wrongdoers and in protecting the innocent and vulnerable. But we must never lose sight of the fact that the sinful nature of mankind means that the power of the state, even when seasoned by love, is a corrupting instrument to those who wield it. In Niebuhr's unforgettable phrase, "Goodness, armed with power, is corrupted." Therefore, all attempts to use government to establish justice must be tempered by an equally strong impulse to keep government small, limited in its functions, and diffuse in its operations. As religious conservatives rise in political influence, they should exercise the power they have gained with prudent restraint and tread carefully when legislating their moral views for the entire society. Whenever possible, social and family policy should be legislated at the community and state levels to protect against the excessive authority of the centralized federal government.

A second important principle in a theology of Christian political involvement is the notion of citizenship as a spiritual obligation. For years, conservative people of faith have resisted direct political activity because they thought it was "dirty," "worldly," and a distraction from the call to evangelism. There is simply no biblical basis for such a belief. In the book of Romans, the apostle Paul instructs that Christians are to render "taxes to whom is due taxes, honor to whom is due honor, respect to whom is due respect." In an ancient society, Paul was advising persons of faith to pay their taxes and honor the king. But in a democracy, we are the kings. That means we literally owe an obligation to ourselves and our fellow citizens to register to vote, become informed on the issues, and go to the polls. These activities are not an option, but an obligation and a biblical injunction.[1]

Thirdly, we must assert our full rights as American citizens. Some have claimed that Christian political activity violates Christ's warning that His followers would be persecuted in this life, and that when Christians are maligned, are called names, and their rights to free speech and to practice their religion are denied, they should gladly endure such persecution as a sign of their faithfulness. But that does a disservice to those who died that we might have those rights. In the book of Acts, the tale is recounted of Paul on his way to preach to the court of Caesar, when his sharing of the gospel sparks a riot in Jerusalem. When a group of Roman soldiers tries to flog him, Paul reminds them of his Roman citizenship and appeals all the way to Caesar, a cherished right of citizens of Rome. As a result of Paul refusing to allow the government to deny his rights under the law, the gospel reached the highest levels of the Roman Empire.

The Bible is filled with the accounts of heroes of the faith who served God and His people through government service. The book of Proverbs recounts that a wise man is one who is "respected at the gates," a reference to the political authority of the community. Joseph delivered his family and the nation of Israel from famine and death by becoming a top official to the Pharaoh of Egypt. Esther became the instrument to deliver the Jews from mass extinction by persuading the king to rescind a decree that allowed the enemies of the Jews to kill them. The words of Mordecai to Esther should ring in the ears of both Jews and Christians today: "And who knows but that you have come to royal position for such a time as this?" To the unborn, the poor, the downtrodden, the persecuted minorities, people with faith who occupy high positions in government can bring mercy and deliverance.

Another important principle in a theology of political activism is grace and humility in speech and deed. Ronald Reagan exemplified this spirit as well as anyone in recent times. One day when I was rifling through some old files, I came across a copy of Reagan's first inaugural address. In reading through it again for the first time in years, I was reminded of Reagan's buoyant optimism, his irrepressible good humor, and his faith in the American people. "Those who say that we're in a time when there are no heroes, they just don't know where to look," he said. Heroes were everywhere: "going in and out of factory gates," on farms, behind diner counters, and among the small-business owners "who create new jobs, new wealth, and opportunity." He added, "Their patriotism is quiet, but deep." It is no accident that religious conservatives burst upon the national political scene and first gained respectability when their values were expressed in Reagan's voice. He spoke charitably towards friend and foe alike. It was his inability to hate those who hated him that made us trust him with our nation's destiny.

We must speak today with that same charity. The apostle Paul wrote, "If I speak with the tongues of men and of angels, but do not have love, I have become a noisy gong or a clanging cymbal." There are two contradictory qualities that faith should bring to politics. The first is an uncompromising sense of right and wrong and a willingness to speak out against injustice and immorality. The second is mercy. Our political witness should reflect not only God's judgment but also His forgiveness. For He loves everyone—including our political foes.

Prior to my own faith commitment, I viewed politics as a form of combat. Within the bounds of what was legal, I did whatever it took to win. I said and did many things toward my political opponents that were hurtful. I viewed this as all part of the game. But after I became a Christian, I wrote letters to many of them and apologized. One such letter went to a young man, a fellow student at the University of Georgia, whom I had opposed when he ran for chairman of the college Republican club. My group's candidate had signed up the entire university swim team as members of the club the day before the election so they could vote for our slate. Muffled laughter filled the room when the swim-team members walked in, in single file, on the day of the election—their chlorine-bleached hair and wet Speedos showing through gym clothes made them an odd sight at a political meeting. Not long afterwards I became a committed Christian, and I wrote my opponent a letter of apology for some of the things I did and said during that campaign. Years later, I bumped into that young man at a meeting on Capitol Hill, where he is now a lobbyist for a major trade association. The look in his eyes told me instantly that he had forgiven me. That meant more to me than all the political victories I had ever won.

Every word we say and every action we take should reflect God's grace. This is easy when dealing with political allies, but the Bible tells us to love our enemies. Nowhere is this principle more important than in our opposition to Bill Clinton. Like an army that overwhelms its enemy but leaves the land uninhabitable, some religious conservatives have come dangerously close to defining themselves in purely anti-Clinton terms. Some of this opposition has been deeply personal, attacking Clinton's character rather than his policies, and in so doing it risks permanent damage to the office he occupies. Other presidents have polarized the country and felt the wrath of a vocal opposition. Virulent opponents of Franklin Delano Roosevelt compared the New Deal to fascism and accused him of aspiring to a dictatorship. Lyndon Johnson, despised by both the John Birch Society and the New Left, saw his presidency drown beneath cries of "Hey, hey, LBJ, how many kids did you kill today?" Richard Nixon polarized the electorate throughout his career, from the Hiss case in 1948 to Watergate, and ultimately left the White House in disgrace. Yet none of these predecessors engendered more personal invective and animosity than Clinton has among his enemies.

Clinton-bashing has become a veritable cottage industry. *The Clinton Chronicles*, a videotape produced by a California conservative group and marketed by Jerry Falwell on his *Old Time Gospel Hour* television program, claims that Clinton ordered the murder of political opponents in Arkansas and that, as governor, he was "hooked on cocaine." The video has sold more than 100,000 copies (at $40 apiece), primarily through religious conservative outlets. A second video bearing the ominous title *Circle of Power* includes a charge by Clinton critic Larry Nichols that people have been killed at the order of the Clintons. "You may also wonder what it's like fighting Bill Clinton," intones Nichols. "People are dead in Arkansas. There are people that are dead." He adds that "countless people [have] mysteriously died that, as it turns out, had some connection to Bill Clinton. I believe this is going on today."[2] David Brock, the investigative journalist who broke the "troopergate" story in *The American Spectator,* is no friend of the Clintons. But he calls the video "an admixture of fact, halftruths, innuendo and outright falsehoods that does nothing to advance the public's knowledge of Clinton."[3] It recycles and exaggerates tales that have floated around for years about Clinton's alleged drug use, partying, womanizing, and money laundering. It ends with a harrowing disclaimer that reads: "If any additional harm comes to anyone connected to this film or their families, the people of America will hold Bill Clinton personally responsible." Tony Campolo, a liberal evangelical Christian and supporter of Clinton with whom I have occasionally clashed, challenged Falwell to grant him air time to refute the charges—an offer that Falwell flatly refused. "These videos are giving the church a bad name," claims Campolo. But liberals are not the only ones who found the tapes distasteful. Bill Bennett called them an inappropriate attempt at character assassination, and even Brandt Gustafson, president of the National Religious Broadcasters, said such practice "has no place in religious broadcasting."[4]

I was recently at a conservative gathering where a speaker railed at length about Clinton, accusing him of murder and embezzlement among other alleged crimes. He called Clinton the most criminal president in our history, and called for his impeachment and imprisonment. The next day I spoke with a successful businessman and devout Christian who was at the dinner. "I felt very uncomfortable about the tone of what he said about Clinton. I have no intention of voting for him. But we should respect the office," he said. I believe this discomfort exists throughout the religious conservative community. Those individuals and organizations that have made demonizing Clinton their *raison d'être* in recent years have largely faded from the scene, and they do not represent the future of the pro-family movement.

A case in point was in 1994 when the Christian Defense Coalition announced the formation of a legal defense fund for Paula Corbin Jones, who has accused the President of sexual harassment.[5] There has been much righteous indignation among conservatives and evangelicals about Jones' allegations against the President. Whether her charges are true or false is in dispute; the matter is now before the courts, and I do not believe the president should be above the law. If he is guilty of sexual harassment, he should be punished like any other citizen, and I disagree with those who claim that he should be immune from prosecution while he remains in office. But I also think it is a mistake for conservatives to build their case against Clinton's reelection around Ms. Jones' charges. When Jones held a news conference at a conservative gathering to air her sexual harassment charges, I declined to participate. I have always deliberately confined my criticism of Clinton to public policy issues, not his character or moral shortcomings.

I oppose President Clinton's policies. But I do not despise him. Nor do I despise Mrs. Clinton, who has also come under a blizzard of attacks in recent times. If Bill Clinton is a sinner, then he is no worse or less than you or me. Questions about character have haunted Clinton since he announced his presidential candidacy in 1991, and they are not likely to go away. The reservations that many voters feel about him are understandable. If the account provided by Pulitzer-prize winning journalist James Stewart in *Blood Sport* can be believed, Bill Clinton has suffered from an ethical blind spot that even many liberals find troublesome. But the Bible teaches that all have fallen short of the glory of God—and that means each and every one of us. Has our version of the gospel become so politicized that we no longer believe that His grace extends to Bill Clinton? I am in no way arguing that legitimate criticism of the president for misconduct in office should be muted or circumscribed, for these are the benefits of a free society. But those who are identified as followers of Christ should temper their disagreements with Clinton with civility and the grace of God, avoiding the temptation to personalize issues or demonize their opponents. This is critical to remember if our movement is to avoid the fate of its predecessors.

Some of the harshest criticisms of Clinton have come from the "Christian nation" or Reconstructionist community, which argues that the purpose of Christian political involvement should be to legislate biblical law. Some of the more unyielding elements even advocate legislating the ancient Jewish law laid out in the Old Testament: stoning adulterers, executing homosexuals, even mandating dietary laws. Led by R. J. Rushdoony, a theologian who serves as the intellectual fountainhead of the movement, they believe that the primary objective of Christian activism should be to perfect society so that it is ready when Christ returns for His millennial reign. Many reject school choice and efforts to reform public education as short-sighted and self-defeating. Instead, they call for the eventual elimination of public schools. There are historical precedents for Reconstructionist ideas stretching back to the millennialistic strains of Puritan thinking, American Revolutionary ideology, and even the anti-slavery movement. But those currents did not reflect the mainstream of Christian thinking then, and they certainly do not today. Reconstructionism is an authoritarian ideology that threatens the most basic civil liberties of a free and democratic society. If the pro-family movement hopes to realize its goals of relimiting government and reinstilling traditional values in our culture and in public policy, it must unequivocally dissociate itself from Reconstructionism and other efforts to use the government to impose biblical law through direct political action. It must firmly and openly exclude the triumphalist and authoritarian elements from the new theology of Christian political involvement.

Abuses of religion are not confined to the right, of course. In late 1995 a group of liberal church leaders associated with the National Council of Churches were ushered into the Oval Office. They huddled in a circle around President Clinton, laid hands on him, and prayed for strength so that he could resist the tyranny of Newt Gingrich and Republican budget cutters on Capitol Hill. Apparently these liberal Christian activists believed that God had a position on the balanced budget, and that opposing Clinton's stand on the GOP budget plan might somehow be "unChristian." This partisan use of intercessory prayer shows how religion is often misused as a political weapon by those on the religious left. It is the very kind of political use of religion that we conservatives are frequently accused of. Religious conservatives must resist the temptation to pray in explicitly political terms. Our prayer should be for peace in our nation and the world, wisdom for our political leaders (including the president), and the healing of our divided nation—not the defeat of one party or a given politician at the polls.

We will be judged by history and by our God not according to the political victories we achieve, but by whether our words and our deeds reflect His love. When one of the nation's leading evangelical preachers suggests that the president may be a murderer, when a pro-life leader says that to vote for Clinton is to sin against God, and when conservative talk-show hosts lampoon the sexual behavior of the leader of the free world, the manner of their speech reflects poorly on the gospel and on our faith. Make no mistake about it: we do ourselves and our nation harm when we sacrifice the principle of respect for those in authority—a principle clearly laid out in Scripture and practiced by Christ—in the interest of short-term political gain. Is it possible that religious conservatives could win the political battle by defeating Bill Clinton in 1996 and yet lose the moral high ground in the process? Lest we become like those on the radical left who tried to smear Robert Bork or Clarence Thomas through character assassination and sleaze, we must meet a higher standard in truth and civility.

Not that people of faith should fall silent in their opposition to Clinton. We must remain faithful to a calling that is uniquely ours—to speak the truth, in season and out of season, no matter how unpopular, and always in love. John the Baptist warned Herod that it was wrong for him to have his brother's wife. To John the Baptist this was not a matter of politics, but a matter of right and wrong. In a 1988 commencement address to Duke University, Ted Koppel noted the importance that biblical standards of conduct still play in our politics. The Iran-Contra scandal was largely about whether members of the Reagan White House staff had told the truth to Congressional committees, a controversy that ultimately relied on the standard of morality laid out in the Old Testament that one should not bear false witness. Gary Hart saw his presidential campaign fall apart after he was accused of violating the Seventh Commandment: Thou shalt not commit adultery.

Old-fashioned values still have relevance today. As Koppel observed, they are the Ten Commandments, not the Ten Suggestions. God's standards still apply against murder, stealing, lying, adultery, coveting the possessions of others, and homosexuality. Some mistakenly believe that when Christians speak out against these practices, they must hate those who commit them. That is not the case. True Christianity loves the sinner, but hates the sin because it is destructive of the human spirit and contrary to God's plan for humanity. But how we criticize is important, as are our motives. Do we chasten in love, seeking repentance and reconciliation? Or do we seek the political destruction of our foes? The answer to that question is a matter of the heart that makes all the difference.

This principle is especially important in our approach to the issue of homosexuality. Americans are of two minds on the issue of homosexuality. They are opposed to persecution of homosexuals, or "gay-bashing," whether it is verbal abuse or physical harm. But they also oppose efforts by the organized liberal gay lobby to seek affirmative government promotion of their lifestyle by granting minority status to gays or teaching homosexuality to children in the schools. As strategist Bill Kristol puts it, "Americans are a tolerant people; we do not want to persecute homosexuals, or make their lives miserable. But we also understand that tolerance of individuals' private behavior is not the same thing as approval of the gay rights agenda." For that reason, I have found some of the religious conservative movement's discourse on homosexuality disturbing. Calling gays "perverts" or announcing that AIDS is "God's judgment" on the gay community are just a few examples of rhetoric that is inconsistent with our Christian call to mercy. Jerry Falwell's Liberty Alliance sent out a fund-raising letter in 1995 which claimed that "THE RADICAL HOMOSEXUAL ONSLAUGHT OF AMERICA IS RAGING!" The evidence? Al and Tipper Gore had opened the vice presidential residence to a "horde of homosexual leaders." The letter went on to assert that "if we do not act now, homosexuals will 'own' America." We have all been guilty of excessive hyperbole in fund-raising letters (the harangues against conservative Christians by groups on the left are notorious), but I would hope that in future both sides will resist attacking individuals and stick to policy differences. We must never retreat from our principled defense of the traditional, marriage-based family as the foundation of our society. But we must always speak and move in love, seeking redemption rather than condemnation.

The Christian view of homosexual practices derives from a belief in the moral principles of human sexuality found in the Bible. From descriptions in the Book of Genesis of the destruction of Sodom and Gomorrah and the injunctions against sexual misconduct in Leviticus to the apostle Paul's letter to the Romans, in both the Old Testament and the New Testament, the Bible makes it clear that homosexuality is a deviation from normative sexual conduct and God's laws. There is a vigorous debate about the meaning of these Scriptural passages, of course, such as those who insist that the great sin of Sodom was its mistreatment of the poor, its inhospitable attitude towards outsiders, and general sexual licentiousness of a heterosexual nature (and there is some justification, particularly elsewhere in the Old Testament, for the interpretation regarding the rights of the poor). But the totality of Scripture is clear in treating homosexuality in the same terms as adultery, incest, and other forms of sexual temptation that deviate from God's plan of heterosexual conduct within the institution of a monogamous marriage. One does not need to believe in a literal interpretation of Scripture or in other tenets of the Christian faith to believe that the government should tolerate but not encourage homosexual conduct. For many Americans, including me, this is a matter of sound public policy, not an attempt to impose Judeo-Christian theology through the power of the state.

Moreover, the deeply-held moral beliefs of Christians regarding this practice do not justify hateful or spite-filled intolerance of homosexuality. We live in a fallen world, among a society of sinners, and sin is an ever-present reality that we tolerate in our daily lives. Therefore, we allow for deviations from our own moral code as a matter of course. This is true not only of gays and lesbians, but of those who divorce the wives of their youth, those who disrespect their parents, and those who cheat on their spouses. Religious conservatives are not seeking as part of their political agenda to arrest those engaged in homosexual practices. But tolerance of homosexuality does not mean approval or government affirmation. Indeed, tolerance by definition implies a corollary attitude of disapproval. Contrary to the liberal view that tolerance means open-minded acceptance of every human preference, tolerance is not in fact synonymous with the suspension of moral judgment. We can tolerate the reality of teenaged girls becoming single mothers, and give those young women and their babies all the love and support they deserve, without accepting single parenthood as morally equivalent to the two-parent family or condoning premarital sex among children. The same distinction applies to homosexuality.[6]

Gays should be afforded the same protections that other citizens enjoy: to register to vote, turn out at the polls, run for office, and affect the public-policy process. And they do so. The Human Rights Campaign Fund, a gay-rights lobbying group, is one of the wealthiest ideological political-action committees in the nation, raising millions of dollars a year and distributing money to candidates who share its views. But the granting of minority status based on one's sexual preference is bad law, pure and simple. The 1993 gay March on Washington called for "legislation to prevent discrimination against Lesbians, Gays, Bisexuals, and Transgendered people in the areas of family diversity, custody, adoption, and foster care, and that the definition of family includes the full diversity of family structures." This is a radical demand that would overturn four centuries of tradition in America. To grant special minority status to gays and lesbians while denying it to other sexual minorities would probably violate the equal-protection clause of the Fourteenth Amendment.

The entire issue is such a Pandora's box that even Andrew Sullivan, the gay editor of the *New Republic*, has called the granting of minority status to gays unnecessary and ill advised. Sullivan has instead called for granting marital status to gay couples. But it is not altogether clear how many gays and lesbians want to be married, or whether their marital status would grant them the right to adopt children or to bear children through artificial means. Historically, family law in the United States has recognized the term "family" as legally applying to those related by blood, marriage, or adoption. Tinkering with the meaning of marriage when the traditional two-parent, marriage-based family is already an endangered species and the divorce rate is highest in the Western industrialized nations is hardly propitious or wise. Like the granting of domestic-partner benefits, this is not a gay-or-straight issue. It is a question of whether traditional marriage is an institution deserving of special protection by the government, or whether it should be redefined to include other relationships. That is why the best policy toward homosexuality should be tolerance but not government-sanctioned approval or promotion.

Unlike some of our predecessors, our deepest hopes for restoring and renewing America do not rest solely on our political involvement. In fact, though it may come as a surprise to some, I believe there are strict limits to what politics can accomplish. In many cases our best agenda may not be a political agenda at all.

That is not a limiting admission but a vital affirmation. It is an affirmation of Christ's pronouncement that "my kingdom is not of this world." Only after we acknowledge how little government and politics can accomplish are we free to roll up our sleeves and enter the fray with a realistic view of what politics *can* achieve. If people of faith pour all of their dreams for the reform of society into their political activity, they will not only be sorely disappointed but could set their movement back by decades. We must resist the temptation to identify our religious convictions with the platform of a political party or the election-year platitudes of favored politicians. As Alexis de Tocqueville warned, "[I]n forming an alliance with a political power, religion augments its authority over a few and forfeits the hope of reigning over all."

What America needs is not political revolution but spiritual renewal. The failure of Prohibition proves this observation. Unlike the temperance movement, which sought some legal restrictions combined with education, Prohibition sought to usher in the millennium through government action. They attempted to use the instrument of government to accomplish what had always been the role of the church: the salvation of the soul and the moral renewal of society. In the words of one Anti-Saloon League lobbyist, "Those things in the way of the progress of the Kingdom of God must get out of the way!" In one sweeping and misguided reformist impulse, the prohibitionist lobby succeeded in passing a constitutional amendment and the draconian Volstead Act, which banned all alcoholic beverages, including beer with an alcohol content as low as 0.5 percent. This strict and exacting standard, if enacted today, would outlaw most nonalcoholic beers on the market.

Prohibition contained the seeds of its own destruction for two main reasons. First, the dogmatism of the dry lobby prevented modest revisions of the law that would have made it enforceable and workable. Like a thirty-mile-an-hour speed limit, Prohibition was a noble idea carried to uncompromising and unworkable excess. But the second and more important lesson is that cultural change is more important than political victory in changing behavior in a free and democratic society. The temperance movement had its greatest influence in churches and schools, shifting attitudes and shaming excessive drinkers so that alcohol consumption actually declined in the years prior to Prohibition. In fact, the greatest reduction in alcohol consumption in American history came not during the legal regime of Prohibition, but during the Second Great Awakening of the 1830s, when per-capita consumption of alcohol declined by 50 percent in a single decade. This was also true to a lesser extent of the civil rights movement. Changes in public attitudes, not the passage of laws alone, ended the reign of Jim Crow and segregation in the South.

And yet social movements have an obligation to resist injustice and advance what is right regardless of public sentiment. Martin Luther King asserted in his famous "Letter from a Birmingham Jail," "A just law is a man-made law that corresponds with the law of nature and the law of God." Public opinion alone cannot dictate the political program of people of faith. It is undeniable that the pro-life movement, the temperance struggle, and the civil rights movement have all called us back to the "better angels of our nature," forcing politicians to confront troubling issues and social injustice that they would have otherwise ignored. The difficult question is how to balance moral suasion with the force of law.

The most dangerous thing that could happen to the pro-family movement would be to gain political power without having first learned to turn the levers of government slowly, deliberately, and cautiously. No amount of lobbying or arm-twisting can take the place of a change in public attitudes through moral persuasion. If religious conservatives are wise, they will re-

sist the temptation to replace the social engineering of the left with the social engineering of the right by forcing compliance with the moral principles that motivate us so deeply.

The most obvious application of this principle is the issue of abortion.
Currently there is a fractious and, I believe, healthy debate within the pro-
life community about whether to pursue a strategy of cultural remedies and
persuasion that will lead to fewer abortions, or whether to seek a legal ban
on abortion. One of the top priorities of the pro-family movement from its
inception has been legal protection for the aged, the disabled, the infirm,
and the unborn. Even Americans describing themselves as "pro-choice"
would not deny that 1.6 million abortions a year is a national tragedy.

Some, like Bill Bennett and scholar Marvin Olasky, argue that adoption and abstinence pose the greatest hope of reducing the number of abortions. "The pro-life movement is asking itself at this point a question that
leads to self-abuse," concludes Olasky. "Why haven't we been able to stop
abortion?" Noemi Emery argued in a controversial article in the *Weekly
Standard* that pro-lifers should pursue a cultural strategy, arguing that abortion is wrong and leaving disputes over how to reduce it to polite differences on tactics.[7] In a similar vein, George McKenna, in a provocative
article in the *Atlantic Monthly,* tried to resolve the predicament by proposing what he called a "Lincolnian" position on abortion. McKenna proposed
accepting the Supreme Court's ruling in *Roe* v. *Wade* (much as Lincoln re-
luctantly conceded the legality of the Dred Scott decision of 1857), but
treating abortion as a grave evil to be discouraged. The most recent anal-
ogy to McKenna's argument would be to smoking, which has not been
legally banned but has been shamed by public attitudes, restricted in public places by local ordinances, and discouraged by the pronouncements of
the U.S. Surgeon General.[8]

Should the pro-life community make abortion the "smoking" issue of
the 1990s, conceding that a legal ban is unworkable, yet using the power of
government to discourage it? I do not believe we should. Abortion is not
smoking or drinking, both of which are adult behaviors that are control-
lable by personal discipline and self-restraint. Abortion is the taking of the

life of an innocent child that cannot defend itself. We ban cigarette smoking for minors because we recognize the distinction between protecting children, as opposed to adults, under the law. The innocence, frailty, and vulnerability of the child requires an affirmative role for the state in protecting its life. For example, we do not say as a society that child abuse is a terrible act that should be discouraged through public shaming and Sunday sermons but not banned by law. Why not? Because child abuse harms the innocent.

The problem with McKenna's argument is that it is unhistorical, freezing Lincoln's evolution on the slavery issue in 1860. His anti-slavery campaign platform was designed to win critical border states and placate the South, and was driven by short-term electoral goals, not the long-term objectives of the Republican party. Three years later Lincoln issued the Emancipation Proclamation, ending slavery in those areas of the South not yet under Union control. Had he lived, Lincoln would have led the fight for the ratification of the Reconstruction constitutional amendments granting blacks the right to vote and equal protection under the law. To call a "pro-choice, anti-abortion" compromise Lincolnian does a great disservice to the historical legacy of the Great Emancipator.

The problem with the "moral suasion" argument posited by Bennett and Olasky is that it is a little like arguing in 1963 that a Civil Rights Act would be unnecessary because people could read *To Kill a Mockingbird*. Do we need moral arguments and changes in public opinion before we end the tragedy of abortion? Of course we do. But the law is also an effective teacher—it is part of a cultural solution, not a substitute for it. My own view is that the division between cultural and political action is a false dichotomy. The cultural versus political debate among pro-lifers today is like the debate that raged in the 1890s within the black community, featuring Booker T. Washington and the "Tuskeegee movement," which argued for self-help and education as the surest road out of poverty for blacks, versus the more radical and overtly political wing under W. E. B. Du Bois and the National Association for the Advancement of Colored People, who advocated direct political action and legal remedies. Both strains remain an important part of the civil rights movement's message to this day. Martin Luther King chose the more political route of protests, petitions, and marches. But he always acknowledged that hearts and souls could not be changed by ballots alone. That must be the strategy of the pro-family movement: a vigorous political strategy tempered by a humble acknowledgement that children will never ultimately be safe in their mothers' wombs until we change people's hearts.

We have made enormous progress. Pro-life political action has had the undeniable effect of culturally stigmatizing abortion. What else would cause President Clinton to promise to make abortion "rare," abortion lobbyist Kate Michelman to admit that it was "a bad thing," the Clinton administration to misstate the number of abortions Dr. Henry Foster had performed prior to his confirmation hearings, and the feminist author Naomi Wolf to denounce the "fetus-is-nothing paradigm of the pro-choice movement"? The truth is that the pro-life movement has already prevailed in people's hearts, and eventually their heads will follow. No one defends abortion as an affirmative good to be encouraged. We may not yet have won the political battle, but we have clearly won the moral argument.

Yet, undeniably, the votes cannot currently be found in Congress for the ultimate goal of the pro-life movement, a constitutional amendment to protect innocent human life. This presents a political dilemma. Until public opinion shifts on a political solution to abortion, outlawing all abortions by constitutional fiat would create the same dilemma for pro-lifers that the prohibitionist movement faced—or that pro-choice advocates have wrestled with after *Roe*. What is the answer? It is a statistical fact that there is no one more vulnerable in America today than an unborn child. This is a matter of principle for us, a principle upon which we cannot and should not compromise. But as a purely tactical matter, while I personally support all measures to protect innocent human life—including legal and constitutional remedies—it has become apparent that amending the Constitution may be the least practical and most remote weapon at our disposal at this time. The best strategy for the near term is a combination of the temperance movement before 1918 and the feminist movement prior to

1972—before it frittered away its energy and political capital on the failed Equal Rights Amendment. The most effective strategy for the pro-family movement is to seek to overturn *Roe* through the appointment of pro-life judges, to pass pro-life laws in every state possible, to eliminate tax subsidies for abortion and the organizations that perform them, and to reduce the incidence of abortion through cultural and moral suasion. At the same time, we must never retreat from reaffirming the fact that our ultimate goal is to see a day when the sanctity of innocent life is enshrined in our laws and in the Constitution. We will never truly be at ease with our conscience as a nation until it is. To change public attitudes, we must also repudiate the demonization of women who are pregnant out of wedlock, condemn violence practiced against abortion clinics in unequivocal terms, and pour our greatest efforts into education, persuasion, and prayer—not politics alone.

The Republican Party's pro-life position is a winning position that has given the party landslides in three of the past four presidential elections. It has served the party well and should not be retreated from, not only a moral principle, but as a purely political matter—because it would cost the party the support of millions of pro-family citizens. But the pro-life community's hopes for the protection of innocent human life do not ultimately hinge on the existing wording of the GOP platform. They lie with the noble principle behind it. I have supported the existing pro-life plank since its inclusion in the platform in 1980, and would enthusiastically support it again. However, in the interest of making it clear that our objective should be upholding principle rather than language, here is my effort at a pro-life plank:

> We are a party that respects the sanctity of innocent human life as the basis of all civil rights. We will seek by all legal and constitutional means to protect the right to life for the elderly, the infirm, the unborn, and the disabled. We oppose physician-assisted suicide, euthanasia, and the rationing of health care because they threaten the lives of the elderly. We deplore abortion on demand as a grave evil and a national tragedy. We oppose the taxpayer subsidies for abortion and those organizations that promote and perform them, a prac-

tice that millions of our citizens believe is the taking of an innocent human life. We agree with Mother Teresa's statement: "Abortion is the greatest destroyer of peace in the world today." We seek compassionate and humane alternatives to abortion, such as adoption services, and favor reforms of our foster-care and adoption system, such as greater facilitation of transracial adoptions, to provide loving homes for children who need them. We urge all Americans to work together to create what Pope John Paul II has called a "culture of life."

Let me be clear: these words are my own, and do not necessarily reflect the official policy of the Christian Coalition. Further, the final decision on the Republican party platform will be made by the 107 members of the platform committee, who represent the varying views and the diversity of the grassroots of the party. But it is my personal hope that the pro-family and pro-life community will ultimately find its values codified in the platforms of both political parties, in words that celebrate cultural solutions as well as legal and constitutional protections.

To many critics, our pursuit of laws to protect innocent human life are really the product of a hidden desire to "oppress" women and establish a theocracy. Nothing could be further from the truth. These critics will probably be equally unwilling to acknowledge that what really motivates our movement is a passionate concern for social justice. As I have argued earlier, the religious impulse has always been on the side of reform, and that is why it so easily becomes confused with liberal politics. Liberals have often understandably seen religious enthusiasm for "progressive" causes as reflecting an agreement with their own secular radical outlook. Those liberals are now stunned to learn that religious folk who were "liberal" on civil rights and labor are now "conservative" on issues affecting the family and the culture. This is because religious people are not motivated by partisan ideology but rather by a transcendent ethic of moral concerns that are grounded in faith.

In fact, though liberals regard our focus on abortion and school prayer as aspects of a theocratic agenda, they are best understood as the modern form of a perennial Christian concern for justice and equality. Our goal has been and remains to help those who have been cast down, despised, or rejected. With abortion, our concern is a matter of caring for a mother facing the trauma of an unplanned pregnancy and caring for a child who has no voice of its own. In the reform of a broken educational system, our concern means giving the poor and minorities the opportunity to send their children to safer, better schools. In the area of welfare, our concern seeks to end the disaster of federal programs from Washington that have ended up hurting the very people they were supposed to help. In trying to pass tax relief for middle-class families, we are seeking to relieve the crushing financial pressure that can lead to family breakup. In each case, our goal is not to legislate our theology. It is to strengthen the family, protect the children, and defend the rights of the poor and marginalized.

Where do we go from here? Probably where many of our predecessors have gone—to care for the poor. In my Methodist upbringing, I was taught that fiery preaching alone rarely reached the hungry or the homeless unless it was preceded by compassion. A hot meal, a blanket, and a warm cot pave the way and soften hearts for the message of the gospel. Religious conservatives in recent decades have neglected this work, to our detriment and to the great loss of the nation. But compassion for the poor was not invented by modern liberals. It was practiced by the Puritans, codified in the charity laws of the American colonies, and remains a vital work among conservative people of faith today.

Our movement is not just the social and political heir of the Social Gospel, with its focus on the least among us, but also of the War on Poverty. Few biblical mandates are as clear as our requirement to care for those in need. As followers of an itinerant carpenter from Bethlehem, Christians have long felt a responsibility to care for those whom the larger society has shunned. It was the early church's love of the unloved that drew so many to the faith and led the emperor Julian to ask: "Why do we not observe that it is in their benevolence to strangers, their care for the graves of the dead, and the apparent holiness of their lives that they have done most to increase [Christianity]?" And it is the revitalization of this by today's religious conservatives that will draw many more to their side.

LOOKING AHEAD

In practice, this effort will be rather different from the government-centered campaigns that came to define the Social Gospel and the Great Society. Our efforts will not commence with massive government programs or with grand promises of sure-fire solutions hatched in Washington, D.C. The failure of this approach is undeniable: rather than rolling up their sleeves to actually care for people, the liberals preferred instead to legislate measures from Washington that would somehow make it all go away. But those honorable intentions spawned a hierarchical, uncaring bureaucracy driven by powerful interest groups, and a downward spiral of hopelessness and despair that has led many to conclude that things today are actually worse than when Lyndon Johnson declared war on poverty a generation ago.

Unlike our liberal counterparts, we have tempered our goals, cautioned by the failure of the welfare state. We have heeded the church doctrine that Roman Catholics refer to as subsidiarity, the idea that charity is best practiced by those closest to the problem. Echoing the teaching of Pope Pius XI, we believe that when money intended to feed children and house the homeless ends up in government bureaucracy, that is not only inefficient, but immoral and evil.

Yet our vision for a compassionate society does not exclude a role for government. Under our guidelines, local and state government assistance for orphans, widows, the disabled, and those unable to work would continue, but churches, synagogues, and the faith community would be called upon to help more, and the tax code would be rewritten to provide greater incentives for charitable giving. An excellent blueprint has been provided by Senator Dan Coats' Project for American Renewal, which allows taxpayers to earmark up to $500 of their income taxes currently going to fund government public-assistance programs toward a charity working among the poor. I envision a new partnership between government and the faith community in which the sacred aspect is no longer excluded from welfare work.

The outlines of this new, compassion-centered conservatism are already emerging. Under Governor John Engler, the state of Michigan cushioned reductions in its welfare rolls with grants to the Salvation Army to house the homeless. In Mississippi, a literacy program sponsored by the Christian Broadcasting Network in partnership with Governor Kirk Fordice and state agencies taught thousands in the poorest regions of the state how to read and write. Ninety percent of our nation's homeless shelters are already operated by churches or synagogues, many of which reject government funding because of the red tape that comes with it. And an effort is also underway to launch an explicitly Christian and conservative version of United Way, so that many of the struggling ministries working in the inner city can receive charitable funding adequate to pay for their work.

When I hear some conservatives proposing that we eliminate government welfare programs altogether, I fear they do not understand the full consequences of their proposal. Charitable giving in the United States in 1995 totaled approximately $124 billion, but only a fraction of that finds its way to the poor. A truly Christian approach would be to gradually phase out many government welfare programs over a period of years, with an adequate transition period for private and faith-based charities to pick up the slack. Even after that transition, there should always be local government assistance for the truly disabled and for abandoned children. Otherwise, lives that are already hanging precariously by a thread could fall by the wayside, and the already crime-ridden, tension-filled urban centers could likely explode. This is not a defense of the existing welfare system or of federal entitlements, but it is a warning not to go too far too fast.

A second area that must move higher among the priorities of the religious conservative movement is the issue of race relations. As people of faith have sought to re-enter the political arena, they have been hamstrung by the painful legacy of Jim Crow, a history which remains shackled to their culture like a ball and chain. The past complicity of the white evangelical community in the mistreatment of blacks under the regime of segregation cannot be denied. White evangelicals stood in the front lines defending segregation and invoking Scripture to justify its cruelty. I believe that our moral authority on issues such as abortion and religious freedom will never carry sufficient weight to change the nation's culture until we thoroughly remove the stain of past racism from our own culture. Dan T. Carter argues in his recent biography of George C. Wallace that today's religious conservative message is an outgrowth of Wallace's anti-government, traditional values message stripped of its now disreputable racial appeal. That charge is overdrawn. Yes, there are some white racists on the right. But they do not speak for our movement, any more than Louis Farrakhan speaks for liberal African-Americans. Where were many of today's conservative leaders when Wallace was standing in the school-house door? Pat Robertson was integrating white churches in Virginia at the height of massive resistance, Newt Gingrich supported Rockefeller against Nixon in 1968 solely because of the race issue, and William F. Buckley's *National Review* argued that a vote for Wallace was the least de-fensible ballot that could be cast that year. In more recent times, Pat Robertson has condemned David Duke on his nationally televised news program. This hardly qualifies as a veiled appeal to race.

But the pro-family movement must do more. The Promisekeepers, a movement to encourage men to be better husbands and fathers, have made racial reconciliation a major priority. In February, 1996, the Christ-ian Coalition joined other pro-family groups in urging Congress to hold hearings on the recent rash of bombings directed against black churches in the South. I later wrote a letter to Attorney General Janet Reno urging that the FBI put the investigation and prosecution of the arsonists and vandals of black churches at the top of its list of pending cases. The domi-nant media predictably ignored these appeals to racial justice, but the evo-lution of our movement from a lily-white phenomenon to a multi-racial community is occurring slowly but surely. Most religious conservative groups have also been slow to take a formal position on reforming affirma-tive action, primarily because they fear that it could inflame racial tensions and divide the American people. But what is needed today is a major effort to build bridges with the African-American community based on our many shared values. That effort must be preceded by a genuine, public repen-tance for past racism. Only when our community is thoroughly cleansed of that taint can we move forward and heal the body politic.

These efforts will keep us honest and faithful to the true call of faith.

Because in the end, the pursuit of social justice in the political arena requires more than passing laws or winning elections. It requires a turning of the soul of a nation. It requires repentence, renewal, and reconciliation. No man-made law can substitute for the higher law that transforms the human heart.

When we took our first tentative steps on the political battlefield, we religious conservatives combined the skill of a novice with the temperament of a zealot. But times have changed. We now know that politics is not the sole or even the primary answer to our nation's moral decay, and that the best standard for government is still John Stuart Mill's principle of allowing the greatest liberty possible until someone else's life or liberty is jeopardized. Thus, in the view of religious conservatives the use of alcohol in moderation may be left to personal choice, but getting behind the wheel of a car while inebriated, thereby threatening the lives of others, may not. Reasonable persons of good will can disagree about how damaging pornography is to a person's soul. But the exploitation of women and children by hard-core and child pornography, its proven tendency to lead to rape and other sexual crimes, and the exposure of children to it on the Internet invade the rights of others. Likewise legal barriers to an official state church or government-sponsored religion are perfectly consistent with the intent of the Founders and with Mill's standard, until they restrict (as they do all too often today) the rights of citizens to express their faith in the public square. However, to compel individuals to participate in a prayer with which they don't agree is a form of tyranny; therefore I would oppose any statute or constitutional amendment that mandates prayers composed or led by teachers, principals, or other school officials. Finally, while the freedom guaranteed by our Bill of Rights to speak freely and express our ideas is a uniquely American right, even the Supreme Court has recognized clear limits to that right, and has ruled that speech which is prurient, slanderous, or outright deceptive is forbidden. Nevertheless, I believe that restricting speech—moral censorship—is ultimately destructive to the body politic and to our society.

The revitalized participation of people of faith in American politics is an overwhelmingly positive phenomenon. But in these and other matters, the recognition that politics has its limits and that it can be corrosive both to our faith and to the social peace in our large and diverse nation is every bit as important. It is this recognition that will allow us to thrive in the future and not perish. This understanding is crucial: we have no more intention of allowing the worldly concerns of the political process and government to overwhelm and pollute our church than we have to remake the United States as a theocracy. Our religion necessarily informs and molds our politics, but the two must still remain separate.

As I pointed out in Chapter 3, religion was once the driving force of liberalism. Today it is a mere appendage. Most of the time, liberals are uncomfortable using religious language or religious arguments to support their political agenda. When religion is employed at all, it is trotted out at election time as a get-out-the-vote tool, no different from phone banks or attack ads. The sad truth is that involvement in politics has corrupted the religious faith of liberals. Today, mainstream churches and liberal religious lobbies like the National Council of Churches are mere shells of their former greatness. Since World War II, membership in these denominations has hemorrhaged, and their share of total church membership has declined by 50 percent. Why? Because they confused their liberal politics with the gospel, causing a mass exodus from the pews. As religious conservatives increase in their political involvement and clout, we must be wary of this pitfall. The pro-family movement must not become the Republican party at prayer. Instead, it must seek to transcend both political parties by reaching out to Roman Catholics, Jews, African-Americans, and blue-collar workers with a positive message that speaks for a cause larger than partisan politics.

If we want to avoid the fate of the religious left, there are times when we will have to resist the temptation of political power instead of blindly pursuing it. At those times we must be ministers of grace. Our critics do not believe me when I say we desire a place at the table. They assume we wish to sit at the head of the table, carving up the spoils. They do not understand us. The truth is that we eschew political power—not to protect them but to protect ourselves. No amount of political gain by religious conservatives is worth having our churches become mere means to a partisan end.

These are not easy scales to balance. There will be times when we find ourselves too engaged in the political and will need to pull back. There will be other times when we have to be even more politically forceful than we have been. But in our times of questioning, we still have a history to look back on. It is a history that teaches us the importance of being politically sophisticated—of knowing that there are times to fight harder, times to speak loudly, times to say nothing. It is a history that teaches us the importance of remembering where we are going—to a place where families are valued, children are educated, and hope and opportunity abound. We are proud to stand on the shoulders of those who have come before us—and we wish to ensure that our movement will be viewed in the years to come not as a flash in the pan, but as a long-term participant in American public life. History has shown that people of faith can follow two paths in politics. Either we can become inflamed with zeal, and make much sound and fury before our fervor and influence ultimately dissipate; or we can assume the role of a responsible player within the democratic polity, so that the voices of Christians will always be heard in public discourse. The latter vision requires religious conservatives to understand our movement's purpose, and to comprehend the role of each individual within the movement and the larger society.

As it happens, I draw much of my own inspiration from the example of Martin Luther King, Jr. He faced this difficult dilemma of balancing a movement's passionate faith with the requirements of political sophistication. His response varied, but one of the things he did say in no uncertain terms was that his must be a movement defined by love. To ensure that everyone was clear about what this meant, each and every volunteer in his SCLC signed a pledge card mandating that they would:

1. *Meditate* daily on the teachings and life of Jesus.
2. *Remember* always that the . . . movement . . . seeks justice and reconciliation, not victory.

3. *Walk* and *talk* in the manner of love, for God is love.
4. *Pray* daily to be used by God in order that all men might be free.
5. *Sacrifice* personal wishes in order that all men might be free.
6. *Observe* with both friend and foe the ordinary rules of courtesy.
7. *Seek* to perform regular service for others and for the world.
8. *Refrain* from the violence of fist, tongue, or heart.

With this solemn promise in place, King and his army were able to move out in love, transforming the country and bringing to fruition the dreams of tens of millions of Americans—a transformation whose spirit has outlived both King and the movement he led. I am not comparing our movement to King's. We can never know the indignity, suffering, violence, and death that the civil rights pioneers experienced. But we can seek to make this creed our own, and hope to wield a fraction of the influence that they had on the hearts of their fellow citizens.

A century from now, when some student leafs through the yellowed pages of books talking about the religious conservative movement led by the Christian Coalition—as I did looking back on the populists and the Progressives while writing this book—it is my hope that he or she will be amazed. Not because of our political power, our grassroots strength, or our ability to turn out a huge vote on Election Day, though I am proud of all those things, but because our movement of common people had an uncommon commitment to caring for those in need, loving those who attacked us, and displaying the love, dignity, and decency that are the hallmarks of an active faith.

NOTES

1. How We Got There

1. Robert Booth Fowler, "The Failure of the Religious Right," in Michael Cromartie, ed., *No Longer Exiles: The Religious New Right in American Politics* (Washington, DC: Ethics and Public Policy Center, 1993), pp. 57, 60.
2. Matthew C. Moen, *The Transformation of the Christian Right,* (University of Alabama Press, Tuscaloosa, 1992). See Margaret Edds, "Reshaping American," Norfolk *Virginian-Pilot,* June 18, 1995, p. J1, for this and similar quotations cited in this paragraph.
3. Richard N. Ostling, "A Jerry Built Coalition Regroups," *Time,* November 16, 1987, p. 68.
4. David Frum, *Dead Right* (New York: Basic Books, 1994), p. 169.
5. Lee Atwater, "Lee Atwater's Campaign," *Life,* February 1991, p. 65.

2. All God's Children

1. Robert Fogel, Bradley Lecture Series, American Enterprise Institute, University of Chicago, September 11, 1995
2. Samuel Eliot Morison, *Oxford History of the American People* (New York: Penguin Books, 1961), p. 210.
3. Bernard Bailyn, *The Ideological Origins of the American Revolution* (Cambridge, MA: Harvard University Press, 1967), p. 187.

4. Whitney R. Cross, *Burned-over District: The Social and Intellectual History of Enthusiastic Religion in Western New York, 1800–1850* (Ithaca, NY: Cornell University Press, 1950/1981), p. 224.

5. Melvin K. Bruss, "History of Oakland College (Mississippi), 1830–1871," M.A. thesis, Louisiana State University, 1965, pp. 62–65; Charles S. Sydnor, *Slavery in Mississippi* (New York, 1933), pp. 208–9, 217–18.

6. Whitney R. Cross, *Burned-over District*, p. 223.

7. Ronald G. Walters, *American Reformers, 1815–1860* (New York: Hill & Wang, 1978), p. 23.

8. Jack S. Blocker, Jr., *American Temperance Movements: Cycles of Reform* (Boston: Twayne Publishers, 1989), p. 3.

9. Joel Bernard, "From Fasting to Abstinence: The Origins of the American Temperance Movement," in Susanna Barrows and Robin Room, eds., *Drinking: Behavior and Belief in Modern History* (Berkeley: University of California Press, 1992), pp. 337–51.

10. A. James Reichley, *The Life of the Parties: A History of American Political Parties* (New York: Free Press, 1992), p. 187.

11. Francis Russell, *The Shadow of Blooming Grove: Warren G. Harding and His Times* (New York: McGraw-Hill, 1968), p. 299.

12. Arthur S. Link and William B. Catton, *American Epoch: A History of the United States Since 1900* (New York: Knopf, 1955, 1980), p. 285.

13. Kobler, pp. 198–200.

14. Washington Gladden, *Recollections*, (Boston: Houghton Mifflin, 1909), pp. 90–91, cited in Ronald C. White, Jr., and C. Howard Hopkins, *The Social Gospel: Religion and Reform in Changing America* (Philadelphia: Temple University Press, 1976), p. xv.

15. Shailer Matthews, "Social Gospel," in *Dictionary of Religion and Ethics* (New York, 1921), p. 416, quoted in Ronald C. White, Jr., and C. Howard Hopkins, *The Social Gospel: Religion and Reform in Changing America* (Philadelphia: Temple University Press, 1976), p. xi.

16. Ibid., p. xx.

17. Michael Novak, "Morality: How It Became a Four-letter Word," *Rising Tide*, September–October 1995.

18. Paul Carter, *The Decline and Revival of the Social Gospel: Social and Political Liberalism in American Protestant Churches, 1920–1940* (Ithaca, NY: Cornell University Press, 1956), p. 4.

19. Ronald C. White and C. Howard Hopkins, *The Social Gospel*, p. xv.

20. A. James Reichley, *The Life of the Parties*, p. 207.

21. William M. Ramsay, *Four Modern Prophets* (Atlanta: John Knox Press, 1986), pp. 12–17.

NOTES

22. Walter Rauschenbusch, *Christianity and the Social Crisis* (New York: Macmillan, 1907), pp. 414–22, quoted in White and Hopkins, *Social Gospel,* p. 46.

23. A. James Reichley, *The Life of the Parties,* p. 201 (Roosevelt quotation); Reichley, *Religion in American Public Life* (Washington, DC: Brookings Institution, 1985), p. 214 (Addams quotation).

24. Garry Wills, *Under God: Religion and American Politics* (New York: Simon & Schuster, 1990), p. 99.

25. David D. Anderson, *William Jennings Bryan* (Boston: Hall, 1981), p. 190.

26. A. James Reichley, *Religion in American Public Life,* p. 210.

27. Garry Wills, *Under God: Religion and American Politics* (New York: Simon and Schuster, 1990), pp. 102–104.

28. Edwin Gaustad, ed. *A Documentary History of Religion in America: Since 1965* (Grand Rapids, MI: William B. Eerdmans, 1983), p. 117.

29. Ronald C. White and C. Howard Hopkins, *The Social Gospel,* pp. 63–64.

30. Walter Rauschenbusch, "Christianity and the Social Crisis," in Edwin Gaustad, *Documentary History of Religion in America,* p. 120.

31. Page Smith. *Rediscovering Christianity: A History of Modern Democracy and the Christian Ethic* (New York: St. Martin's Press, 1994), pp. 155–56.

32. Ronald C. White and C. Howard Hopkins, *The Social Gospel,* pp. 65, 68.

33. Elizabeth and Kenneth Fones-Wolf, "Trade-Union Evangelism: Religion and the AFL in the Labor Forward Movement, 1912–1916," in Michael H. Fisch and Daviel J. Walkowitz, eds., *Working Class America: Essays on Labor, Community, and American Society* (Urbana: University of Illinois Press, 1983), pp. 153–84 (p. 169 for quotation).

34. Edwin Gaustad, *A Documentary History of Religion in America,* p. 122.

35. Paul Carter, *The Decline and Revival of the Social Gospel: Social and Political Liberalism in American Protestant Churches, 1920–1940* (Hamden, CT: Archon Books, 1971), p. 20.

36. Ibid., p. 21.

37. Rexford Guy Tugwell, *In Search of Roosevelt,* p. 122, found in Page Smith, *Rediscovering Christianity* (New York: St. Martin's Press, 1994).

38. Kenneth Davis. *FDR, The New Deal Years, 1933–37* (New York: Random House, 1986), p. 212.

39. Kenneth Davis. *FDR, The New York Years, 1928–1933* (New York: Random House 1986), p. 19.

40. Kenneth Davis, *FDR, The New Deal Years, 1933–1937* (New York: Random House, 1986), p. 19.

41. Ibid., p. 446.

42. Ibid.

43. William Safire, ed., *Lend Me Your Ears: Great Speeches in History* (New York: Norton, 1992).

44. Ibid., p. 780.

45. Page Smith. *Rediscovering Christianity: A History of Modern Democracy and the Christian Ethic* (New York: St. Martin's Press, 1994), p. 181.

46. Suzanne M. Daughton, "Metaphorical Transcendence: Images of the Holy War in Franklin Roosevelt's First Inaugural," *Quarterly Journal of Speech,* 79 (1993): 434.

47. Paul Carter, *The Decline and Revival of the Social Gospel,* p. 166.

48. Eugene Genovese, *The Southern Front: History and Politics in the Cultural War* (Columbia, MO: University of Missouri Press, 1995), p. 171.

49. Taylor Branch, *Parting the Waters: America in the King Years 1954–1963* (New York: Touchstone Books/Simon & Schuster, 1988), p. 3.

50. Richard Lischer, *The Preacher King: Martin Luther King, Jr., and the Word that Moved America* (New York: Oxford University Press, 1995).

51. Ibid.

52. Eugene Genovese, *Roll, Jordan, Roll: The World the Slaves Made* (New York: Viking Press, 1976).

53. Stephen B. Oates, *Let the Trumpet Sound: A Life of Martin Luther King, Jr.* (New York: Harper Perennial, 1982), p. 17.

54. Ibid., p. 57.

55. Taylor Branch, *Parting the Waters: America in the King Years 1954–1963* (New York: Touchstone Books, 1989), p. 74.

56. Stephen B. Oates, *Let the Trumpet Sound,* p. 26.

57. Ibid., p. 50.

58. Taylor Branch, *Parting the Waters,* pp. 131–35.

59. Ibid., pp. 140–41.

60. Ibid., pp. 228–33. Quotation is on p. 275.

61. Theodore H. White, *The Making of the President, 1960* (New York: Atheneum, 1961); Taylor Branch, *Parting the Waters,* pp. 366–75.

62. Martin Luther King, Jr. "Our Struggle," in James M. Washington, ed., *A Testament of Hope: The Essential Writings of Martin Luther King, Jr.* (San Francisco: Harper & Row, 1986), p. 80.

63. William Manchester, *The Glory and the Dream: A Narrative History of America, 1932–1972* (New York: Bantam, 1984), p. 977.

64. Stephen L. Carter, *The Culture of Disbelief: How American Law and Politics Trivialize Religious Devotion* (New York: Doubleday, 1994), p. 228.

65. A. James Reichley, *Religion in American Public Life* (Washington, DC: Brookings Institution, 1985), p. 246.

66. Ibid., p. 248.

67. Ibid., p. 402.

68. Theodore H. White, *America in Search of Itself: The Making of the President 1956–1980* (New York: Harper & Row, 1982), p. 125.
69. Michael Barone, *Our Country: The Shaping of America from Roosevelt to Reagan* (New York: Free Press, 1990), p. 402.
70. Robert M. Crunden, *Ministers of Reform: The Progressives' Achievement in American Civilization 1889–1920* (New York: Basic Books, Inc., 1982), p. *ix*.

3. Liberalism's Hollow Core

1. Harvey Cox, "The Transcendent Dimension," *The Nation*, January 1, 1996, p. 20.
2. Jim Wallis, *The Soul of Politics: Discovering a Practical and Prophetic Vision for Change* (Maryknoll, NY: Orbis Books, 1994).
3. Theodore H. White, *The Making of the President, 1964* (New York: Atheneum, 1965). White described Lyndon Johnson's victory as "the greatest vote, the greatest margin, and the greatest percentage (61 percent) that a President had ever drawn from the American people," p. 400. In addition, the Democrats increased their already impressive control of Congress, winning 259 seats in the House and leaving the Republicans with only 32 members of the Senate. White described the Republicans as suffering from a "continuing failure to capture the imagination of the American people" and noted that the number of Americans identifying themselves as Republicans had declined from 38 percent in 1940 to 25 percent by 1964.
4. President-elect John F. Kennedy, Address to Massachusetts Legislature, January 9, 1961, in *Congressional Record*, January 10, 1961, vol. 207, Appendix, p. A169.
5. Richard N. Goodwin, *Remembering America: A Voice from the Sixties* (Boston: Little, Brown, 1988), pp. 426, 417.
6. Vic Fazio, "National Press Club Morning Newsmaker," June 21, 1994: "Statement by Ralph Reed, Jr.," June 21, 1994; Dan Balz, "Fazio Says Religious Right Is Pushing GOP to Extremes," *Washington Post*, June 22, 1994, p. A1.
7. In polls taken in 1962, for instance, nearly three-quarters of all Americans opposed legal abortion if a family couldn't afford to have another child. Throughout the 1960s, polling indicates that while there was certainly a percentage of Americans who believed that abortion should be legal to save a mother's life or in the event of severe physical deformities, and even in the first three months of pregnancy, there is absolutely no evidence of political support for the kind of extreme abortion positions that liberals started taking in the 1970s. In fact, by 1969, when asked a straight question on whether abortion should be legal for a woman in the first three months of pregnancy, a majority said, "No."
8. Edward M. Kennedy, letter dated and signed August 3, 1971.

9. Stephen L. Carter, *The Culture of Disbelief: How American Law and Politics Trivialize Religious Devotion* (New York: Doubleday, 1994), pp. 253–54.

10. Just a few years earlier, this was hardly a controversial position. In 1984, for instance, Senator Al Gore of Tennessee wrote to a constituent, "As you know, I have strongly opposed federal funding of abortions. In my opinion, it is wrong to spend federal funds for what is arguably the taking of a human life. . . . It is my deep personal conviction that abortion is wrong. . . . Let me assure you that I share your belief that innocent human life must be protected and I have an open mind on how to further this goal."

   In 1977, during debate over whether to prohibit the use of Medicaid funding for abortion, the Reverend Jesse Jackson sent "an open letter to Congress," saying: "As a matter of conscience I must oppose the use of federal funds for a policy of killing infants. The money would much better be spent to meet human needs."

11. The party's platform, meanwhile, has undergone a dramatic shift to the extreme. Where the party's platform had been silent on abortion for all of its history, by 1976 the official platform said, "We fully recognize and religious and ethical nature of the concerns which many Americans have on the subject of abortion. We feel, however, that it is undesirable to attempt to amend the U.S. Constitution to overturn the Supreme Court decision in this area." That position evolved, four years later, into a similar but bolder statement, "We fully recognize the religious and ethical concerns which many Americans have about abortion. We also recognize the belief of many Americans that a woman has a right to choose whether and when to have a child. The Democratic Party supports the 1973 Supreme Court decision on abortion rights as the law of the land and opposes any constitutional amendment to restrict or overturn that decision."

   By 1992, all mention of the serious religious and ethical problems posed by abortion had been eliminated. In its place, the party boldly declared: "Democrats stand behind the right of every woman to choose, consistent with *Roe* v. *Wade*, regardless of ability to pay, and support a national law [Freedom of Choice Act] to protect that right. It is a fundamental constitutional liberty . . . ." It was the first time in American history that a major party favored codifying abortion rights in federal law.

12. Mario M. Cuomo, *More Than Words: The Speeches of Mario Cuomo* (New York: St. Martin's Press, 1994), p. 41.

13. Ibid., p. 41.

14. Ibid., p. 39.

15. *New York Times*, July 14, 1994, and elsewhere.

16. "Pennsylvania Gov. Casey Seeks to Address Democratic Convention," *PR Newswire*, July 7, 1992.

17. One of his friends, and later Roosevelt's Secretary of Labor, Frances Perkins, said this: "He says his prayers. I would rather have a man in the White House who says his prayers than one who doesn't pay any attention to religion." George Martin, *Madam Secretary: Frances Perkins* (Boston: Houghton Mifflin, 1976), p. 198.

18. Ibid., p. 203.

19. Terry Catchpole, "A Short History of Political Dirty Tricks," *Playboy*, November 1992, p. 86.

20. So great was the defeat and the bigotry that the historian Richard Hofstadter notes that "the election inflicted upon American Catholics, in their civic capacity, a trauma from which they never fully recovered and the consequences of which still haunt the nation." Richard Hofstadter, *The Age of Reform* (New York: Knopf, 1963), p. 298.

21. Michael Barone and Katia Hetter, "The Lost World of John Kennedy," *U.S. News and World Report*, November 15, 1993, p. 38.

22. Allen J. Matusow, *The Unraveling of America: A History of Liberalism in the 1960s* (New York: Harper & Row, 1984), p. 22.

23. Theodore Sorenson, ed., *"Let the Word Go Forth": The Speeches, Statements, and Writings of John F. Kennedy, 1947 to 1963* (New York: Delacorte Press, 1988), p. 131.

24. Ibid., pp. 133–34.

25. Scott Lehigh and Frank Philips, "Romney Hits Kennedy on Faith Issue: Says Senator Is Betraying JFK's Stand," *Boston Globe*, September 28, 1994, p. 1.

26. Tom Mathews, with Eleanor Clift, "Carter: Early Bird," *Newsweek*, December 1, 1975, p. 41.

27. Ibid.

28. Susan Fraker, with Eleanor Clift and James Doyle, "Carter and the God Issue," *Newsweek*, April 5, 1976, p. 19.

29. Ibid.

30. Ibid.

31. Jules Witcover, *Marathon: The Pursuit of the Presidency, 1972–1976* (New York: Viking Press, 1977), pp. 208–9.

32. Garland Haas, *Jimmy Carter and the Politics of Frustration* (Jefferson, NC: McFarland & Co., 1992, p. 49.

33. A. James Reichley, *Religion in American Public Life* (Washington, DC: The Brookings Institution, 1985), p. 318.

34. Part of the fault lay with the evangelical right, whose political naïveté in supporting Carter in the first place was remarkable. Anyone familiar with his career knew that he was allied with the moderate-liberal wing of his denomination, spoke more the language of Martin Luther King than of Billy Graham,

and held liberal theological views on issues like evolution and abortion. But Carter was the most conspicuously evangelical candidate for president since William Jennings Bryan. Many of his coreligionists viewed his moralistic rhetoric and evangelical campaign style as a validation of their own views. They blithely ignored deep and abiding theological differences. For that reason, when Carter failed them, they felt doubly betrayed.

Perhaps the lowest point for Carter and for the Democratic party came during his fight with Kennedy for the presidential nomination. Going into the convention in New York City, Carter had more than enough delegates to secure renomination. However, Kennedy refused to quit. He sought revision of obscure party rules that would have allowed for "delegates to vote their consciences" in an "open convention." After that effort failed, and following a stirring speech by Kennedy to the delegates, Carter felt compelled to capitulate. He made a backroom deal with Kennedy to adopt several of his key issues as part of the platform. One of those issues was the pledge to pursue a civil rights act for homosexuals. This final decision, which would not come to full light until late in the campaign, was important not for the role it played in Carter's crushing by Reagan in 1980 but as a commentary on how a grand party had become the captive of outside interest groups.

35. Dinesh D'Souza, "Out of the Wilderness: The Political Education of the Christian Right," *Policy Review,* Summer 1987, p. 54.

36. Garry Wills, *Under God: Religion and American Politics* (New York: Simon & Schuster, 1990), p. 85.

37. The Reverend J. Philip Wogaman, the minister of Foundry Methodist, is an outspoken liberal who has attacked "laissez-faire capitalism" as responsible for drug abuse, murder, and homelessness in the United States while praising socialist regimes in Cuba and China for "modest but real economic success." Cal Thomas, "Politics and the President's Pastor," *Los Angeles Times* Syndicate, April 19, 1995.

38. Priscilla Painton, "Clinton's Spiritual Journey," *Time,* April 5, 1993, p. 49.

39. Gustav Niebuhr, "Clinton Says Psalms Bring Him Relief," *New York Times,* February 3, 1995, p. B9.

40. Statement by Bill Clinton, November 16, 1993, White House Press Office; Peter Steinvels, "Clinton Signs Law Protecting Religious Practices," *New York Times,* November 17, 1993.

41. Remarks by the president to the Eighty-Sixth Annual Holy Convocation of the Church of God in Christ, Mason Temple, Church of God in Christ, Memphis, TN, November 13, 1993.

42. Al From, the Democratic Leadership Council director, predicted, "Clinton can carry out another Democratic realignment like Roosevelt's, and fashion a new majority." Howard Fineman, "Knowing When the Party's Over," *Newsweek,* November 16, 1992, 38.

43. Ben Wattenberg, *Values Matter Most: How Republicans or Democrats or a Third Party Can Win and Renew the American Way of Life* (New York: Free Press, 1995), pp. 45–46.
44. "A New Covenant with the American People," 1992 Democratic Platform, pp. 3, 5 (for quotations).
45. E. J. Dionne, "Clinton's Blend of Liberal and Conservative Themes," *Washington Post*, June 30, 1992, p. A18.
46. Paul Taylor, "Democrats' New Centrists Preen for '88," *Washington Post*, November 10, 1985; Dan Balz, "Southern and Western Democrats Launch New Leadership Council," *Washington Post*, March 1, 1985; Laurence Barrett, "Rising Stars of the Sunbelt: The Democratic Leadership Council is Redefining the Party," *Time*, March 31, 1986, p. 31; Richard Shifter and Thomas Sowell, "Have the Democrats Really Changed?" *Commentary*, September 1992, pp. 23–32.
47. As Clinton stated in 1991 when he served as chairman of the Democratic Leadership Council, it "plainly rejects the old ideologies and the false choices they impose. Our agenda isn't liberal or conservative. It is both, and it is different." The best example of this synthesis is Clinton's "reinventing government" initiative, designed to make government more responsive by eliminating bureaucracy and waste. One achievement about which Clinton has boasted is the computerization of tax filings by small businesses, saving billions of dollars a year in paperwork and overhead. What Clinton fails to grasp is that his liberal base is unimpressed by a more streamlined welfare state, while conservative voters are more interested in lowering taxes, not making their collection more efficient. The "third way" is no way at all when it comes to mobilizing the voters necessary to win elections and govern.

Like "new" Coke versus "old" Coke, no one is buying Clinton's new recipe for liberalism. Instead of acting as liberalism's most energetic reformer, Clinton has become its most weak-kneed apologist. William Kristol, *Standard* editor and Republican strategist, has argued, "With Clinton in power, liberalism now has no excuse, and also no exit. In this sense the election of Bill Clinton may yet prove to be, for liberals, a deeply Pyrrhic victory."

Events have confirmed this prediction. By supporting the North American Free Trade Agreement and GATT, Clinton angered the labor unions that once provided the money and ground troops for Democratic candidates. The result: the biggest drop in union donations to Democratic campaigns in history, contributing to a Republican landslide in 1994. The Clinton health care plan, which embraced "managed competition" and split the difference between big-government and free market solutions, alienated both conservatives and liberals. In the end, it collapsed in a center that did not hold. By declining to oppose a Colorado anti-gay-rights law before the Supreme Court, Clinton alienated homosexual and lesbian groups. (A meeting at the White House intended to smooth over relations with gay officials backfired when Secret Service agents manning metal detectors donned rubber gloves.) In promising a "reevaluation" of affirmative action, he invited a third-party challenge by Jesse Jackson and incurred the wrath of the Congressional Black Caucus. Jackson has called Clinton an example of "Republican Lite" and has all but announced that he does not consider him a true Democrat. "Mr. Clinton is really operating at this point as an independent," Jackson claimed, adding that "a growing number of Democrats feel that perhaps they should be independent of him." This threat sent Clinton lurching back to the left, embracing affirmative action in its current form while pledging to tinker around the edges.

His deficit reduction plan of 1993 included $250 billion in taxes but delayed most spending cuts until after his first term; it sent moderate Democrats into open revolt. When Clinton followed that performance by proposing a budget in 1995 that reduced Medicare spending and eliminated the deficit over ten years, he angered Congressional liberals who had made opposition to Republican cuts in Medicare the centerpiece of their reelection campaigns. If Clinton tacked left, he lost the center; if he tacked right, his left flank exploded in protest. The result was a president who could not lead his own party in Congress. David Obey of Wisconsin, the ranking Democrat on the House Appropriations Committee, denounced Clinton's budget proposal: "Most of us learned some time ago that if you don't like the president's position on a particular issue, you simply need to wait a few weeks." Not since Richard Nixon's presidency unraveled during Watergate has an incumbent President enjoyed such little support from leaders of his own party.

48. Clinton's sway over Democrats has become so tenuous that even the DLC has distanced itself from its former leader. The issue is more political survival than ideological purity. "The DLC worries about dying off if the President is defeated," explained Elaine Kamark of the Progressive Policy Institute, a centrist think tank affiliated with the DLC. For if Clinton "loses, liberals will claim that the DLC's centrist views were responsible and should be tossed aside completely." The DLC put out a full-length issues "manifesto" to differentiate itself from Clinton, just in case he should be rejected at the polls in 1996.

49. George J. Church, "The Education of Mikhail Sergeyevich Gorbachev," *Time*, January 4, 1988, p. 18.

50. William R. Doerner, "The Call to Reform," *Time*, February 9, 1987, p. 28.

51. Mikhail Gorbachev, *Perestroika: New Thinking for Our Country and the World* (New York: Harper & Row), 1987, p. 119; Walter Isaacson, "The Gorbachev Challenge," *Time*, December 19, 1988, p. 16; Bruce W. Nelan, "His Vision Thing," *Time*, October 2, 1989, p. 22.

52. Dinesh D'Souza, "Out of the Wilderness: The Political Education of the Christian Right," *Policy Review*, Summer 1987, p. 54.

4. Rising from the Ashes

1. Frank B. Atkinson, *The Dynamic Dominion: Realignment and the Rise of Virginia's Republican Party Since 1945* (Fairfax, VA: George Mason University Press, 1992), p. 362.
2. Michael Tackett, "Middle-Class Catholics Shun the Democrats," *Chicago Tribune*, December 27, 1995, p. N1.
3. John B. Donovan, *Pat Robertson: The Authorized Biography* (New York: Macmillan, 1988), pp. 152–53.
4. Richard Viguerie, *The New Right: We're Ready to Lead* (White Plains, NY: Caroline House/Longman, 1981), pp. 123–36.
5. Jerry Falwell, *Strength for the Journey* (New York: Simon & Schuster, 1987), pp. 358–65.
6. Cal Thomas, *Uncommon Sense: A Layman's Briefing Book on the Issues* (New York: Scribner's, 1990).
7. Richard Viguerie, *The New Right: We're Ready to Lead*, p. 128.
8. Michael Lienesch, *Redeeming America: Piety and Politics in the New Christian Right* (Chapel Hill: University of North Carolina Press, 1993), p. 2.
9. Rowland Evans and Robert Novak, *The Reagan Revolution* (New York: E. P. Dutton, 1981), pp. 215–21.
10. Dinesh D'Souza, "Out of the Wilderness: The Political Education of the Christian Right," *Policy Review*, Summer 1987, p. 54.
11. Quoted in Charles R. Stith, *Political Religion: A Liberal Answers the Question Should Religion and Politics Mix* (Nashville: Abingdon Press, 1995), p. 148.
12. Jerome L. Himmelstein, *To the Right: The Transformation of American Conservatism* (Berkeley: University of California Press, 1990), p. 117.
13. "Basic rules of politics [include] respect for opposing views, an emphasis on coalition-building and compromise, and careful rhetoric," Tom Atwood, a former staffer of the Robertson presidential campaign, observes. "They often came across an authoritiarian, intolerant, and boastful, even to natural constituents." Thomas C. Atwood, "Through a Glass Darkly," *Policy Review*, Fall 1990, p. 45.
14. Ed Dobson, a former top official of the Moral Majority, acknowledged in his 1988 book *The Seduction of Power* that many of his fellow evangelicals suffered from "that mentality that overstates one's success or influence . . . the attitude of wanting to announce the score when our team has won and to change the conversation when we have lost." Ed Dobson and Ed Hindson, *The Seduction of Power* (Old Tappan, NJ: Revell/Guideposts, 1988), p. 141, cited in Michael Lienesch, *Redeeming America*, p. 249.
15. Dinesh D'Souza, "Out of the Wilderness," p. 59. D'Souza, a former Reagan White House staff member and author of a biography of Falwell, argued in

1987 that the pro-family movement's "best hope for change lies in the decentralization, localization, and privatization of power. More ground can be gained by influencing the moral tenor of their home towns and communities than on such presently futile battles at the federal level as the Human Life Amendment and a School Prayer Amendment."

16. David Shribman, "Marlene Elwell story," *Boston Globe*, August 4, 1995.

17. Remarks by Pat Robertson, *Proceedings of the Thirty-Fifth Republican National Convention*.

18. Remarks by Mary Fisher, *Proceedings of the Thirty-Fifth Republican National Conventation*.

19. David Gergen, "A Fight for the Soul of the Party," *U.S. News and World Report*, August 31, 1992, p. 58.

20. Curtis Wilke, "GOP Compass Direction: The Far Right," *Boston Globe*, August 18, 1992, p. 10, cited in David Frum, *Dead Right* (New York: Basic Books, 1994), p. 15.

21. Editorial, "Mr. Bush, Crossing the Line," *New York Times*, August 26, 1992, p. A20.

22. Michael D'Antonio, "Bedeviling the GOP," *Los Angeles Times Magazine*, November 29, 1992, p. 28.

23. Jim Lobe, "Grand Old Party Finds Itself in Shambles," Interpress Service, November 18, 1992.

5. *Christian Coalition: After the Fall*

1. Thomas Friedman, "To the Mat: Now Clinton Decides Which Promises Come First," *New York Times*, November 15, 1992.

2. David Nyhan, "Clinton's Talkfest Was Terrific," *Boston Globe*, December 17, 1992.

3. Eliza Newlin Carney, "Family Time," *National Journal*, July 29, 1995, pp. 1947–51.

4. Ralph Reed, Memorandum to Conservative Friends and Leaders, November 21, 1992, p. 1.

5. Ibid., p. 2.

6. Peter Stone, "Rallying the Troops," *National Journal*, September 2, 1995, pp. 2152–56.

7. Walter Mears, "Once Again, GOP Governors Sifting Through Rubble of Defeat," Associated Press, November 14, 1992.

8. Michael Weisskopf, "Energized by Pulpit or Passion, the Public Is Calling," *Washington Post*, February 1, 1993, p. A1.

9. James A. Barnes, "Revival Time," *National Journal*, January 23, 1993, pp. 189–92.

10. *American Enterprise*, November/December 1992.
11. Ralph Reed, Jr., "Casting a Wider Net: Religious Conservatives Move Beyond Abortion and Homosexuality," *Policy Review*, Summer 1993, pp. 31, 33.
12. David S. Broder, "Christian Coalition, Shifting Tactics to Lobby Against Clinton Budget," *Washington Post*, July 18, 1993; E. J. Dionne, "The New Ideas Republicans," *Washington Post*, July 6, 1993.
13. *Congressional Record*, July 23, 1993, p. H5047.
14. *Congressional Record*, July 29, 1993, p. H5459.
15. Martin Mawyer, "God and the GOP: Will We on the Christian Right Go Wrong?" *Washington Post*, September 1993, p. C1.
16. Randall Terry, "Selling Out the Law of Heaven, *Washington Post*, September 18, 1994, p. C9.
17. Ibid.
18. Jon Meacham, "What the Religious Right Can Teach the New Democrats," *Washington Monthly*, vol. 25, no. 4, p. 43; Charles Mahtesian, "The Christian Right Turns Pro," *Governing*, September 1994.
19. David Brudnoy et al., "Gurus of Gab: Talk Radio Stars Are Changing America," *Policy Review*, Summer 1994, pp. 60–63.
20. Associated Press, "Home Schoolers Oppose Teacher Certification Bill," *Chicago Tribune*, February 20, 1994, p. A4.
21. Jean Christensen, "Ears Ringing, Legislators Clarify School Bill," Minneapolis *Star-Tribune*, February 25, 1994, p. A10.
22. Associated Press, "Home Schooling Wins Emphatic Assurance from House," in *New York Times*, February 25, 1994.
23. Carolyn Curtis, "High Tech Activists," *Christian American*, October 1995, p. 21.
24. Ibid.
25. Ann Reilly Dowd, "The Net's Surprising Swing to the Right," *Fortune*, July 10, 1995, p. 113.
26. Dane Smith, "Bounced by the Right, the Left Aims for Rebound," Minneapolis *Star-Tribune*, June 25, 1995, p. A1.
27. Carolyn Curtis, "High Tech Activists."
28. "Whither Reform? Your Congress Remains in the Lobbyists' Pockets," editorial, *Houston Post*, October 10, 1994, p. A16.
29. Katharine Q. Seelye, "All-Out Strategy Hobbled Lobby Bill," *New York Times*, October 7, 1994, p. A22.
30. Eliza Carney, "In the Enemy Camp on Lobby Reform," *National Journal*, October 8, 1994, p. 2354.
31. Graeme Browning, "Zapping the Capitol," *National Journal*, October 22, 1994, p. 2446.
32. *Congressional Record*, October 6, 1994, p. S14285.
33. *Congressional Record*, October 7, 1994, p. S14607.

34. Adam Clymer, "G.O.P. Filibuster Deals a Setback to Lobbying Bill," *New York Times,* October 7, 1994, p. A1.
35. *Congressional Record,* October 7, 1994, p. S14613.
36. "Truth, Trust, and Lobbying Reform," editorial, *New York Times,* October 4, 1994, p. A20.
37. Howard Fineman. "The Brave New World of Cybertribes," *Newsweek,* February 27, 1995, p. 30.

6. *No More Stealth: The Real Agenda*

 1. Ralph Reed, "The Christian Coalition: An Agenda for the New Congress," address before the Economic Club of Detroit, January 17, 1995; John Harwood, "Religious Right Plans to Use Tax, Budget Battles to Start Reshaping the Nation's Moral Landscape," *Wall Street Journal,* January 17, 1995, p. A18.
 2. Nat Hentoff, "A Zero for Jesus in a Public School," *Washington Post,* January 26, 1996 sec. A.
 3. Christian Coalition, *Contract with the American Family* (Nashville: Moorings, 1995), p. xi.
 4. Mark O'Keefe, "The Christian Coalition Comes to Congress with a Potent Bid for a Pragmatic Social Agenda," *The Oregonian,* May 18, 1995.
 5. Amy Waldman, "Why We Need a Religious Left," *Washington Monthly,* December 1995, p. 38.
 6. Tom Shales, "Putting the Fear of God in America," *Washington Post,* September 6, 1995, p. D1.
 7. Ralph Hallow, "Family Contract Too Mild for Many," *Washington Times,* May 20, 1995, p. A1.
 8. Kate Michelman, "The New Anti-Abortion Strategy," *San Francisco Chronicle,* August 3, 1995, p. A21.
 9. Dennis Farney, "As Caucuses Near, Iowa's Christian Conservatives Feel Like Insiders But Lack a Unifying Candidate," *Wall Street Journal,* January 12, 1996, p. A18.
10. Abe Foxman to Pat Robertson in Anti-Defamation League, *The Religious Right: The Assault on Tolerance and Pluralism in America,* 1994, pp. 18–22; Christian Coalition, "A Campaign of Falsehoods: The Anti-Defamation League's Defamation of Religious Conservatives," July 28, 1994, pp. 7–10, 22 (for quotation); Midge Decter, "The ADL vs. the 'Religious Right,' " *Commentary,* September 1994. For a good overview of the controversy, see Thomas L. Jipping, "The Explanation for Shoddy Research at the ADL," *Washington Times,* September 29, 1994, p. A19.
11. Michael Lind, "Rev. Robertson's Grand International Conspiracy Theory," *The New York Review of Books,* February 2, 1995, pp. 21–25.

12. Lind repeats an ADL assertion that Robertson once said at a "Christian Broadcasting Network prayer meeting" that "Jews were 'spiritually deaf' and 'spiritually blind' but that in the climactic end times many would be converted." Robertson never made such a statement. Lind also repeats a statement previously attributed to me elsewhere: "What Christians have got to do is take back this country, one precinct at a time, one neighborhood at a time and one state at a time." I never made this statement.

13. Pat Robertson, *The New World Order* (Dallas: Word Publishing, 1991), p. 256.

14. Statement by Pat Robertson on *The New World Order*, March 3, 1995; Gustav Niebuhr, "Pat Robertson Says He Intended No Anti-Semitism in Book He Wrote Four Years Ago," *New York Times*, March 4, 1995, p. A10.

15. Pat Robertson, "A Reply to My Critics," *Wall Street Journal*, April 12, 1995, p. 12.

16. William F. Buckley, "In Defense of Pat Robertson," *Cincinnati Enquirer*, April 25, 1995, p. A10; Norman Podhoretz, "In the Matter of Pat Robertson," *Commentary*, August 1995, pp. 27–32 (pp. 28–29 for quotations).

17. "Remarks to the Anti-Defamation League of B'nai B'rith," April 3, 1995, pp. 2–4; Gustav Niebuhr, "Olive Branch to Jews from Conservative Christian," *New York Times*, April 4, 1995, p. A1; Laurie Goodstein, "Christian Coalition Leader Extends Olive Branch to American Jews," *Washington Post*, April 5, 1995, p. A3.

18. Frank Rich, "Bait and Switch II," *New York Times*, April 6, 1995, p. A31; Samuel Francis, "Groveling Is Always Bad Politics," *Washington Times*, April 11, 1995, p. A17.

19. Ira Rifkin (Religious News Service), "Jews, Conservative Christians Defuse War of Words," *Los Angeles Times*, December 3, 1994, p. B4.

20. Abe Foxman, Letter to the Editor, "Sorry Spectacle," *Metro West Jewish Community News*, December 14, 1995.

21. Frank Wolf, statement on "National Gambling Impact and Policy Act of 1995," September 29, 1995.

22. Ibid.

23. Ibid.

24. Ibid.

7. Looking Ahead

1. C. S. Lewis, "Membership," in C. S. Lewis, *The Weight of Glory and Other Addresses* (New York: Macmillan, 1980), pp. 113–114.

2. E. J. Dionne, Jr., "Sleaze on the Right," *Washington Post*, June 28, 1994, sec. A.

3. David Brock, "Falwell's False Witness," *Forbes Media Critic* (Winter 1995), pp. 45, 49.

4. Associated Press, "Evangelical Leader Petitions to Rebut Anti-Clinton Tapes," *Washington Post*, January 27, 1995, p. A2.
5. George J. Church, "The Clinton Hater's Video Library," *Time*, August 1, 1994, p. 21; Michael Isikoff, "Christian Coalition Forms Legal Expenses Fund for Clinton Accuser," *Time*, May 13, 1994.
6. Readers interested in the idea of tolerance are referred to an excellent essay by Oxford professor John Gray, "Toleration and the Currently Offensive Implication of Judgment," in *The Loss of Virtue: Moral Confusion and Social Disorder in Britain and America* (New York: The Social Affairs Unit/National Review Books, 1992), pp. 31–48.
7. Marvin Olasky, *Abortion Rites: A Social History of Abortion in America* (Washington, DC: Regnery, 1995).
8. George McKenna, "On Abortion: A Lincolnian Position," *Atlantic Monthly*, September 1995, pp. 51–64.

INDEX

Abbott, Lyman, 48
Abolitionism, 32–34, 85–86, 261
Abortion: Alexander's position on, 3; Bush's position on, 7, 84, 138–39, 144, 147; *Casey* decision, 38; Catholic position on, 84–85, 216, 218; Clinton's position on, 84, 99, 228–29, 270; Coverdell's position on, 158; cultural remedies and persuasion versus legal ban on, 269–74; Democratic platform on, 286n11; Dole's position on, 242; Falwell's position on, 108; funding for, 76, 286n10; and Hyde Amendment, 171–72, 184; liberals' position on, 74, 81–88; and Operation Rescue, 171; opposition to, by religious conservatives, 81; partial-birth abortion ban, 40, 96, 201, 228–29; Prather's position on, 80; priority of, with voters, 166; public opinion on, 285–86n7; *Roe v. Wade*, 81, 82, 84, 104, 134, 158, 203, 216, 269, 271, 286n11; statistics on, 269; *Webster* decision on, 38, 132. *See also* Pro-life movement
Abraham, Spence, 158–59
Abramoff, Jack, 22
Achtenberg, Roberta, 166, 181
ACLU. *See* American Civil Liberties Union (ACLU)
Acton Institute, 218
Adams, John, 53
Addams, Jane, 44, 49
ADL. *See* Anti-Defamation League of B'nai B'rith (ADL)
Adoption laws, 75
AFL-CIO, 5, 72. *See also* American Federation of Labor (AFL)
African Americans. *See* Blacks; Civil rights movement; Slavery
Agnew, Spiro, 255
AIDS, 147, 264

Alcohol use. *See* Prohibition; Temperance movement
Alexander, Lamar, 3–4
"America First" message, 145, 209
American Antislavery Society, 33
American Cause, 155
American Center for Law and Justice, 216
American Civil Liberties Union (ACLU), 173, 181
American Congress of Christian Citizens, 12, 14, 17
American Family Association, 13, 124, 203
American Federation of Labor (AFL), 46, 49, 50. *See also* AFL-CIO
American Israeli Political Action Committee, 212
American Jewish Committee, 212
American Jewish Congress, 212
American Life League, 203
American Revolution, 31–32, 262
American Spectator, 259
Americans United for the Separation of Church and State, 202
Anderson, John, 112
Anti-Communist movement, 55–56, 73
Anti-Defamation League of B'nai B'rith (ADL), 207–14, 295n13
Anti-Saloon League (ASL), 36, 38–39, 267
Anti-Semitism, 47, 86, 91, 191, 208–10, 212–14, 248–49, 295n13
Antislavery movement, 32–34, 85–86, 262, 270
Antiwar movement, 28, 29, 99, 140, 259
Armey, Dick, 168, 176, 178–79, 184–86
Ashcroft, John, 158–59
ASL. *See* Anti-Saloon League (ASL)
Atlantic Monthly, 269
Atwater, Lee, 22, 23, 103, 125, 143
Atwood, Tom, 291n13

299

INDEX

INDEX

INDEX